VICTORIAN TYPES, VICTORIAN SHADOWS

VICTORIAN TYPES
VICTORIAN SHADOWS

BIBLICAL TYPOLOGY IN VICTORIAN LITERATURE, ART, AND THOUGHT

GEORGE P. LANDOW

ROUTLEDGE & KEGAN PAUL
BOSTON, LONDON AND HENLEY

First published in 1980
by Routledge & Kegan Paul Ltd
9 Park Street,
Boston, Mass. 02108, USA
39 Store Street,
London WC1E 7DD and
Broadway House,
Newtown Road,
Henley-on-Thames,
Oxon RG9 1EN
Photoset in 10 on 12 Bembo by
Kelly Typesetting Limited, Bradford-on-Avon, Wiltshire
and printed in the United States of America by
Vail Ballou Press Inc, Binghamton, New York
Copyright George P. Landow 1980

British Library Cataloguing in Publication Data

Landow, George P

Victorian types, Victorian shadows.
1. Arts, English
2. Arts, Modern – 19th century – England
3. Typology (Theology)
4. Arts and religion – England
I. Title
700'942   NX544.A1   80–40970

ISBN 0 7100 0598 9

For My Father
H. I. Landow, MD

CONTENTS

ILLUSTRATIONS

(between pages 146 and 147)

PREFACE

In proper Victorian fashion this study of the art and literature of the period will begin with a tale of conversion. I was originally, before my second birth, quite skeptical about the importance of this mode of biblical symbolism to any Victorian writer but John Ruskin, whom I considered an anomaly. I have since realized that typology helps us to understand other major figures in both Victorian literature and art. Although students of English and American literature of the seventeenth century have demonstrated the importance of biblical typology in their fields for more than a decade, students of Victorian culture have paid little attention to it. Typology (or typological symbolism) is a Christian form of biblical interpretation that proceeds on the assumption that God placed anticipations of Christ in the laws, events, and people of the Old Testament. When I wrote *The Aesthetic and Critical Theories of John Ruskin* (1971), I was most concerned to explain the basic nature of the Evangelical Anglican form of this exegetical mode and then demonstrate how Ruskin moved from it to his own peculiar kind of allegory. While writing this book about Ruskin in 1968, I became aware that it was the critic's emphasis upon elaborate symbolism that so excited Hunt and his Pre-Raphaelite associates, and this recognition led to an essay on William Holman Hunt's *The Shadow of Death* in the 1972 *Rylands Library Bulletin* (and later to *William Holman Hunt and Typological Symbolism*, 1979). By the time I began to work on Pre-Raphaelite theories of realistic symbolism, I saw that Ruskin, Hunt, Rossetti, Millais, Collins, and other members of their circle drew heavily upon this supposedly arcane theological matter, and I concluded that it possessed more importance than I had earlier thought possible.

Earl Miner's gracious invitation to take part in the 1974 Princeton conference on literary typology, which took place while I was at work on *William Holman Hunt and Typological Symbolism*, encouraged me to look more widely than I had done for evidence of typology in Victorian literature. By the time I wrote my position paper, which later appeared in Professor Miner's *Literary Uses of Typology from the Late Middle Ages to the Present* (1977), I had become convinced that, with the obvious exception of Arnold, every major Victorian poet employs typology in some manner.

When I first began to investigate this subject some fifteen years ago, there was little available to the literary student other than essays by William Madsen and Northrop Frye on Milton. Such lack of studies of literary typology has proved an unexpected benefit – albeit in a rather backhanded sort of way. Since I was unable to learn much about typological readings of the Bible during the Victorian period from histories of theology or from accounts of the Evangelical movement, I began a course of reading sermons, tracts, hymns, biblical commentaries, and devotional poetry. Although this manner of proceeding required a great deal of time, it had the obvious advantage of forcing me to confront Victorian materials directly before formulating any broad generalizations. Fortunately, Ruskin's favorite preacher (whom, as I later learned, Browning and Gladstone also admired) was Henry Melvill, Canon of St Paul's, sometime chaplain to the Queen, and one of the most popular preachers of his time. My more recent investigations have required that I make myself acquainted with a far wider range of dissenting, Broad Church, and High Anglican applications of this exegetical mode. The advantage of going directly to major Victorian preachers and Bible commentators is not only that one makes some unexpected discoveries of unexpected talents – Melvill, for instance, often writes finer sermons than Newman – but that one does not risk basing assumptions about Victorian typology upon the theory and practice of other ages and other arts. One can learn much about typology in Gothic architecture from Emile Mâle's *The Gothic Image: Religious Art in France of the Thirteenth Century* and also much about its appearance in Northern Renaissance painting in Erwin Panofsky's *Early Netherlandish Painting, Its Origins and Character*, both brilliant works that mark new epochs in scholarship. One can also learn about literary applications of typology in many recent studies of seventeenth-century work, including those by my colleague Barbara Kiefer Lewalski. Such studies are especially useful if one already has a fairly clear idea of Victorian orthodox and extended applications of this exegetical mode. Otherwise, the student of Victorian literature will find himself looking at Browning, Ruskin, and Keble through preconceptions formed by mediaeval or seventeenth-century practice. Therefore, we must first discover how the Victorians defined and applied typology, and in this manner we can also understand how such apparently arcane theological matters influenced so much Victorian art, literature, and thought. After some basic questions about Victorian uses of this interpretive mode have been answered, one hopes that students of the period will begin to examine its nineteenth-century appearances in relation to earlier manifestations.

Portions of this work have appeared in different form in Earl Miner's *Literary Uses of Typology from the Late Middle Ages to the Present, Studies in Romanticism*, and *Victorian Newsletter*, and I would like to thank Princeton University Press and the editors of these two periodicals for granting permission to reprint these materials. I would also like to thank the Scuola di San Rocco, Venice, the Tate Gallery, the Birmingham City Museums and Art Gallery, Manchester City Art Gallery, Llandaff Cathedral, and Jesus College, Oxford, for granting permission to reproduce works of art in their possession.

I would like to thank the John Simon Guggenheim Memorial Foundation and its president, Dr Gordon N. Ray, for another Fellowship that allowed me to complete a study of Victorian typology. I would also like to thank, for their assistance and encouragement, John L. Bradley, James Boulger, Stephen Brook, Jerome Bump, David J. DeLaura, William E. Fredeman, Ernest Frerichs, E. D. H. Johnson, U. C. Koepflmacher, Earl Miner, Linda H. Peterson, Andrew Saint, Frank Taylor, G. B. Tennyson, and Hugh Witemeyer.I would also like to thank Terry Hackford, Kenneth Johnson, Shoshana M. Landow, Stephen Murray, and Sarah Webster for helping me read proof.

My greatest debt is to my wife Ruth whose presence encouraged this study to take form more quickly than it otherwise would have done. Her continued support, good humor, and enthusiasm for the project made it much easier to carry out, and her generosity in lavishing her skills as a professional copy editor upon the manuscript is responsible for much that seems clear and much that does not seem awkward.

Providence, Rhode Island

WORKS FREQUENTLY CITED

Quotations from these editions are identified in the main text by author, title of work, and, following the passage quoted, citation within parentheses of volume and page number:

Thomas Carlyle, *The Works* ('Centenary Edition'), ed. H. D. Traill, 30 vols (London, 1896–9).

Patrick Fairbairn, *The Typology of Scripture viewed in connection with the whole series of . . . The Divine Dispensations*, 2 vols (Grand Rapids, 1975, reprint of N. Y., 1900 edition).

Thomas Hartwell Horne, *An Introduction to the Critical Study and Knowledge of the Holy Scriptures*, 7th ed., 4 vols (London, 1834).

John Keble, *Sermons for the Christian Year*, 7 vols (Oxford, 1879–80).

John Henry Newman, *Parochial and Plain Sermons*, 8 vols (London, 1891).

John Ruskin, *The Works* ('The Library Edition'), eds E. T. Cook and Alexander Wedderburn, 39 vols (London, 1903–12).

Charles Haddon Spurgeon, *Sermons*, 20 vols (London, 1856).

INTRODUCTION

Although writers before the Reformation thoroughly understood both typology and tropology, they believed that tropology – moral allegory – should play a more central role in their writings. Or, to put it differently, although post-Reformation writers were also thoroughly acquainted with tropology, to them typology was more important. . . . The change in balance seems to me to involve the crucial Protestant concern with hermeneutics, with the active attempt by all the faithful – lay as well as clerical – to interpret the Bible. As soon as exegesis of the Old Testament becomes an issue necessary to daily reading of Scripture, typology becomes of far greater importance than tropology. Of course Catholics as well as Protestants were exegetes, but by elevating Scripture to the Rule of Faith and by deposing Church tradition as its handmaiden, Protestants inevitably became a hermeneutically minded group. . . . The Protestants did something else: they stumbled into the discovery of a more modern idea of history. To them Christendom was not simply timeless, nor was it some kind of temporally vague contrast between the miserable now and blissful then which required an attitude of contempt for the world.

– Earl Miner, 'Afterword', *Literary Uses
of Typology from the Late Middle Ages to
the Present* (1977)

INTRODUCTION

With the obvious exception of studies of the Oxford movement and
the valuable work of Hoxie N. Fairchild and Robert Lee Wolff,
when literary and cultural historians have considered Victorian
religion, they have focused narrowly on themes of honest doubt and
consequent loss of belief.[1] This focus has been particularly unfor-
tunate since the first two-thirds of the nineteenth century saw a
great, almost astonishing, revival of biblical typology, which left its
firm impress upon Victorian literature, art, and thought.

Although it is a commonplace that we have lost the intimate
knowledge of the Bible that characterized literate people of the last
century, we have yet to perceive the full implications of our loss. In
the Victorian age – to go back no farther – any person who could
read, whether or not a believer, was likely to recognize scriptural
allusions. Equally important, he was also likely to recognize
allusions to typological interpretations of the scriptures. Typology is
a Christian form of scriptural interpretation that claims to discover
divinely intended anticipations of Christ and His dispensation in the
laws, events, and people of the Old Testament. When we modern
readers fail to recognize allusions to such typology, we deprive
many Victorian works of a large part of their context. Having thus
impoverished them, we then find ourselves in a situation compar-
able to that of the reader trying to understand a poem in a foreign
language after someone has gone through his dictionary deleting
important words. Ignorant of typology, we under-read and misread
many works, and the danger is that the greater the work, the more
our ignorance will distort and inevitably reduce it.

The writings of John Ruskin, the great Victorian critic of art and
society, well exemplify major works which have thus fallen victim
to modern inabilities to supply a once obvious context. Typological
symbolism and the habits of mind derived from it provide a major, if
little-noticed source of unity in his thought, informing both his
interpretations of art and his theories of beauty, imagination, and
ideal art.[2] Drawing upon his knowledge of Evangelical typology,
Ruskin explicates Giotto and Tintoretto; and, sounding like any
Victorian preacher, he uses typological interpretations of the
Levitical sacrifice to argue that men of the nineteenth century should
lavish money upon their houses of worship. Typology, in fact,
permeates Ruskin's thought, appearing in the most unexpected
places, not only in his readings of individual paintings and buildings

but also in his discussions of geology, history, and aesthetics. The emphasis of this form of biblical interpretation on the reality of both type and antitype – of signifier and signified – left a particularly heavy impress upon his thought. For example, such an emphasis lies at the heart of Ruskin's theory of typical beauty, which asserts that men instinctively enjoy certain visual qualities, such as proportion and balance, because they are the material embodiment of divine qualities. Ever a polemical author, he uses this conception of beauty, as he does many of his other aesthetic theories, as a means of avoiding a crude didacticism; and he can do so because he believes that typical beauty, like types of Christ, exists simultaneously on two levels or in two different contexts: the aesthetic surface of nature (or of a painting) has its own reality, but, Ruskin emphasized, this reality is completed only by reference to God. Since he believed that the perception of beauty is thus intrinsically a religious and moral act, the art which records or creates it necessarily possesses great value. This simultaneous emphasis upon two poles of meaning, or two levels of existence, appears again in Ruskin's notions of an ideal art that combines a realistic style with complex symbolic intentions as a way of reconciling fact and imagination, materialism and idealism.

Students of the Pre-Raphaelites have long realized that Ruskin had a major influence upon the program of these painters and poets. Few have realized, however, that William Holman Hunt and his associates read, not the first volume of *Modern Painters*, which emphasized truth to nature, but the second volume, which contained Ruskin's theories of beauty and imagination.[3] As Hunt several times points out in *Pre-Raphaelitism and the Pre-Raphaelite Brotherhood* (1905), he gained inspiration from the critic's description of the way Tintoretto used typology to reconcile the demands of realistic technique with the need for spiritual truths.[4] The painter obviously believed that the search to create a suitable Victorian equivalent to such earlier forms of symbolic realism unified the diverse members of the Pre-Raphaelite Brotherhood. Hunt, who always resented claims that Dante Gabriel Rossetti or Ford Madox Brown founded the movement, convinced Millais of the artistic value of such Ruskinian high art based on typology. Certainly, Hunt's interpretation of early Pre-Raphaelitism, which places Millais and him at the center, is supported by the large number of Pre-Raphaelite paintings and poems that employ this form of symbolism: Millais's *Christ in the House of His Parents* (1850) and *The Blind Girl* (1856); Rossetti's paintings of the Virgin Mary and the poems that accompany them, his *Passover in the Holy Family* (1856) and its companion poem, the Llandaff triptych (1860–4); Hunt's own *The Scapegoat* (1854–6), *The Finding of the Saviour in the Temple* (1854–60), *The Shadow of Death* (1873), *The Triumph of the Innocents* (1876–83, 1884), and *May Morning on Magdalen Tower* (1888–91); Collins's *The Pedlar* (1850); and poems by Collinson and Christina Rossetti. Recognizing the essential validity of Hunt's claims about the origin and nature of early Pre-Raphaelitism has the unexpected effect of resolving various disagreements about the movement. Most important, Rossetti, who clearly provided the inspiration for so-called Aesthetic Pre-Raphaelitism, remains a seminal figure in the art and literature of the period, but his role in the actual Brotherhood becomes more understandable. Thus, it appears that Hunt and Millais, who were the more advanced students at the time the Brotherhood formed, first led the way in Pre-Raphaelite attempts to create a fully integrated symbolic realism. Rossetti, whose interests lay elsewhere, continued to employ elaborate scriptural typology for religious commissions, but he soon began to develop his own experimental art that concentrated on extremely personal symbolism and often moved beyond subject painting.

Although Dante Gabriel Rossetti was fully aware of typology's capacity to create a richly symbolic painterly realism in the manner of Van Eyck and Memling, he was chiefly attracted to this symbolic mode because it provided an order and significance to human time. Typology connects two times, the second of which is said to 'complete' or 'fulfill' the first, and therefore it provides a meaningful structure to human history.[5] Rossetti, who frequently concerns himself in his poetry with the problems of time and loss, tried to solve them by creating secular equivalents to christological typology. Typology, in fact, had several important influences upon the work of this non-believer. First, it furnished his early painting and poetry with imagery; second, typology permitted him, like the other Pre-Raphaelites, to experiment with a form of symbolic realism; third, it allowed him to make poetry and painting into sister arts; and, fourth, it shaped the tone, structure, and ideas of his major poetry.[6]

Sounding strikingly like Hunt and Ruskin, Elizabeth Barrett Browning founds a theory of the arts upon typology. In the eighth book of *Aurora Leigh* (1856), her heroine thus asserts that one must emphasize both

> natural things
> And spiritual, – who separates those two
> In art, in morals, or the social drift,
> Tears up the bond of nature and brings death,
> Paints futile pictures, writes unreal verse.

Combining scriptural allusion, Platonism, and standard Augustinian explanations of symbolism, she argues that without the spiritual,

> The natural's impossible, – no form,
> No motion: without sensuous, spiritual
> Is inappreciable, – no beauty or power:
> And in this twofold sphere the twofold man
> (For still the artist is intensely a man)
> Holds firmly by the natural, to reach
> The spiritual beyond it, – *fixes still*
> *The type with mortal vision, to pierce through,*
> *With eyes immortal, to the antetype*
> Some call the ideal, better called the real,
> And certainly to be called so presently
> When things shall have their names.[7] [My emphasis]

As one might expect from a poet who advances such an artistic program, Mrs Browning makes use of typological symbolism in her own works, and she is also drawn to its connection of two times, the second of which fulfills the first. Thus, in 'The Lost Bower', one of many Victorian paradises lost, the speaker's inability to rediscover an idyllic forest retreat prefigures all the losses that come about with adulthood and immersion in everyday existence. In contrast, 'Italy and the World' borrows the notion of prefiguration for an overtly political poem, as, like Swinburne, she presents the Risorgimento in typological and religious terms.[8]

The poetry of Gerard Manley Hopkins, which frequently makes

use of typological allusion, has intentions strangely similar to those of Hunt, Ruskin, and Mrs Browning. The persistent inability of critics to perceive how deeply Hopkins is rooted in his Victorian environment appears nowhere more clearly than in their failure to perceive the genesis of his most characteristic poems in typology. Like Ruskin and Browning – here almost certainly major influences – the poet continually seeks a means of combining a rich, aesthetic surface with a carefully articulated symbolism. Furthermore, as Jerome Bump has recently demonstrated, the poet also draws upon both mediaeval and Tractarian conceptions of typology that extend this kind of symbolism to include natural objects, such as the sun and seasons.[9] It is not so much that Hopkins's 'The Windhover' and similar poems exemplify Ruskin's aesthetic theories which derive from typology, though of course they do, but rather that his entire conception of inscape and its relation to the structure of a poem seems to develop from a mind accustomed to seeking types and figures of Christ. A poem such as 'The Windhover' elaborately presents the sensuous, visible details of a really existing thing – here the hawk – and then makes us realize the elaborate Christian signifi-cance of each detail, as (like a type) the image of the bird is 'com-pleted' only by reference to Christ. Hopkins prompts the reader to carry out such an interpretive procedure by employing both commonplace types and subtle echoes of them. 'Barnfloor and Winepress' and 'New Readings', for instance, make explicit reference to biblical types in the same way that do poems by Tennyson, Browning, and Christina Rossetti. 'The Windhover', 'God's Grandeur', and other later works by Hopkins instead employ characteristically distant echoes of commonplace typological images. For example, the basic or generating conceit of 'The Windhover' is that higher beauty and higher victory come forth only when something – say, a hawk, an ember, or clump of soil – is subjected to great pressure and crushed or bruised. This conceit is in fact an extension of the standard typological interpretation of that passage in Genesis where God tells the serpent: 'And I will put enmity between thee and the woman, and between thy seed and her seed; it shall bruise thy head, and thou shalt bruise his heel' (3:15). According to the conventional typological reading of this passage, Christ was the seed Who would bruise the serpent's head, and He in turn would be bruised – crucified – in thus conquering evil. As

7

preachers often emphasized, one chief truth contained in this type is that Christ achieves His highest victory by submitting Himself to be bruised or crushed. In this manner, He permits His true power and beauty to shine forth.

A rather different, if equally important influence of biblical typology appears in Tennyson's *In Memoriam*. Here it is typology's linking of times and events, rather than its equal emphasis upon signifier and signified, that is important. Organizing his poem in terms of plays upon the word 'type', the poet closes the elegy with the now calm assurance that Hallam

> was a noble type
> Appearing ere the times were ripe,
> That friend of mine who lives in God,
>
> That God, which ever lives and loves,
> One God, one law, one element,
> And one far-off divine event,
> To which the whole creation moves.

As John D. Rosenberg has commented of these lines, 'Hallam is at once the noble type of evolution's crowning race and forerunner of "the Christ that is to be." . . . With the "one far-off divine event" we confront Tennyson's final effort at uniting evolutionary science and Christian faith. For that event holds out the promise both of the Kingdom of Heaven, when all shall "live in God," and the Kingdom of Earth, when all shall have evolved into gods'.[10] Rephrasing Professor Rosenberg's point, we can observe that Tennyson has resolved the crisis of faith precipitated by Hallam's death by assuming that his friend is doubly a type, one which foreshadows both the second appearance of Christ and also that of the higher race of men. In making this characteristically Victorian – that is, charac- teristically idiosyncratic – use of typology, Tennyson 'solves' the problem raised earlier in the poem by his other uses of the word 'type' where it means 'biological species'. The central sections 54 through 56, which dramatize his groping for consolation, show how the poet's doubts raised increasingly appalling specters. He thus begins section 54 with trust that when God's plan is understood, all will see that not one life is 'cast as rubbish to the void', but even as he tries to assert this hopeful view, his doubts wear away his confidence. Retreating, he tries in the next section to find consolation in the fact that while nature may be careless of the individual life, she is none the less 'careful of the type'. In response to this last desperate hope that nature preserves the species if not the individual, section 56 immediately replies:

> 'So careful of the type?' but no.
>   From scarpèd cliff and quarried stone
>   She cries, 'A thousand types are gone:
> I care for nothing, all shall go.'

Thus, his friend's death, which first made the poet experience the emotional reality of loss, soon forced him to realize the possibility that not only man-the-individual but also man-the-species could die out. But, as the final lines of the poem make clear, Tennyson can accept this once terrifying possibility – that man the 'type' may disappear from the earth – precisely because he believes that Hallam, the original cause of this investigation, is a dual type. In other words, Tennyson can accept the possibility that man will become extinct, because he believes that such extinction would occur only when God was ready to replace man with a higher, more spiritual descendant. At the close of the poem, then, theological type replaces biological type, or rather encompasses it, because faith reveals that God's eternal plan includes purposeful biological development.

Robert Browning, one may point out, makes a surprisingly similar use of typology in *The Ring and the Book*, where Pompilia is also seen as a type both of Christ and the highest in human nature. Wondering at the ignorant girl's magnificence of spirit, the Pope observes how she could

>   rise from law to law,
> The old to the new, promoted at one cry
> O' the trump of God to the new service, not
> To longer bear, but henceforth fight, be found
> Sublime in new impatience with the foe!
> Endure man and obey God: plant firm foot
> On neck of man, tread man into the hell
> Meet for him, and obey God all the more! (1050–7)

9

In the Pope's description of Pompilia's nature, Browning alludes to Genesis 3:15, and the poet thus shows that his heroine both rose to a higher form of the human, acting fully as a Christian, and served as a type of Christ Who will finally tread Satan into Hell.

The chief difference in terms of typological imagery between Tennyson's presentation of Hallam and Browning's presentation of Pompilia is that the author of *The Ring and the Book* does not so confidently assume his heroine is necessarily a type of a coming higher humanity. This use of typology to describe a higher form of the human race does, however, appear earlier in Browning's poetry. *Paracelsus*, for example, proclaims:

> All tended to mankind,
> And, man produced, all has its end thus far:
> But in completed man begins anew
> A tendency to God. Prognostics told
> Man's near approach; so in man's self arise
> August anticipations, symbols, types
> Of a dim splendour ever on before
> In that eternal circle life pursues. (5, 770–7)

Both Browning and Tennyson, in other words, find typological symbolism capable of describing – and sacralizing – their conceptions of human evolution.

Typology thus provided these poets with a means of talking about the future of man in a particularly reassuring manner. Tennyson and Browning, however, did not make any very original synthesis of biblical exegetics and evolutionary biology when they advanced their similar conceptions of developing species, for such had already been suggested by typologists. Students of Victorian culture have been so accustomed to considering Evangelicalism and evolutionary theory as inevitably conflicting with each other that it may come as a shock to discover Patrick Fairbairn, the great Victorian expert on scriptural typology, claiming that the Book of the Earth, like the Bible, was arranged by God according to the principles of progressive revelation:

> It has been found by a wide and satisfactory induction, that the *human* is here the pattern-form – the archetype of the vertebrate

division of animated being. In the structure of all other animal forms there are observable striking resemblances to that of man, and resemblances of a kind that seemed designed to assimilate the lower, as near circumstances would admit, to the higher . . . . For, as geology has now learned to read with sufficient accuracy the stony records of the past, to be able to tell of successive creations of vertebrate animals, from fish, the first and lowest, up to man, the last and highest; so here we also have a kind of typical history – the less perfect animal productions of nature having throughout those earlier geological periods borne a prospective reference to man, as the complete and ultimate form of animal existence. In the language of theology, they were the types, and he is the antitype, in the mundane system. . . . In this view of the matter, what a striking analogy does the history of God's operations in nature furnish to His plan in providence, as exhibited in the history of redemption! Here, in like manner, there is found in the person and kingdom of Christ a grand archetypal idea, towards which, for successive ages, the divine plan was continually working.[11]

Broad Churchmen and other liberal thinkers habitually thought in terms of various kinds of spiritualized human development, but, as the Evangelical Fairbairn makes clear, even more conservative believers long saw no conflict between biology and the Bible. Since typology is essentially a system of progressive revelation, any attempt to apply it to the natural world inevitably leads to some sort of theory of evolution. Typologically based theories of biological evolution, which are intrinsically teleological, of course have no room for Darwin's principle of natural selection. But however unpalatable later evolutionary theory became to many Victorian believers – particularly after the appearance of *The Descent of Man* in 1871 – conceptions of biological development were originally supported by basic Victorian attitudes towards the scriptures.

Typology, which thus provided a means of formulating a history of man the species, also offered Victorian autobiographers a means of presenting the histories of individual people. One of the most basic ways of ordering the experiences of that problematic, elusive entity the autobiographer seeks is to choose a metaphor of the self and then expand it into a narrative (or what Avrom Fleishman terms 'a *personal* myth').[12] Typology, as Linda H. Peterson has shown, provided Victorian autobiographers with an important source of such personal myths.[13] Furthermore, as one might expect, it also influenced fiction that purports to be the self-history of the narrator. Such autobiographical application of typological symbolism thus appears in straightforward autobiography (Ruskin's *Praeterita*), autobiographical fiction (Carlyle's *Sartor Resartus*), and novels taking the form of fictionalized autobiographies (Brontë's *Jane Eyre* and Kingsley's *Alton Locke*).

In order to explain how biblical typology had such pervasive influence upon Victorian culture, Chapter One will first look at the ways in which the average believer learned to read his Bible in terms of types and shadows of Christ, after which it will examine in detail received Victorian opinion about typology's nature, use, and implications. Chapter Two focuses upon the literary uses of a single type, that of the smitten rock, in order to set forth the various ways Victorian poetry and hymnody used such imagery. Chapter Three extends the investigation of the literary effects of typological symbolism by observing its use in narrative poetry, prose fiction, dramatic monologue, and non-fiction; and Chapter Four examines typology's appearance in the visual arts of the period and attempts to explain some of its different uses in painting, stained glass, sculpture, mosaic, and ecclesiastical metalwork. Chapter Five, which surveys applications of types to politics at home and abroad, shows its orthodox, extended, and secularized forms. Chapter Six uses the example of Rossetti and Hopkins to demonstrate the way in which two major Victorian poets employed structures based upon typology in their work, while the concluding chapter, which examines the Pisgah Sight, investigates a particularly complex combination of typological image and structure. Here again the attempt is to reveal the influence upon Victorian culture of a wide range of uses of a single passage from the Bible.

CHAPTER ONE

TYPOLOGICAL INTERPRETATION IN THE VICTORIAN PERIOD

How the Victorians learned to read the Bible for types and shadows of Christ

To understand the many important ways that typology shaped Victorian ideas, one must determine how the received authorities of the time defined and applied it, and one must also explain how such a seemingly arcane theological matter could have influenced secular thought at all. In particular, one wants to know precisely which points of doctrine and which interpretive rules encouraged so many Victorians to transfer habits of mind derived from interpreting the Bible to theories of evolution, contemporary politics, literary characterization, painterly symbolism, and other areas of thought apparently far distant from theological studies.

But even before attempting this crucial process of definition, one can explain how something so seemingly specialized as typology had such general effect by recognizing that typology formed the reading and interpretive habits of many Victorians. Anyone who has looked at much Victorian art and literary criticism knows that, with few exceptions (such as that provided by Ruskin's reading of 'Lycidas' in *Sesame and Lilies*), one looks in vain for close readings of individual works.[1] The difficulty therefore arises of determining how most Victorians read a book, a picture, or a building. It is not difficult, however, to determine how many Victorians read their Bibles, because sermons, tracts, commentaries, hymns, and guides to scriptural exegesis show how they did so quite clearly and in abundant detail.

All the major Protestant denominations devoted a great deal of time and effort to teaching the individual believer how to read the scriptures. Both the various parties in the Church of England and the dissenting groups outside this established church made large use of sermons in educating worshippers in the subtle points of scriptural interpretation. Two sermons were the rule each Sunday – one in the morning and one in the afternoon – and during the reign of Victoria, which seems to have been a golden age of preaching, people would often travel long distances to hear famous ministers. Although that rivalry between Church and Dissent which characterizes Amos Barton's Shepperton certainly existed in many areas, members of one denomination would still attend services of some other group if that other group's minister had acquired a reputation as a preacher. In the 1850s and 1860s, for instance, a Londoner might attend the morning service of Henry Melvill (1798–1871), the Evangelical Anglican whom many, including Ruskin, Browning, and Gladstone, considered the greatest preacher of his day. After taking part in a service at which this Chaplain to the Queen had preached, our Londoner might either return home until it was time for the afternoon service or else head for the Metropolitan Tabernacle, where he would be one of 5,000 people assembled to hear the self-educated Baptist, Charles Haddon Spurgeon (1834–92), the most famous preacher of the age, who had already established his reputation in his twentieth year.

What kind of a sermon was the average English churchgoer likely to encounter on a Sunday at mid-century? An official government religious census conducted on Sunday, 30 March 1853 showed that in England and Wales fewer than 400,000 attended Roman Catholic services, while 5,300,000 attended those of the Church of England and another 4,500,000 those of the various dissenting sects. Since one out of every fourteen parishes refused to respond to this state inquiry, one can justifiably conclude that the Church of England could claim an even greater number of adherents. Although determining the party affiliation of ministers within the Established Church is particularly difficult, contemporary estimates suggest that far more than half belonged to the Evangelical branch and that the rest were divided among the High Church, Broad Church, and old High-and-Dry groups.[2] Since almost all dissenting groups shared the basic doctrines of Evangelical Anglicanism, more than three-quarters of the congregations assembled on a Sunday in the 1850s and 1860s would have heard some form of Evangelical doctrine. Certainly, one still encountered parsons in the Church of England like George Eliot's Gilfil and Farebrother throughout the century, but in general it had become an age of doctrinal clergy and doctrinal preaching, and the Evangelicals were largely responsible for this change.

The Evangelicals within the Church, who conceived of themselves as the proper heirs of the Reformation and seventeenth-century Puritan divines, placed relatively little importance upon either ecclesiastical tradition or hierarchy. Instead, their version of Protestantism emphasized that the individual, who must strive for an emotional conversion, had to attain an emotional, imaginative experience of Christ. In practice, such an experience required that the believer recognize his own innate depravity and then both project himself imaginatively into his Saviour's agonies and feel their saving effect upon himself. As John Charles Ryle, the great Evangelical Anglican writer of tracts, urged:

> You may know a good deal about Christ, by a kind of head knowledge. You may know who He was, and where He was born, and what He did. You may know His miracles, His sayings, His prophecies, and His ordinances. You may know how he lived, and how He suffered, and how He died. But unless you know the power of Christ's Cross by experience – unless you know and feel within that the blood shed on that cross has washed away your own particular sins, – unless you are willing to confess that your salvation depends entirely on the work that Christ did upon the Cross, – unless this be the case, Christ will profit you nothing . . . . You must know His Cross, and His Blood, or else you will die in your sins.[3]

The Evangelicals, who were convinced of man's essential depravity, practiced a strict morality and placed great importance upon rigid Sabbath observance. Although they believed that good works could not save a person from Hell, they accepted that their performance was both a Christian duty and a sign that one had been converted. Their central emphasis upon preaching the Gospel, which produced so many great Evangelical writers of sermons and tracts, also prompted their organization of missionary endeavors and Bible societies. The members of this church party often cooperated with dissenters in sponsoring such missionary activities, and they were therefore often accused of being 'Methodists in the Church'. Since they wished to raise the moral condition and tone of England by making vice unfashionable in the upper classes, the Evangelical Anglicans often appeared to curry favor with the rich and powerful, and the practice, which was originated by the great Cambridge Evangelical Charles Simeon (1759–1836), of raising money to purchase benefices held by laymen for worthy Evangelical clergy, struck many in other portions of the Church as savoring too much of worldly practice.

The twentieth-century reader of Victorian novels who has encountered Mr Stiggins of *Pickwick Papers* and the odious Mr Slope

17

of *Barchester Towers* might well wonder how Evangelicals within and without the Church of England ever attracted such a large number of devoted adherents. Certainly, after reading the novels of Dickens, Trollope, Kingsley, and many lesser figures, we would be tempted to assume that all Evangelical clergymen had oily, florid complexions, damp handshakes, and portly stomachs waiting to be filled with tea-cakes. Furthermore, these unappealing creatures, who seem to have made their way through this life by preying upon emotional females, expended most of their energies upon the rigors of Sabbath observance.[4] When they did bestir themselves on the behalf of others, their benevolence (if we can believe the novelists) always took the form of sending flannel waistcoats to the inhabitants of tropical Africa and Bibles to the starving victims of flood and famine.

The often self-righteous Evangelicals, who advocated zeal and earnestness in promoting the Gospel, were easy to mock, and, in fact, they welcomed such mockery as a sign that infidels persecuted them for serving Christ. Furthermore, since the stricter Evangelicals looked upon novels as the devil's invention, practitioners of this literary form had yet another reason for directing their satire at these heirs of the Puritan tradition. None the less, Evangelicals dominated British religion from the last decade of the eighteenth century through the 1860s and beyond; for even though the Tractarian-led High Church revival of the 1830s and 1840s and the later Broad Church movement gradually rivaled this party in the Church, most English men and women, as well as those in Scotland and Wales, remained Evangelicals. The Evangelical Anglicans and related groups, such as the Baptists, Methodists, and Presbyterians, first gained and then long kept their leading position in British life because they brought vital heartfelt religion to the nation. Although the severity and puritanic zeal of the Evangelicals were easy to mock, many who came to jeer at Wesley, Whitefield, Newton, Simeon, and other great preachers found themselves deeply moved.[5] At a time when the Established Church had seemingly lost all sense of its mission, the late eighteenth-century Evangelical revival brought spiritual sustenance to people high and low. The Evangelical emphasis upon an imaginative and emotional experience of Christ, which made this form of Protestantism a religious equivalent (and stimulus) of English romanticism, made belief a living factor in men's lives. Although we are used to considering Evangelical puritanism a dour, inhumanely restrictive force on English life, the fact is, rather, that it provided an emotional, imaginative form of belief that endowed its adherents with a sense of their own identities.

In contrast, High Anglicanism – which is also known as Puseyism, Newmanism, and Tractarianism – opposed Evangelical emotional religion and its emphasis upon the experiences of the individual lay believer with an emphasis upon reserve, and it derived this notion of reserve from what its adherents took to be a central principle of God's dealings with man. As Isaac Williams argued on the opening page of Tract 80, *On Reserve in Communicating Religious Knowledge* (1837):

> There appears in God's manifestations of Himself to mankind, in conjunction with an exceeding desire to communicate that knowledge, a tendency to conceal, and throw a veil over it, as if it were injurious to us, unless we were of a certain disposition to receive it.

Similarly, looking at the early Church's practice of concealing points of doctrine from the uninitiate so that they would not sully them, Williams and the other Tractarians found ample precedent for emphasizing the higher spiritual status of the ordained clergy. In opposition to the Evangelicals, who placed comparatively little importance on sacraments or ecclesiastical hierarchy, the High Church found the essence of Christianity to lie in an ordained priesthood that descended in an unbroken succession from the Apostles to the present. Their emphasis upon Church tradition also prompted them to revive both ritual and elaborate ecclesiastical decoration. Whereas the Evangelicals, who often worshipped in relatively bare, unadorned churches, provided the believer with emotional and aesthetic satisfaction in the form of preaching and hymns, the High Anglicans, who rejected hymns and emotional sermons, provided their congregations with the aesthetic pleasures of ritual and rich surroundings. Without too much exaggeration, one might claim that the Evangelicals sought the pleasures of the ear and the High Anglicans those of the eye.[6]

Although High and Low Churchmen disagreed about major points of doctrine, we must be careful not to exaggerate their differences. Both parties handled the Bible in very similar ways, and, indeed, when an individual preacher is not specifically concerning himself to advocate a particular doctrine, such as a need for conversion or the Apostolic succession, he usually sounds like proponents of the other side.[7] The elaborate typological interpretations of Newman and Keble, for instance, strongly resemble those of Melvill. Of course, one reason why Tractarians had much in common with the Evangelical wing of the Church (and with dissenters outside of it) is that many High Churchmen had at one time been Evangelicals. Once they became adherents of the High Church party, they rarely abandoned all their former attitudes and habits of mind.[8]

In contrast to the other two factions in the Established Church, the liberal one known as the Broad Church movement willingly trusted to reason in matters of faith. These followers of Coleridge included Thomas Arnold, Henry Hart Milman, F. W. Robertson, F. D. Maurice, and Charles Kingsley. The members of this comparatively small and loosely organized section of the Church of England emphasized the humanity of Jesus, and, unlike the other Church and dissenting groups, they accepted that the Bible was divinely inspired only in some rather free and figurative manner. In fact, if any one procedure characterizes these progressive theologians it is the reinterpretation of traditional Christianity, its doctrines, and terminology in very personal ways. In essence, they tried to preserve Christianity against the increasing onslaught of modern ideas, particularly those from the continent, by abandoning points of belief easily disproved on rational grounds and replacing them with mythic or symbolic interpretations of the Bible. Although Broad Church attitudes towards the scriptures inevitably undercut typological exegesis, which is based on the axiom that the Bible is literally true, many Broad Churchmen still continued to use extended versions of typology because both they and their audiences had become accustomed to it. This section of the Established Church has justifiably received a considerable amount of attention from literary scholars, both because it prefigured important developments in English Christianity and because many of its adherents were literary figures. None the less, these progressive theologians and preachers, who were relatively few in number, had very little influence on the average English believer at mid-century and for long afterwards.

To answer our first question, then, the average worshipper would be most likely to attend some sort of an Evangelical service, and the reputation of a particular minister as a preacher might well guide him or her to choose which service to attend. If one was ill, attended another service, lived too far from London or other large cities, or was temporarily away from home, one could read the sermons of famous preachers in the pages of *The Homilist*, *The Pulpit*, and *The Penny Pulpit* – weekly periodicals that published sermons of renowned preachers and thereby extended their influence not only throughout all England but throughout the English-speaking world.[9]

Upon returning home, our devout Victorian would be likely to read selections from a wide choice of religious writings. Members of strict Evangelical households, in which all light reading and secular entertainment was forbidden on Sunday, might devote themselves to studying the Bible, published sermons, religious periodicals, and well-established devotional works of former times, such as Bunyan's *Pilgrim's Progress* and Milton's *Paradise Lost*. Picking up the family Bible, our Victorian religionist, if an Evangelical, would very likely encounter the detailed annotation of famed Evangelical scriptural commentator Thomas Scott (1747–1821), whose commentaries first appeared in weekly parts in the 1790s, after which they were gathered in volume form and later printed with the scriptures themselves. The individual might read the Bible and relevant commentary aloud to the entire family, meditate upon them himself, or even take extensive notes upon them, as Ruskin's Evangelical mother required him to do from the age of nine.

Others who wished to go beyond these substantial commentaries in their search for Christ in the Old Testament might turn to one of many commentaries on individual books, such as Revelation or Psalms. If one sympathized with the Hutchinsonians – followers of John Hutchinson (1674–1737) who characterized themselves by elaborate, often wildly far-fetched typological and allegorical readings of the Bible – the believer might pick up Samuel Eyles Pierce's *The Book of Psalms, an Epitome of the Old Testament Scripture, Opened. In which the Plan of Each Psalm is Given, the Subject-Matter Expressly Stated, and the Whole Set forth as Prophetic of Christ, and His*

Church (1817). The more orthodox, on the other hand, might turn to the Anglican John Morison's three-volume guide, whose title makes clear that it was directed at the layman: *An Exposition of the Book of Psalms, Explanatory, Critical, and Devotional. Intended Chiefly to Aid Private Christians in the Enlightened Perusal of Compositions, in which the National History of the Jews, and the Personal Experience of David, are often blended with the Spirit of Prophecy* (1832). Later in the century those of any denomination might have consulted the Baptist Charles Haddon Spurgeon's *The Treasury of David* (1870), whose three volumes contain an anthology of several hundred years' comments on individual psalms.

In many dissenting, Evangelical, and High Church families, fathers would often read a printed sermon and a Bible passage to the assembled family and servants, both on Sundays and on weekdays before the household retired for the evening. Throughout the week many English men and women also read devotional poetry, which could range in quality from Tennyson's *In Memoriam* (1850), the Evangelical Edward Henry Bickersteth's visionary epic, *Yesterday, To-day, and For Ever* (1866), and the Tractarian Keble's *The Christian Year* (1827) to efforts of Frances Ridley Havergall and Charlotte Elizabeth Tonna. Many such poems made heavy use of biblical types, paraphrase, and allusion, thus providing yet another means of inculcating habits of Bible reading.

Types: historical, legal, and prophetical

A type is an anticipation of Christ. Thus, Samson, who sacrificed his life for God's people, partially anticipates Christ, who repeats the action, endowing it with a deeper, more complete, more spiritual significance. Similarly, the scapegoat and the animals sacrificed in the Temple at Jerusalem, both of which atoned for man's sins, and Aaron, God's priest, are types. As Thomas Hartwell Horne explains in *An Introduction to the Critical Study and Knowledge of the Holy Scriptures*, the text which was standard reading for British divinity students:

A type, in its primary and literal meaning, simply denotes a rough draught, or less accurate model, from which a more perfect image is made; but, in the sacred or theological sense of the term, a type may be defined to be a symbol of something future and distant, or an example prepared and evidently designed by God to prefigure that future thing. What is thus prefigured is called the *antitype*.

Horne further explains that the Bible contains three kinds of types: the historical, the legal, and the prophetical.

Historical types, such as those provided by Moses, Samson, David, and Melchizedek, 'are the characters, actions, and fortunes of some eminent persons recorded in the Old Testament, so ordered by Divine Providence as to be exact prefigurations of the characters, actions, and fortunes of future persons who should arise under the Gospel dispensation' (2.529). For example, as Newman explains in 'Moses the Type of Christ', this first great prophet of the Jews prefigured Christ as redeemer, prophet, and intercessor for guilty man.

Newman begins this sermon by asserting that 'The history of Moses is valuable to Christians, not only as giving us a pattern of fidelity towards God, of great firmness, and great meekness, but also as affording us a type or figure of our Saviour Christ'. He next emphasizes the authority and authenticity of Moses' status as a type by pointing out that 'no prophet arose in Israel like Moses, till Christ came, when the promise in the text was fulfilled. "The Lord thy God," says Moses, "shall raise unto thee a Prophet like unto me:" that was Christ' (*Sermons*, 7.118). Then, having thus identified and authenticated a divinely instituted parallel, Newman proceeds to examine 'in what respects Moses resembled Christ' (*Sermons*, 7.118). First, however, he makes the commonplace assertion, which was accepted by all typologists, that the history of the Jews recorded in the Old Testament was intended to serve as an anticipatory image of later eras, so 'if we survey the general history of the Israelites, we shall find that it is a picture of man's history, as the dispensation of the Gospel displays it to us, and that in it Moses takes the place of Christ' (*Sermons*, 7.118). To begin with, Moses prefigures Christ the redeemer, for he rescued the Israelites, the particular children of God, from Egyptian slavery and led them to the promised land. Newman says:

How clearly this prefigures to us the condition of the Christian

Church! We are by nature in a strange country; God was our first Father, and His Presence our dwelling-place: but we were cast out of Paradise for sinning, and are in a dreary land, a valley of darkness and the shadow of death. We are born in this spiritual Egypt, the land of strangers . . . [and] by nature slaves we are, slaves to the Devil. He is our hard task-master, as Pharaoh oppressed the Israelites. (*Sermons*, 7.119)

Fortunately for the Israelites, God sent Moses, armed with His power, to lead them forth from slavery. 'And who is it that has done this for us Christians? Who but the Eternal Son of God, our Lord and Saviour, whose name in consequence we bear' (*Sermons*, 7.120). Christ leads us out of the slavery of sin, guides us through apparently unsurmountable difficulties, and, at last, brings us to the true Promised Land. 'Christ, then, is a second Moses, and greater than he, inasmuch as Christ leads from hell to heaven, as Moses led the Israelites from Egypt to Canaan' (*Sermons*, 7.121–2).

The second function of Moses as a type is to prefigure Christ as prophet and giver of the New Law of grace. 'Christ reveals to us the will of God, as Moses to the Israelites. He is our Prophet, as well as our Redeemer' (*Sermons*, 7.122). As Newman points out, no other Old Testament prophet 'was so favoured as Moses', since 'before Christ came, Moses alone saw God face to face; all prophets after him but heard His voice or saw Him in vision' (*Sermons*, 7.122). Moses returned from the mount with the Ten Commandments and the Levitical law of sacrifices by which men could make atonement for breaking them; Christ, who incomparably surpasses His type, brings the New Law of salvation.

The 'third point of resemblance between Moses and Christ' was that both interceded on behalf of their people in order to save them from a deserved punishment for sinning. 'Moses was the great intercessor when the Israelites sinned' (*Sermons*, 7.127), for after the Jews had corrupted themselves with worshipping idols while Moses was on the mount receiving the tablets of the law, God would have cut them off from the Promised Land had not Moses interposed himself. Moses first begged God to delay His punishment and he then told his wayward people, 'Ye have sinned a great sin; but now I will go unto the Lord; peradventure I shall make an atonement for your sin' (Exodus 32:30). According to Newman, 'Here Moses, as is obvious, shadows out the true Mediator between God and man, who is ever at the right hand of God making intercession for us; but the parallel is closer still than appears at first sight' (*Sermons*, 7.128), since when Moses interceded on behalf of the Jews, he offered to sacrifice his own portion of blessedness in order to save theirs. 'The exchange was accepted. He was excluded, dying in sight, not in enjoyment of Canaan, while the people went in under Joshua. This was a figure of Him that was to come' (*Sermons*, 7.128).

Having thus emphasized that the historical Moses closely pre-figures Christ as redeemer, prophet, and intercessor, Newman next proceeds to show how far short Moses none the less falls of his divine antitype. Since the purpose of typological exegesis of the Bible was always in part to demonstrate the way all sacred history centers upon Christ, the interpreter necessarily pointed out the many ways in which some person or thing in the Old Testament anticipated Christ or His Church. But once the interpreter had demonstrated that God had graciously provided anticipations of Christ in His dealings with those who lived in Old Testament times, he frequently went on to emphasize the essential incompleteness of such types and their essential inadequacy to save man. Newman, for example, points out that Moses 'was not taken instead of Israel, except in figure' (*Sermons*, 7.129), and that, in spite of the prophet's willingness to sacrifice himself, the sinners died of the plague and only their children entered Canaan. In other words, the historical Moses was adequate as a means of suggesting man's universal need for intercession, but he was inadequate as an intercessor: Moses, who possessed his own historical reality, can function only as a symbol of Christ; he cannot be the reality of Christ.

Furthermore, argues Newman, Moses, whose nature falls far below that of Christ, actually 'suffered for his own sins' and not for the sins of his people. 'True, he was shut out from Canaan. But why? Not in spite of his having "done nothing amiss," as the Divine Sufferer on the cross' (*Sermons*, 7.129), but because he disobeyed God's instructions during the desert wanderings and struck the rock a second time. It is important for the Christian to perceive 'how apparently slight a fault it was for which Moses suffered; for this shows us the infinite difference between the best of a sinful race and Him who was sinless, – the least taint of human corruption having in it an unspeakable evil' (*Sermons*, 7.129). In other words, the history of Moses can lead the Christian to his saviour in two ways: first, perceiving the significant resemblances of Moses to Christ enables the believer to see the essential human need for a redeemer, lawgiver, and intercessor; second, perceiving the differences between type and antitype enables him to see how much greater Christ is than Moses. Essentially Moses, like all other types, functions as an elaborate trope that permits man to begin to understand something otherwise too great for his comprehension by first providing a historical analogy to make that truth accessible and then emphasizing that the true reality vastly surpasses its historical image.

The second major branch of prefigurative symbolism is that provided by what Horne calls the '*Legal types*, or those contained in the Mosaic law' (2.528) of ritual observance. According to Horne, who offers the standard explanation of these legal types, the entire ritual law 'was typical of the Messiah and the Gospel blessings . . . and this point has been . . . clearly established by the great apostle of the Gentiles in his Epistle to the Hebrews' (2.528). All interpreters of the Bible therefore follow St Paul in holding that the legal types prefigured Christ by conveying the fundamental idea that only the sacrifice of innocent blood could atone for man's sinning against God.

> Thus, the entire constitution, and offerings of the Levitical priesthood, typically prefigured Christ the great high priest (Heb. v. vii. viii.); and especially the ceremonies observed on the great day of atonement. (Lev. xvi. with Heb. ix. throughout, and x. 1–22.) So, the passover and the paschal lamb typified the sacrifice of Jesus Christ (Exod. xii. 3 *et seq.* with John xix. 36 and 1 Cor. v. 7). (2.528)

These legal types (which were also known as ritual, ceremonial, and Levitical types) provided a particularly popular occasion for the exercise of this form of scriptural interpretaion. At first glance, the Book of Leviticus, which contains detailed instructions for rituals which even the Jews had not practiced for almost two millennia, hardly seemed relevant to Christians. Typology, however, demonstrated that these arcane rituals of an alien religion in fact contain continual glimpses of Christian truth, and in so doing it also demonstrated that the eye of faith could transform even the most apparently barren ground into fields lush with gospel flowers.

But since scriptural interpretation always implicitly follows the rule 'Seek and ye shall find', each Church party caught sight of its own gospel flower. For example, the Evangelicals within and without the Church of England, who stressed the primacy of Christ's atonement, urged that the believer meditate upon this central event in human history until it came imaginatively alive and the believer attained an 'experimental' knowledge of Christ; by imaginatively experiencing Christ's sufferings, one could move toward a heartfelt conversion and then intensify one's faith. Evangelical Anglicans, Methodists, Baptists, and Presbyterians thus read the Levitical types as divinely intended prefigurations of Christ's passion and death. According to the extraordinarily popular Bible commentary of Thomas Scott, the burnt-offerings mentioned in Leviticus 1:3 'especially typified Christ, in the intenseness of his sufferings, both of body and soul, when he gave himself a sacrifice for our sins . . . and they likewise shewed forth the perfection of zeal and love, with which he voluntarily went through his inexpressible sufferings'. One may remark in passing that precisely such an Evangelical conception of the Levitical types informs William Holman Hunt's *The Scapegoat* (1856), which stands as a powerful meditative image of suffering innocence.

In contrast to the Evangelicals who placed their chief emphasis upon the individual believer's personal relation to Christ and thereby downgraded the Church as an institution, members of the High Church party stressed the centrality of the sacraments and the Church hierarchy. Consequently, Keble, Newman, and their followers interpreted the legal types as prefiguring both the priesthood and the sacrament of Holy Communion which it administers. For example, in 'The Gospel Feast', Newman explains how the legal types provide part of a chain or series of types reaching from patriarchal times into Christ's life to prefigure Holy Communion.

> Not in the miracle of the loaves only, though in that especially, but in all parts of Scripture, in history, and in precept, and in promise, and in prophecy, is it given to see the Gospel Feast typified and prefigured, and that immortal and never-failing Supper in the

visible presence of the Lamb which will follow upon it at the end. (*Sermons*, 7.162)

According to Newman, then, the ceremonial types of the Passover ritual, animal sacrifice, and first-fruits – like the historical types of manna and Melchizedek's bread and wine – all prefigure 'that banquet which is to last for ever and ever' (*Sermons*, 8.178).

John Keble's 'Our Sacrifice of Praise and Thanksgiving' similarly shows how a chain of linked types leads to fulfillment in the sacrament of Communion. Using a slightly different set of types from Newman's, Keble traces this gospel antitype of sacrifice through its various prefigurations in the firstlings of Abel's flock, the encounter of Abram and Melchizedek, and the sacrifices of Noah, Abraham, Isaac, and Jacob. He then shows how the Levitical burnt-, free-will-, and sin-offerings, which were in part sacrifices of praise, were types of Holy Communion. Rightly understood, these three types show the Christian that his Church, like that of Moses, has its means of commemoration and praise. Indeed, since the believers under the Old Covenant had such opportunity, the Christian must also have 'sacrifice of praise and thanksgiving: and what was that Sacrifice? Chiefly, and before all else, it was the Holy Eucharist, the Bread and Wine first, and then the Lord's Body and Blood, offered up on the Christian altar by the priest in the Name of Jesus Christ, for this among other great purposes: that it may be a solemn and perfect acknowledgment of the Great God, and what He has done for us' (*Sermons*, 2.343).

In 'The Priesthood of all Christians, and the Sacrifices they should offer', Keble provides an example of the second High Church interpretation of the ceremonial types, which is as prefiguring Christ-the-priest. According to him, Christ 'is the only true Priest, of Whom all other priests, whatsoever their time and order, whether they followed Aaron or Melchizedek, whether they came before or after their Lord, are nothing more than shadows and types. He is a High Priest for ever, and therefore His people and members, in their measure and degree, are priests also' (*Sermons*, 2.319). Since each Christian is a priest, he must, concludes Keble, have something to sacrifice to the Lord, just as had priests of the Old Law. But since 'we are spiritual, i.e. Christian priests, we must bring spiritual, i.e., Christian Sacrifices: not carnal sacrifices, such as were those of the

Jews, appointed for a time, as figures and shadows, until Christ the True Sacrifice should come: but spiritual, Christian, Gospel-Sacrifices: such as these we must have, every one of us, Spiritual, Christian, Gospel, priests' (*Sermons*, 2.320). This High Church-man's emphasis upon the priesthood of every believer, like his heated rhetoric, makes him sound much like an Evangelical. For example, he seems to be making exactly the same point as does Ruskin, writing during his early Evangelical phase, when the author of *Modern Painters* argued that no Christian priesthood exists separate from that composed of all believers. According to Ruskin:

> the whole function of Priesthood was, on Christmas morning, at once and for ever gathered into His Person who was born at Bethlehem; and thenceforward, all who are united with Him, and who with Him make sacrifices of themselves; that is to say, all members of the Invisible Church become, at the instant of their conversion, Priests; and are so called in 1 Peter ii. 5, and Rev. i. 6, and xx. 6, where, observe, there is no possibility of limiting the expression to the Clergy, the conditions of Priesthood being simply having been loved by Christ, and washed in His blood. ('Notes on the Construction of Sheepfolds', 1851; 12.537)

Having possibly suggested that he holds an extreme Protestant position which necessarily downgrades the Church hierarchy, Keble wastes no time in reassuring his High Anglican congregation that he means nothing of the sort. In fact, he begins his explanation by wondering how St Peter could have affirmed that all Christians constitute a priesthood 'seeing that there are priests according to our Lord's own law, to whom, through His Apostles, He said, Do this – offer the Holy Communion, "in remembrance of Me" ' (*Sermons*, 2.320). He quickly resolves this problem by pointing out that just as the ancient Jews were all 'so far priests to the God of Israel, yet this hindered not but that Aaron's sons had a special commission: so it remains true that the Apostles of our Lord and those who act by authority from them are the only Priests by office in the Church of Christ, yet is each Christian in some sense appointed to somewhat of a priestly work' (*Sermons*, 2.321). As Keble next explains, each Christian turns out to perform 'somewhat of a priestly work' only in so far as he or she receives the sacrament of Communion from a true

Priest, or, as Keble puts it, 'there is no doubt that the chief thing, in which Christian people shew themselves priests, is devoutly joining in the Sacrifice of our Lord's Body and Blood in the Holy Eucharist' (*Sermons*, 2.322).

Granted, Keble had to resolve problems created by a long tradition of contradictory texts, but his use of 'in some sense' and 'somewhat of a priestly work' encourages one to sympathize with Ruskin's attacks on the High Church party's 'bold refusals to read plain English' and 'its elaborate adjustments of tight bandages over the eyes, as wholesome preparation for a walk among tracks and pitfalls'. Interestingly enough, when attacking 'Puseyism', Ruskin singles out for condemnation Keble's attempt in an anonymously published poem to defend his conception of Christian priesthood by referring to sacrifices of the Old Law. Ruskin savagely attacks 'that dangerous compound of halting poetry with hollow Divinity, called the *Lyra Apostolica*', and scornfully rejects Keble's 'suggested parallel between the Christian and Levitical Churches' in his poem 'Korah, Dathan, and Abiram'.[10] On Keble's threat that there are 'Judgment Fires, For high-voiced Korahs in their day', this 'high-voiced' Evangelical comments, 'There are indeed such fires. But when Moses said, "a Prophet shall the Lord raise up unto you, like unto me," did he mean the writer who signs himself in the *Lyra Apostolica*? The office of the Lawgiver and Priest is now for ever gathered into One Mediator between God and man; and THEY are guilty of the sin of Korah who blasphemously would associate themselves in His Mediatorship.' Making the usual Low Church point that High Churchmen tried to arrogate Christ's office to themselves, Ruskin thus dismisses Keble's position – and his reading of the legal types as well.

In contrast to the way in which both Evangelicals and High Anglicans read the legal types as precise prefigurations of identifiable events and rituals, Broad Churchmen, who rarely employed orthodox typology, found these types to be general symbols of basic religious ideas. Thus, F. W. Robertson (1816–53), the popular workingman's preacher at Trinity Chapel, Brighton, from 1847 until his death, argued that the 'Jewish sacrifices' had their origin in a combination of 'two feelings: one human, one divine or inspired'. The true feeling, says Robertson, is that we must surrender something to God, whereas the human, more primitive, feeling adds to it the mistaken notion that 'this sacrifice pleases God because of the loss or pain which it inflicts'. The 'ancient spiritually-minded Jews', such as David, had an

> accurate and even Christian perception of the real meaning of sacrifice. . . . Men like David felt what lay beneath all sacrifice as its ground and meaning was surrender to God's will – that a man's best is himself – and to sacrifice this is the true sacrifice. By degrees they came to see that the sacrifice was but a form – typical; and that it might be superseded.

The sacrifice of Christ, which superseded the Levitical sacrifices, 'satisfied' God, not because 'it was pain, but . . . because for the first time He saw human nature a copy of the Divine nature – the will of Man the Son perfectly coincident with the will of God the Father.'[11] Robertson interprets something in the Old Testament convention-ally taken to be a type, he uses the vocabulary of typological exegesis, and he clearly accepts the theory of progressive revelation which is implicit in typology. None the less, when Robertson writes 'typical', he means 'symbolical' and not 'typological'. He examines these ancient Jewish ceremonies only to show the presence in them of universal spiritual principles, and he does not discover them to be divinely instituted signs of specific events or things. Like many Broad Churchmen, he employs terms figuratively that many among his listeners usually understand literally, and he does so for a variety of reasons: his audience expects to hear discussions of Christianity in such terms and will listen more sympathetically when it does; his audience – particularly the more orthodox – will believe he is more traditional than he in fact is; and his audience by these means can gradually be led to perceive the true 'spiritualized' meaning of older words and ideas. Robertson, in other words, grows out of the long tradition of typological interpretation, but he is no typologist.

The third branch of typology is composed of the 'PROPHET-ICAL TYPES [which] are those, by which the divinely inspired prophets prefigured or signified things either present or future, by means of external symbols. Of this description is the prophet Isaiah's going naked (that is, without his prophetic garment) and barefoot (Isa. xx. 2.), to prefigure the fatal destruction of the Egyptians and Ethiopians'. Perhaps the most important of all prophetic types was that which appears in Genesis 3:15 when God tells the serpent, 'And I will put enmity between thee and the woman, and between thy seed and her seed; it shall bruise thy head, and thou shall bruise his heel'. As Henry Melvill, the great Evangelical Anglican preacher, points out in his sermon 'The First Prophecy', God's words in Eden provide man with a summation of human history; and

> Whether or no the prophecy were intelligible to Adam and Eve, unto ourselves it is a wonderful passage, spreading itself over the whole of time, and giving outlines of the history of this world from the beginning to the final consummation. It is nothing less than a delineation of an unwearied conflict of which this earth shall be the theatre, and which shall issue, though not without partial disaster to man, in the complete discomfiture of Satan and his associates.[12]

Other, non-Evangelical preachers agree that this first prophetic type shadows forth a fundamental battle of good and evil, thus providing believers with a view of the central law of human history. F. W. Robertson, the Broad Churchman, agrees that 'it is the law which governs the conflict with evil. It can only be crushed by suffering from it. . . . The Son of man who puts His naked foot on the serpent's head, crushes it: the fang goes into His heel'.[13]

In addition to shadowing forth an essential principle of human life in this world, this type also announces coming salvation and the means by which it will be purchased. Since the final clause of God's pronouncement, that the serpent shall bruise the heel of the woman's seed, was conventionally taken to prefigure the Crucifixion, this first prophecy was commonly understood to contain the entire so-called 'Gospel scheme' for man's redemption. As John Charles Ryle, the Evangelical Bishop of Liverpool, argued in one of his many tracts, 'one golden chain runs through' the entire Bible:

> no salvation excepting by Jesus Christ. The bruising of the serpent's head, foretold in the day of the fall, – the clothing of our first parents with skins, – the sacrifices of Noah, Abraham, Isaac, and Jacob, – the passover, and all the particulars of the Jewish law, – the high-priest, – the altar, – the daily offering of the lamb, – the

holy of holies entered only by blood, – the scapegoat . . . all preach with one voice, salvation only by Jesus Christ.[14]

Similarly, the High Anglican Keble combines historical and prophetic types when he urges upon his listeners that Christ, 'the true Seed of the woman, God the Son, . . . would, in His own good time, bruise the head of the tempting and corrupting serpent. He, the true David, would cast down the true Goliath, would take from him all his armour wherein he trusted' ('The Deadly Peace of the Unawakened Conscience', *Sermons*, 3.195). In one of his *Short Sermons for Family Reading*, John William Burgon, Fellow of Oriel and Vicar of what had been Newman's church, makes the same point as does Keble when he holds that 'our Saviour therefore slew Satan with his own weapon; – by tasting of Death destroyed the author of Death; – even by dying, bruised, if he did not cut off, the Tempter's head. . . Yes, you are requested to note the prominence given to what befel *the head* of the giant [Goliath]. . . . for indeed it is full of Gospel meaning. . . . What does all this signify but that the true David should hereafter "bruise the serpent's *head*", and then ascend on high, leading captivity captive.'[15] The way in which both High and Low Churchmen link this prophetic type with other prefigurations of Christ reveals that for them it points directly to His presence at the center of human history.

Furthermore, as all Church parties agree, this type also speaks directly to the individual believer. Melvill makes this usual point in 'The First Prophecy' when he holds that 'according to the fair laws of interpretation . . . the prophecy must be fulfilled in more than one individual', and while the seed of the woman is chiefly Christ Himself, this prophetical type necessarily has additional antitypes or fulfillments. Taking Eve as a type of the Church, Melvill points out that this divine institution may be considered from 'three points of view' – 'first, as represented by the head, which is Christ; secondly, collectively as a body; thirdly, as resolved into its separate members'.[16] In setting forth the many ways the individual believer can become an *imitatio Christi* by suffering in the battle against Satan, Victorian preachers pointed to those party doctrines they wished to enforce. Thus, Keble, who advocates fasting as a High Church practice, argues that Adam and Eve 'sinned by eating, He [Christ]

33

overcame sin by fasting, – They began to yield to the serpent by longing after the forbidden tree, He began to bruise the serpent's head by abstaining from food itself lawful and innocent' ('On Fasting', *Sermons*, 3.46). Hence the true believer must continue the bruising by appropriate fasting. Charles Clayton, the Cambridge Evangelical, makes a point characteristic of his party, which urged the major importance of preaching the Gospel, when he claimed that 'This word, "testifying" of "the blood" of Jesus, is now preached everywhere, fully and constantly; and wherever this is done, believers find Satan bruised beneath their feet'.[17] In contrast to these precise fulfillments in party doctrine, the Broad Churchman Robertson, we recall, finds instead a general rule of life – namely, that one must suffer in contending with evil, for only in that way can it be conquered.

Images with the stamp of God

According to Thomas Hartwell Horne's standard definition in *An Introduction to the Critical Study and Knowledge of the Holy Scriptures*, one 'requisite to constitute a type is, THAT IT BE PREPARED AND DESIGNED BY GOD TO REPRESENT ITS ANTITYPE' (2.527). Furthermore, as Patrick Fairbairn, the great Victorian student of typology, points out, this divine origin of 'the relation between type and antitype' implies important things about man, God, and the Bible.

> It implies, first, that the realities of the Gospel, which constitute the antitypes, are the ultimate objects which were contemplated by the mind of God, when planning the economy of His successive dispensations. And it implies, secondly, that to prepare the way for the introduction of these ultimate objects, He placed the Church under a course of training, which included instruction by types, or designed and fitting resemblances of what was to come. (1.47)

The Christian is intended to receive these divinely ordained symbols as even more than a peculiarly adequate means of communicating spiritual truths. Indeed, the very existence of such types – the fact that God condescended to create them for man's benefit – tells us much about the relationship between man and his maker.

For example, the types that prepared human beings for the eventual reception of the Gospel accommodated spiritual truths to fallen men, to beings still existing in a relatively primitive spiritual state. Fairbairn explains that since 'the same great element of truth must of necessity pervade both type and antitype, we must also assuredly believe that in the former they were more simply and palpably exhibited – presented in some shape in which the human mind could more easily and distinctly apprehend them – than in the latter. . . . The transition from the one to the other must clearly have involved a rise in the mode of exhibiting the truth from a lower to a higher territory' (1.51). From this conception of typology as progressive revelation derive important interpretive rules. First of all, types generally exist as physical or material embodiments of spiritual ideas. As Fairbairn explains, whereas the type communicates 'divine truth on a lower stage, exhibited by means of outward relations and terrestrial interests', the antitype presents a loftier stage or form of the same truth, one which possesses 'a more heavenly aspect. What in the one bore immediate respect to the bodily life, must in the other be found to bear immediate respect to the spiritual life' (1.158).

For instance, when Moses acts as a type of Christ by redeeming the Israelites from Egyptian slavery, leading them through their desert wanderings, and preparing them to enter the Promised Land, he prefigures with physical acts what Christ does spiritually. Christ spiritually redeems all the children of God from the Egyptian slavery of sin and death; He leads them through the metaphorical desert of this world; and He prepares them to enter the spiritual, or true, Promised Land of Heaven. At each place of correspondence, what had been physical in regard to Moses has become spiritual in regard to his antitype. This notion of a movement from physical to spiritual does not, however, hold for all typological relations, since – to provide an obvious example – Moses is also a type of Christ because he gave man the Old Law. Likewise, when Christ died physically on the cross, he fulfilled a large number of types provided by physical sacrifices. In both cases, none the less, the movement from type to antitype is a movement from something less spiritual to something more spiritual.

Furthermore, since the fulfillment must always be in some sense higher or more spiritual than its type, the interpreter must recognize the inevitable limitations of any particular typological correspondence or relation. Since Christ is greater than all men – indeed greater than all reality – he must far surpass each of his prefigurations. For example, when David conquered Goliath, or Samson laid down his life for his people, or Aaron the priest interceded for the people, they represented only a small portion of the full reality of the Saviour. Not only does the spiritual reality of Christ's action far surpass that contained in each of his almost countless types, but that antitypical spiritual reality requires a wide variety of such types. Using a spatial analogy, one might say that the reality that is Christ is both wider and deeper than any of his types; and, to suggest that surpassing reality, God has thus employed a wide range of prefigurations. From this essential incapacity of the type to suggest the full nature of the antitype arises the standard interpretive procedure of juxtaposing a number of types to each other and to their fulfillment. In that way the interpreter can demonstrate the nature of the antitype more accurately while at the same time showing how wonderfully God prepared for its eventual fulfillment. This exegetical and homiletic habit of juxtaposing numerous types, which makes it easy for the believer to meditate upon the presence of Christ in all history, had a major effect on hymns and devotional verse. It also appears with a particularly High Church flavor in Victorian stained glass programs, eucharistic vessels, and vestments. William Holman Hunt's *The Triumph of the Innocents*, which embodies an Evangelical emphasis, exemplifies the effect of this exegetical practice on Victorian High Art.

This inadequacy of the type to antitype, which produces such heaping up of prefigurations, also required that the reader of scripture follow several obvious hermeneutic rules. First, as Horne explains, the interpreter must recognize that '*There is often more in the Type than in the Antitype*', by which he means that 'we find many things in the type that are inapplicable to the antitype. The use of this cannon is shown in the Epistle to the Hebrews, in which the ritual and sacrifices of the Old Testament are fairly accommodated to Jesus Christ the antitype, although there are many things in that priesthood which do not accord. Thus the priest was to offer sacrifice for his own sins (Heb. v. 3.), which is in no respect applicable to Christ.

(Heb. vii. 27.)' (2.531). Similarly, the exegete must realize that *'Frequently there is more in the Antitype than in the Type'*. The reason for this rule, as we have already observed, lies in the fact that, 'as no single type can express the life and particular actions of Christ, there is necessarily more in the antitype than can be found in the type itself' (2.531).

In attempting to interpret such a divinely created symbol, the reader of scripture must also observe the apparently obvious rule that, as Horne states it, *'The wicked, as such, are NOT to be made Types of Christ'* (2.531). Patrick Fairbairn similarly urges that 'the wicked as such, and acts of sin as such, must be excluded from the category of types', since nothing can be *'typical of the good things under the Gospel which was itself of a forbidden and sinful nature'* (1.140–41). Horne and Fairbairn place such heavy emphasis upon what might seem to be a particularly obvious point as an explicit corrective to the excesses of earlier typologists. Many earlier writers asserted the existence of absurd, even blasphemous correlations between Old Testament people and events and Christ. Among the more infamous – they are frequently cited by nineteenth-century students of typology – are the claims that idolatrous rites introduced into the Temple at Jerusalem prefigured the Gospel, and that when evil Absalom hung by his hair from a tree he prefigured Christ on the cross. Since what Horne calls such *'extravagant typifications'* (2.531n) had done much to discredit biblical typology, its defenders had to show they were not types at all.

None the less, although one must be careful not to take something evil as a type of something good, one can still interpret it as a type, since, as Fairbairn explains, 'it is perfectly warrantable and scriptural to regard the form of evil which from time to time confronted the type, as itself the type of something similar, which should after-wards arise as a counter-form of evil to the antitype. Antichrist, therefore, may be said to have had his types as well as Christ'. It is not that Satan (or Antichrist) governs a scheme of types in a manner parallel to the christological one, but simply that 'all the manifestations of truth have their corresponding and antagonistic manifestations of error' (1.145); so that where one encounters a type of Christ, one may often also encounter something suggesting His great opponent.

In other words, Old Testament history is given a structure by the presence of these divinely instituted types. Furthermore, according to Henry Melvill, the typological significance of a particular fact often explains why God included it in the sacred narrative:

> We are not to regard the Scriptural histories as mere registers of facts, such as are commonly the histories of eminent men: they are rather selections of facts, suitableness for purposes of instruction having regulated the choice. . . . Perhaps more frequently than is commonly thought, it is because the fact has a typical character that it is selected for insertion: it prefigures, or symbolically represents, something connected with the Scheme of Redemption, and on this account has found space in the sacred volume.

Since typology is thus one of the axes or organizing principles of the Bible, one obviously loses sight of a great deal in the scriptures if one fails to perceive the presence of types and figures of Christ. Conversely, if one has 'a correct knowledge and appreciation of the Typology of ancient scripture', claims Fairbairn, one discovers that the earlier portions of revelation receive 'increased value and importance. . . . The whole of the Old Testament will be found to rise in our esteem as we understand and enter into its typological bearing' (1.177). For example, by perceiving how God accommodated His spiritual truths to man's earlier limitations, one can perceive many instances of divine mercy, and, similarly, one can also observe the continual presence of Christ in history and thus understand the meaning of the Old Testament narrative. None the less, although types had the major function of preparing man for the eventual appearance of Christ, that was not their only function. If it were, one would not want to pay too much attention to them, for their function would have ceased and they would now have become mere historical facts. Of course, anything instituted by God could never thus be a mere historical fact, because it will always bear the valued impress of its divine authorship. Thus Fairbairn can argue that types furnish 'materials of edification and comfort to the end of time' (1.49).

From this point of view, which was very popular during the reign of Victoria, one can claim that the types are even more valuable now that they have been fulfilled than they were before. The Christian, unlike the Jew, knows precisely what they mean, and knowing what they mean, the Christian can now understand Old Testament history in the new, higher way. Furthermore, the types, though fulfilled, still contain their earlier epistemological value, and therefore, according to Fairbairn, 'a truly scriptural Typology' provides essential assistance to 'divine knowledge and practice' in 'the *aid it furnishes to help out spiritual ideas in our minds, and enable us to realize them with sufficient clearness and certainty*'. The crucial point here is that although Christians have been privileged by 'a full revelation of the mind of God respecting the truths of salvation . . . it does not thence follow they can in all respects so distinctly apprehend the truth in its naked spirituality, as to be totally independent of some outward exhibition of it' (1.180). In other words, types, which were originally created by God to accommodate truth to man's limited post-lapsarian faculties, still retain their original usefulness.

The one point from which all these hermeneutic emphases derive and to which they always return is that Christ is the central reality of human history. He is the center to which all things move and from which all other things derive their meaning and relative value. This vision of human life and history which perceives Christ as the center of all appears frequently in Victorian writings on typology. Newman, for instance, tells his congregation that 'the Old Testament, as we know, is full of figures and types of the Gospel; types various, and, in their literal wording, contrary to each other, but all meeting and harmoniously fulfilled in Christ and His Church' (8.163). Fairbairn presents essentially the same vision of Christ as divine center when he explains that 'the blessed Redeemer . . . is Himself the beginning and the end of the scheme of God's dispensations; in Him is found alike the centre of Heaven's plan, and the one foundation of human confidence and hope' (1.48). Meditation upon types therefore enabled one to perceive that all the events of Old Testament history form powerful currents sweeping into the future towards the incarnation and sacrifice of Christ, the reign of His Church, and the time – or end of time – when He shall return to make a final judgment on the world. In other words, '*before* His coming into the world', writes Fairbairn, 'all things of necessity pointed toward Him; . . . and *with* His coming, the grand Reality itself came, and the higher purposes of Heaven entered on their fulfillment (1.48). Before Christ, all recorded Old Testament events served as a lens converging upon His appearance; after His death and resurrection, all things simultaneously point backwards towards His earthly life and forwards to His second coming.

According to this conception of things, any single type permits the Christian to observe a complexly ordered cosmos from a privileged position. Having been created in the first place in accordance with the central principle, or core, of history – Christ's conquest of evil by means of His self-sacrifice – the type allows one immediate access to the meaning of the universe. Considered from the point of view of the Bible reader, whether theologian or simple believer, such a conception of things means that any individual type immediately opens into the central meaning of history. Any type, therefore, permits one to meditate upon the whole of God's plan, and any type, furthermore, leads to any other. Considered from the point of view of the writer, whether of hymns or of poems like *The Ring and the Book*, such a powerfully imaginative conception of things means that he may use any type to place the reader in a completely ordered world. Therefore, one of the first things to emphasize about typology for the modern reader is that it is not simply a collection of individual biblical images, the understanding of which helps one better to appreciate Victorian and earlier literatures, arts, and ways of thought. Rather, typology bears with it a powerful, coherent conception of things which any artist, writer, or thinker may conjure into existence by employing a well-known type.

As theorists of the beautiful have emphasized countless times during the past two millennia, beauty depends upon a principle of order. Order, in fact, has often been spoken of as if it were beauty, pure and simple. In any case, typologists clearly took such pleasure, much of it aesthetic, in continually discovering the universal principle of spiritual, moral, and historical order in all things that they often indulged the desire to find Christ in unexpected places to the detriment of the text. Such 'extravagant *typifications*', as Horne termed them, led to the decline of typology's reputation and usefulness, but it also led Patrick Fairbairn to produce *The Typology of Scripture*, probably the finest work written on the subject. Typological exegesis, as we have seen, was so central to nineteenth-century Protestant belief that major theologians, preachers, and commentators tried to formulate sufficient rational canons for its application which would protect it from the obvious abuses of the Hutchinsonians and their seventeenth-century predecessors. Nineteenth-century typologists were so successful that they produced a flowering of typological exegetics which had important influence on Victorian thought.

Even conservative Victorian typologists still ranged more freely than many modern students of the mode would consider permissible, and although the Evangelical denominations outside the Church of England are perhaps best known for abusing typology, High Churchmen, such as Newman and Keble, frequently indulge in the practice of asserting that parallels they have discovered are in fact divinely instituted types. The notion that Christ is to be perceived as the central principle of human history always functioned as a hermeneutic principle as well, for the assumption that Christ is at the center of all things encouraged the Bible reader to find Christ in the most unexpected places. As we have already observed, Victorian interpreters took particular pleasure in pointing out the typological meaning of Leviticus, and the Book of Psalms provided another stimulus for such imaginative interpretations.

As one might expect, the later followers of Hutchinson exemplify such nineteenth-century readings of the Old Testament in terms of Christ at their most extreme. Samuel Eyles Pierce, an avowed follower of 'the learned Mr Hutchinson', quotes his leader's opinion that the Psalms were intended by God to supplement the Gospel record of Christ's life on earth:

> The Psalms contain all the circumstances of our Lord's private employment, on which the Evangelists are silent. His meditation on the law day and night. His firm trust in Jehovah. His fervent prayers, and mournful ejaculations. They refer to all the emblematical institutions, typical sacrifices, deliverances, and persons, and apply them to the gospel state with as much assurance, and with the present tense, as if certainly and already transacted.[18]

Thus, according to the Hutchinsonians, although the Psalms are ostensibly spoken in the historical past of the Old Testament, many of them are in fact the direct pronouncements of Christ speaking

through David. Pierce's Psalm commentaries, for example, hold
that

> Every one of the sacred poems, recorded in this part of Scriptures
> entitled the Book of Psalms, is founded on this revelation of
> Christ, expressed in the representations of the Messiah. In each of
> them we have a new and distinct part of this revelation of Christ
> given us. They are as so many optic glasses, in which we may see
> and behold the similitude of our Lord. (1.181)

When the interpreter emphasizes too much the Christian message
of the Old Testament, he always risks suggesting that the Old
already contained everything of essential value in the New.
Hutchinsonians, like Pierce, often succumb to such risks. This
author of a commentary on the Book of Psalms thus claims that the
scriptures of the Old Testament saints

> were as full of Christ as ours are. Yes, the whole book of Psalms is
> as full of Christ as the whole New Testament put together. For
> what is the latter, but quotations from Psalms, with full proof and
> realization of the accomplishment of the same, in the person of our
> glorious Immanuel, the Lord Jesus Christ? (1.134)

Obviously, when one has stated that the Gospel is 'but quotations
from the Psalms' with relevant proofs of them in the person of
Christ, the attempt to demonstrate the essential unity of Old and
New Testaments has got out of control!

Even though more orthodox commentators were careful not to
carry their search for Christ in the Psalms to such outlandish
extremes, they too found Him in many of these ancient prayers and
hymns of praise. For example, the Anglican John Morison's *An
Exposition of the Book of Psalms* (1832), which occasionally
looks askance at the Hutchinsonians, begins with the recognition
that

> The most vital inquiry, perhaps, involved in the legitimate
> interpretation of this inspired book is that which relates to it as a
> prophecy of Messiah and the times of the Gentiles. To deny its
> prophetic character would be to repudiate the express authority of

the New Testament, and to dim that lustre by which, through the spirit of prophecy, it has been so sweetly irradiated.[19]

Therefore, the chief problems which the interpreter must solve are, first, to what extent 'is the Book of Psalms to be regarded as prophetic?' and, second, 'what are the rules of interpretation by which we are to determine this question?' The answer to both questions, says Morison, must be to rely upon 'the comments and appropriations of Christ and his apostles,' for 'where they have set the example of recognizing the prophetic spirit, we are safe in following in their footsteps; beyond this all is doubt and uncertainty' (1. viii–ix). Morison is here simply restating the old hermeneutic rule that the interpreter can only take something to be a type when he has the authority of the New Testament to do so. As Thomas Hartwell Horne explains in relation to historical types, persons 'declared by Jehovah himself to be typical, long before the events which they prefigured came to pass . . . have been termed *innate*, or natural historical types; and these may be safely admitted. But *inferred* types, or those in which typical persons were not known to be such, until after the things which they typified had actually happened . . . cannot be too carefully avoided . . . because they are not supported by the authority of the inspired writers of the New Testament' (2.529–30). Morison, like many another Anglican, observes the letter, if not the spirit, of this rule in what seems to be a characteristic Victorian approach to typology, against which few writers on the subject protest: he will only interpret something from the Old Testament when he has a specific New Testament warrant to do so, but once he begins to set forth the typological significance of such an authenticated type, he gives his imagination free rein. Morison, Melvill, Scott, Newman, and Keble all indulge in the practice of transforming innate, or authenticated, types into inferred ones. In fact, Morison, who was commended in the sixth edition of Horne's *Introduction to the Critical Study and Knowledge of the Holy Scriptures* for paying proper attention to both the literal and typological meanings of Psalms, often sounds strangely like a follower of Hutchinson.

Like Pierce, he accepts that many Psalms have a double sense because they contain types: 'Belonging literally to David and the nation of Israel, they have at the same time, a mystical or spiritual reference to Christ and the vicissitudes of the New Testament Church. This double sense has its foundations in the well-established fact, that the patriarchs, prophets, priests, and kings, of the former dispensation, were, in their persons, offices, and history, appointed types' of Christ (1. ix). Accepting in the usual orthodox manner that the Psalms contain many divinely instituted types, he assures his reader that anyone who 'would study the Book of Psalms with profit, must accustom himself to look for Christ and the Church. In doing so, however, let him not force his way through every opposing barrier' (1.xi) – as apparently the Hutchinsonians had done. In his introductory comments to Psalm 34, Morison claims that Hutchinson argued on very shaky grounds that the entire Psalm refers to Christ:

> His great maxim is, that wherever a single sentence is found, in any psalm, applicable to the mystic David [Christ], that sentence must determine the force and bearing of the whole psalm. Such canons of interpretation are, to say the least, very arbitrary, and ought to be received with becoming caution on the part of all sound biblical students'. (1.418)

Stating that he himself has ' "been looking unto Jesus", yet not in such a sense as to wrest scripture from its original design', Morison sets forth three distinct classes of prophecies in the Psalms. First are those 'in which the inspired writer personates the Messiah, and identifies himself with the suffering or triumphant church of the redeemed.' Psalms 2, 8, 16, 19, 22, 110, 118 exemplify this first group, while 45, 72, and 132 exemplify the second: 'those in which something is predicated of a third person, who from inspired comment is proved to be Immanuel'. The third class, which is exemplified by Psalms 24 and 68, is formed by those 'in which from the literal and the typical, the mind is carried forward to the great spiritual antitypes furnished by Christ and the gospel' (1.xi).

Despite taking such care to set forth interpretive rules, Morison sounds much like Pierce and the Hutchinsonians at times, although, to be sure, he never bases wide-ranging allegorizations upon the initial assumption that everything in the Psalms must refer to Christ. While discussing the first verse of Psalm 16 – 'Preserve me, O God: for in thee do I put my trust' – he informs his lay audience that

There is not a single scene in the Redeemer's history, from the manger in Bethlehem to the cross on Calvary, which does not illustrate the peculiar adumbration of this prayer. . . . In these circumstances, the incarnate Redeemer is here represented as pouring forth a prayer to his divine Father, for the interposition of his sustaining and preserving influence. (1.167)

This Psalm, one of the class in which David 'personates' Christ, is authenticated for Morison by Acts 2:25–31 and 13:35–7; and once he has this assurance, he feels free to exercise his considerable ingenuity. Thus, when he encounters the fifth verse – 'The Lord *is* the portion of mine inheritance and of my cup: thou maintainest my lot' – he comments that this 'language evidently belongs to the Messiah in his character as an High Priest; and seems borrowed from the ancient Jewish ritual, according to which it was ordained that the Priesthood should have no patrimony with the other people of the land, because the Lord was, in an especial sense, their portion, their inheritance' (1.174). Similarly, about Psalms 22:16, which closes with the statement that 'they pierced my hands and my feet', Morison expectedly comments that 'Here we almost forget the prophecy of the narrative; so minute and circumstantial are the references of this Psalm to the suffering Messiah' (1.304), and continues with a long account of the Crucifixion itself.

In Psalms 5 and 24, which allude to the legal types, these types, rather than any prophetic statement, carry the reader into the future time of the antitype. Thus Morison explains that Psalm 24, which opens with 'The earth is the Lord's, and the fulness thereof', makes an elaborate allusion to Temple rituals which, in turn, had various fulfillments. According to Morison,

The tabernacle, temple, and ark, were significant symbols of Christ and the Church, and of the heavenly state: and hence we find David, under the afflatus of the prophetic spirit, embracing an allusion to the whole. The language is evidently adapted to the temple, though not at that time reared, – to the events of gospel history, though then far distant, – and to the celestial sanctuary, though the pervading image is simply the introduction of the ark into the sacred tent which had been erected for its reception. (1.335)

In fact, the image of the temple which supposedly pervades this brief Psalm appears nowhere in it, and apparently only a tradition that it was composed for the occasion of placing the ark 'in some position of distinction and security' (1.335) prompts such a typological interpretation. Thus, on the assumption that Psalm 24 was written for the occasion of moving the ark, this commentator based the further assumption that an inspired David actually speaks of a temple not yet built, and this unbuilt temple in turn was known by David to prefigure distant Gospel events and those even farther off at the end of time.

Type and temporality

According to Thomas Hartwell Horne, 'Our definition of a type includes also that the OBJECT REPRESENTED BY IT IS SOMETHING FUTURE.' It is fundamental to a type that it adumbrate or represent something which has not yet come into existence – at least not into earthly existence – and here it differs even from divinely instituted symbols, which represent 'a thing, past, present, or future; whereas the object represented by a type is invariably future' (2.528). Typology therefore relates on real existing thing or event to at least one other later thing or event. Paradoxically, despite the fact that it is of the essence of a type that it be a real, existing thing, it still exists as a type only in its relation to something which has not yet come into being.

Although a great many types, such as Joseph and Moses, reached fulfillment when Christ lived on earth, not all types have thus seen completion. In particular, those prefigurations which refer to Christ's Church or its individual members obviously could not have been fulfilled during Christ's earthly career, and these types take three forms. First of all, there are the Old Testament types which apply only to the Church and the people of Christ. 'The rite of circumcision, for example, the passage through the Red Sea, the judgments in the wilderness, the eating of manna, and many similar things, must obviously have their antitypes', explains Fairbairn, 'in the heirs of salvation rather than in Him, who in this respect stood alone; He was personally free from sin, and He did not Himself need the blessings He provided for others' (1.157–8). Second, there are those types, such as the reference to 'bruising' in Genesis 3:15, which demand fulfillment both in the life of Christ and subsequently in the lives of His worshippers. Third, there are the comparatively rare types which appear, not in the Old Testament narrative, but rather within the life of Christ, and these can attain fulfillment only after Christ's death and resurrection.

In preaching on Matthew 27:32, which relates that Simon, a man of Cyrene, was compelled to take up Christ's cross when He faltered on the way to Calvary, Henry Melvill elucidates such a New Testament type. This favorite preacher of Ruskin and Browning begins by reminding his listener that Christ struggling beneath the cross fulfilled the type provided ages before by Isaac.

> There is no more illustrious type of the Redeemer, presented in sacrifice to God, than Isaac, whom, at the Divine command, his father Abraham prepared to offer on Moriah. We have every reason for supposing that, in and through this typical oblation, God instructed the patriarch in the great truth of human redemption; so that it was as he stood by the altar and lifted up his knife to slay his son, that Abraham discerned the shinings of Christ's day, and rejoiced in the knowledge of a propitiation for sin. . . . Herein was accurately portrayed the sacrifice of Christ – the sacrifice presented in fulness of time, on the very spot where Abraham was directed to immolate his son.[20]

Following his standard exegetical practice, Melvill next points out that, since it was one of 'the most significant, and certainly the most affecting, parts of the typical transaction, that Isaac was made to carry the wood on which he was to be presented in sacrifice to God', there must be a particular reason for Simon's having assisted Christ, since otherwise this action mars the symbolic correlation. In other words, Melvill, like all exegetes, makes it standard procedure to center his interpretations on troublesome, apparently contradictory details. Such procedure has the advantage of forestalling possible difficulties while it also permits the interpreter to win his audience by resolving interesting paradoxes. Such procedure, which characterizes many of the finest Victorian sermons, obviously left its mark on the writings of Carlyle, Ruskin, and other 'Victorian sages'.

Melvill, a master of such tactics, here concludes that Simon's assistance demonstrates to the believer that Christ, who has assumed a full human nature, suffered terribly. This proof of Christ's nature and consequent terrible suffering in turn permits the believer to empathize with his Saviour and relive the Passion imaginatively. Having thus related Simon's deed both to the ancient type and to the actual (and antitypical) sufferings of Christ, Melvill then proceeds to treat 'the incident as itself typical', since, he assures his listeners, one 'can hardly doubt than an event, which has apparently so much of significance, was designed to be received by us as a parable, and interpreted as a lesson to the Church' (274). He thereupon reminds his audience 'that, on more than one occasion, Christ had spoken of taking up and carrying the cross, when He wished to represent what would be required of his disciples' (274), and then, on 'that day of wonder and fear, when He was delivered to the will of His enemies . . . was it ordered that the truth, so often urged in discourse, should be displayed in significant action: when the Redeemer has literally a cross to bear, that cross is literally borne by one of his adherents' (275–6). This bold interpretive leap, which ignores the fact that Simon may not have been one of Christ's followers, leads to Melvill's main point, that Simon's taking up Christ's cross functions typologically as the prefiguration of all believers who would attain salvation in Christ and therefore as an instruction to all who would thus be saved. Melvill advises his audience that it is Christ's cross and not their own which must be taken up. 'Many a cross is of our own manufacture: our troubles are often but the consequences of our sins, and we may not dignify these by supposing them the cross which is to distinguish the Christian. . . . The cross of Christ is endurance for the glory of God, and the furtherance of the Gospel' (279). Finally, Melvill tentatively suggests that, since it is possible Simon the Cyrenian may have been a pagan, he may also have 'typified the conversion of idolatrous nations which either have been or will be brought to a profession of faith in our Lord' (283–4).

According to Melvill, then, this comparatively minor episode during Christ's progress towards Calvary points towards the future, just as the anciently instituted types, such as that provided by Isaac, pointed to the initial appearance, actions, and sacrifice of Christ. Moreover, as he makes clear both here and in other sermons, various types must receive their antitypes within the lives of individual believers, so that many types, including the earliest instituted, will not see completion until the end of time. What Melvill has done, of course, is to so widen the application of the individual type that he finds in it something very like the old tropological (or moral) sense of scripture; that is, by joining typology to the notion that the believer must make himself into an imitation of Christ, Melvill discovers moral instruction in scriptural history which supposedly has divine authentication stamped upon it.

Melvill's common practice of thus identifying types within the life of Christ, which is an obvious example of inferred as opposed to innate typology, also appears in the sermons of High Churchmen. Keble, for example, holds that 'the coming of the Wise men of the East, to worship our Lord in His Mother's arms, was, as we all know, a type and token of the conversion of the Gentile Church' ('The Priesthood of all Christians', *Sermons*, 2.316); and his poem from *The Christian Year* on 'The Circumcision of Christ' similarly applies types found within Christ's life. Such habits of identifying types within the life of Christ had an important effect upon Victorian religious art, since they offered a way of approaching sacred subjects in a new way. Thus, Hunt's *The Shadow of Death* (1873), which presents Christ in the carpenter's shop at the end of a long day's labor, makes the shadow cast by the Saviour's outstretched arms represent a prefiguration of the Crucifixion. By thus employing a type within the life of the Messiah, Hunt could simultaneously indulge his love for imaginative recreation of the physical details of Christ's life and yet also provide Victorian believers with a new version of the Crucifixion. Similarly, John Everett Millais's *Christ in the House of His Parents* (1850), which embodies a High Church theme, depicts the young Jesus holding up a wounded palm, as a variety of symbolic details instructs the viewer that this action prefigures the Crucifixion and Resurrection of Christ. The specifically High Church interpretation appears in the fact that Millais has set the young Jesus before a workbench which prefigures the high altar in a church, thus presenting an image of Christ as priest, and he has also separated the sheep, who symbolize the laity, from the sacred space of the main action, thus following this party's doctrinal emphasis.

In addition to locating types within the life of Christ, Keble, like the Evangelical Melvill, also perceives their fulfillment within the lives of individual believers. High and Low Churchman alike accept that types are still being fulfilled in the nineteenth century as they were in the time of Christ. For instance, in his sermon on 'The Priesthood of all Christians' in which he reads the coming of the Magi as a type of the conversion 'of the Gentile Church', he also explains that his listeners are included in that term. God intended 'the gathering together of all nations to Him: and among the rest, of us Englishmen. For we also are Gentiles, naturally "without hope, and without God in the world," but chosen and called, by God's especial mercy, to be Christians' (*Sermons*, 2.316). Similarly, like Melvill, Keble also transforms the typological into the tropological sense of scripture, for, like the interpretations of his Evangelical counterpart, Keble's reading of the antitype demonstrates that he perceived moral instruction to be an essential component of a divinely instituted type. For example, when he discusses the typological significance of David's prayer of contrition in 'How to receive the judgments of Almighty God', he does so in order to instruct the believer how to behave under hardship. David's offer to suffer and thus spare others

> was no doubt a type and figure of our Lord so devoting Himself: and when he went on and made mention of his kindred also, saying not only, let Thine hand be upon me, but likewise, on my father's house; was he not a type of our own Lord offering to His Father not only His own sufferings, but also, in some lower yet very true sense, the sufferings of His saints and martyrs, and of His whole mystical Body, the Church?

According to Keble, this typological significance informs us about the proper form of contrition. Thus, if God put it in the heart of any person to pray and wish as David did, ' "Let Thy hand, I pray Thee, be on me and on my father's house:" devoting himself, and giving himself up, to suffer, if so it might be, rather than others', this action would be an 'acceptable token' of one's 'earnest and true contrition, and would greatly help, through the mercy of Christ, towards the entire forgiveness of past sins'. In fact, says Keble, 'this would be, so far, taking the Cross upon yourself ' (*Sermons*, 1.242).

This widespread belief that scriptural types could be fulfilled in the individual's own life proves to have been a crucial factor in the influence of typology on Victorian literature and the arts. Even without such a notion, typological symbolism might still have appeared in Evangelical hymns and High Church church art, just as it also might have been employed in paintings, such as Hunt's *The Scapegoat* (1856), which portrayed Old Testament types, and poems, such as Browning's 'Saul', which portrayed biblical subjects. Similarly, although types could always be used in devotional verse and hymns simply as prefigurations of Gospel truth, without the popular Victorian belief that antitypes existed within the believer's own life, one could not have the kind of religious poetry written by Christina Rossetti, Hopkins, or Tennyson. Furthermore, without such a belief in the idea that types are fulfilled in individual lives, there could be no poetry, such as Browning's *The Ring and the Book* and Owen Meredith's *Lucile*, which uses types within fictional narrative. For without such a belief, an author would have had to have made a radically unorthodox transfer of ideas from religious to secular discourse, and then the likelihood is that those most able to comprehend such allusions would have found it blasphemous.

The reality of types

Another defining characteristic of typology which has important implications for its use and interpretation is that both the symbolizing element and what it represents— type and antitype – are real. The essential, radical historicity of the type, which both constitutes much of its appeal and creates problems for its interpreters, distinguishes it from other forms of symbolism. According to Horne, 'a type differs from a parable, in being grounded in a matter of fact, not on a fictitious narrative', and it is thus 'much of the same nature in actions, or things or persons, as an allegory is in words' (2.528). Hence a type must not only have (1) a futuristic element and (2) be divinely instituted, but (3) it must also be a real, historical existing thing or person. Therefore, unlike allegory, which interprets one thing as in reality signifying another, typology interprets something existing in its own right as also symbolizing or prefiguring another.

This historical reality of the type distinguished it fundamentally from allegory. Patrick Fairbairn, who has more to say on this subject than does Horne, explains that 'an allegory is a narrative, either expressly feigned for the purpose, or— if describing facts which really took place– describing them only for the purpose of representing certain higher truths or principles than the narrative, in its literal aspect, whether real or fictitious, could possibly have taught' (1.2). In typology, on the other hand, the literal sense or level is true and has an historical existence, whereas in allegory the literal meaning, even if not invented, is used 'simply as a cover for the higher sense' (1.2).

According to Fairbairn, this distinction between allegory and typology has major implications for the student of the Bible, largely because allegory implies that the literal meaning of a text is not historically true. He therefore argues that one employs allegorical interpretation only 'when the scriptural representation is actually held to have had no foundation in fact – to be a mere myth, or fabulous description, invented for the sole purpose of exhibiting the mysteries of divine truth; or . . . when the representation, even if wearing the appearance of a real transaction, is considered incapable as it stands of yielding any adequate or satisfactory sense, and is consequently employed, *precisely as if it had been fabulous*, to convey some meaning of a quite diverse and higher kind' (1.2). Allegory and allegorical interpretation pertain to the Bible only when the passage in question possesses no historical reality or must be treated *as if* it possessed no historical reality. Typology, urges Fairbairn, thus possesses two qualities which distinguish it from allegory:

> Typical interpretations of Scripture differ from allegorical ones of the first or fabulous kind, in that they indispensably require the reality of the facts or circumstances stated in the original narrative. And they differ also from the other, in requiring, beside this, that the same truth or principle be embodied alike in the type and the antitype. *The typical is not properly a different or higher sense, but a different or higher application of the same sense.* (1.2–3)

Whereas in typology both signifier and signified are real, in allegory the signifier can be cast off like an empty husk once its meaning has been understood. The literal, historical, and narrative level of the type remains important.

From this central emphasis upon the historical reality of the type derives the hermeneutic rule that, as Horne states, 'the TYPE *must in the first instance be explained according to its literal sense; and if any part of it appear to be obscure, such obscurity must be removed*' (2.531). As Melvill similarly tells his congregation, 'we should never spiritualize any narrative of facts, till the facts have been carefully examined as facts, and the lessons extracted from them which their record may have been designed to convey'.[21] Fairbairn further explains that the interpreter must pay close attention to the details of each type in its full historical context precisely because such details provide crucial links to the antitype. Therefore, a major 'principle of interpretation is, that we must always, in the first instance, *be careful to make ourselves acquainted with the truths or ideas exhibited in the types, considered merely as providential transactions or religious institutions*. In other words, we are to find in what they were in their immediate relation to the patriarchal or Jewish worshipper, the foundation and substance of what they typically present to the Christian Church' (1.150). The typologist must pay close attention to the type in its full historical setting both because, being a real thing, it possesses such a meaning, and also because that meaning provides valuable clues to the significance of the antitype. In fact, the religious ideas and truths contained in 'the typical events and institutions of former times, must be regarded as forming the ground and limit of their prospective reference to the affairs of Christ's kingdom. That they had a moral, political, or religious end to serve for the time then present, so far from interfering with their destination to typify the spiritual things of the Gospel, forms the very ground and substance of their typical bearing'. In other words, the details of the immediate, literal, historical existence of the type provide the 'essential key' to the remote antitype (1.150–1). In fact, as we have already observed, it was precisely these kinds of limiting clues which the Hutchinsonians like Pierce neglected in creating their free-wheeling interpretations.

The better and more influential Victorian typologists, such as Melvill, Spurgeon, Keble, Newman, and Fairbairn, avoided 'extravagant *typifications*' in part by paying such close attention to the historical sense of the type. One characteristic of Victorian typological exegetics was consequently that the interpreter directed the Bible reader to the literal and the historical. Evangelicals, who were devoted to typology, often as a consequence made contributions to Hebraic studies and studies of the Old Testament lands. Another effect of this emphasis upon the literal appears in theories of a symbolic or typological realism shared by Ruskin and the early Pre-Raphaelites which required both artist and audience to devote particular attention to material and spiritual, realistic and metaphorical, formal and iconographical aspects of painting.

Despite the fundamental importance to the whole notion of typology of this emphasis upon the literal, historical meaning of the prefiguration, from its very earliest days typology has encountered pressures that tended to drive it in the direction of allegory. As Erich Auerbach has shown, Augustine and other early Church Fathers successfully defended 'figural realism, that is, the maintenance of the basic historical reality of figures, against all attempts at spiritually allegorical interpretation'[22] in the Hellenic manner. But without a fully developed historical sense, men of the Middle Ages frequently transformed typology into allegory, for they essentially denatured the literal. Whenever spirituality is equated with reality, the historical, the literal, the here and now will seem of less importance – will appear to be less real – than the world of the spirit and idea. What is perhaps unique about Victorian typology is that it comes into being during an age when men have increasingly come to accept that reality inheres in present fact and not in a realm of ideas, forms, or spirituality. In fact, it is about the middle of the nineteenth century when 'realism', a term formerly employed to designate philosophies which propounded that ideas are most real, becomes used to designate aesthetic and other philosophies which hold that reality inheres in present fact. As should be obvious, a theory of symbolism and biblical interpretation like typology which purports to locate reality in both spheres is well suited to Victorian times. Typology's emphasis upon the essential historicity of the type allows and even encourages that characteristically nineteenth-century fascination with historiography to play a major role in interpretation. At the same time, typology's implicit theory of progressive revelation similarly allows and even encourages meliorist theories of historical development. But perhaps most interesting to the student of Victorian culture is the fact that typology promises a means of linking two conceptions of the real within a coherent intellectual framework.

Ultimately, the very historical pressures which made typology so appealing to many Victorians made it intellectually untenable. Like the Evangelical emphasis upon the centrality of the scriptures, typology was based upon a non-canonical belief that God had dictated every word of the Bible. This belief, which is known as 'Verbal Inspiration', was characteristically set forth by Thomas Scott in the preface to his annotated edition of the Bible, where he informs his reader that

> THE BIBLE IS THE WORD OF GOD. . . . Let it be here carefully observed, that the DIVINE INSPIRATION, and not merely the *authenticity*, or *genuineness*, of each of the sacred writings, is intended. . . . By 'the divine inspiration of the Scriptures,' the Author would be understood to mean, 'Such a complete and immediate communication, by the Holy Spirit, to the minds of the sacred writers, of those things which could not have otherwise been known; and such an effectual superintendency, as to those particulars, concerning which they might otherwise obtain information; as sufficed absolutely to preserve them from every degree of error, in all things, which could in the least affect any of the doctrines or precepts contained in their writings, or mislead any person, who considered them as divine and infallible standard of truth and duty.' Every sentence, in this view, must be considered as 'the sure testimony of God'.[23]

Scott's statement of Verbal Inspiration was neither unique nor particularly extreme. For example, John William Colenso quoted the more extreme version of the doctrine from Burgon's *Inspiration and Interpretation*, which he pointed out was a standard work for ministerial students:

> The BIBLE is none other than the *Voice of Him that sitteth upon the Throne*! Every book of it – every chapter of it – every verse of it – every word of it – every syllable of it – (where are we to stop?) every *letter* of it – is the direct utterance of the Most High! The Bible is none other than the word of God – not some part of it more, some part of it less, but all alike, the utterance of Him, who sitteth upon the Throne – absolute – faultless – unerring – supreme.[24]

By 1860 when the Broad Church volume *Essays and Reviews*

appeared, it had become an open secret that such beliefs in the absolute veracity of the scriptures were driving many out of the Church. Colenso in fact published his controversial *The Pentateuch and the Book of Joshua Critically Examined* two years later precisely because he wished to relieve the spiritual anguish of many who had already come to the conclusion that the Mosaic account is not historically true. By simple calculations this controversial missionary bishop demonstrated that the biblical accounts of the Exodus cannot be accurate.

Colenso, of course, struck but one of the many blows that destroyed widespread belief in Verbal Inspiration and consequently made typology increasingly untenable: the natural sciences, biblical criticism, and comparative philology all contributed to the realization that the Bible could not be historically true. Geology, which showed that the earth was far older than stated in the biblical accounts, and Darwinism, which much later undermined scriptural accounts of the creation, made it impossible to accept such assumptions about the Bible, while German demonstrations that the scriptures had evolved over a long period of time had the same effect. Similarly, comparisons of Hebrew with other languages revealed that it was not, as many Evangelicals had supposed, a unique tongue designed by God as the medium of His truth. A belief in Verbal Inspiration permitted Evangelicals and many High Churchmen to practice typology well into the nineteenth century. The intellectual conservatism of the Church parties and dissenting denominations which employed typological exegesis permitted them to maintain a belief in the absolute historical truth of the Bible long after leading continental thinkers had abandoned such possibilities. But even though many believers found it impossible to accept the doctrine of Verbal Inspiration by the 1860s and 1870s, the influence of typology upon Victorian thought did not cease then, since, as the examples of Ruskin and Browning demonstrate, many men and women retained habits of mind associated with typology long after its initial religious basis had changed or vanished.

Of course, these questions concern the final demise of typology as an intellectual and cultural force, and they do much to clarify how something that had sufficient influence to warrant a book-length study should, after such a comparatively brief period, have been so forgotten by the average educated person as to require such a study to have been begun at all. But even during the heyday of typology, various pressures attempted to deform it into allegory and emblem. First of all, although preachers, tract writers, and guides to biblical interpretation all emphasize the historical nature of the type, they often undermine that historical reality when they refer the type to something more spiritual than itself. For example, although one usually emphasizes that type and antitype – Moses and Christ – are equally real, in precisely what sense are both equally real or even real? Obviously, Moses and Christ are both real only in so far as they both existed in historical time. But in addition to possessing this kind of reality, Christ, who both existed before time and will continue to do so after time has ceased, exists on some higher level of reality than does Moses – even though the prophet may now be in heaven with Christ or in the future will be. The problem of course is that 'Christ' means two different beings or two different aspects of the same being. He is the incarnate, historically existent, physical being, who possesses reality 'equal' to that of Moses and His other types, and He is Christ spiritual, who possesses a higher, more complete reality. Typology, which links these two orders of reality, inevitably contains an uneasy, though often invisible tension.

Problems appear when the believer's understandable delight in emphasizing Christ's transcending reality and importance down-grades the reality possessed by the type. As the popular Evangelical devotional poet, Frances Ridley Havergall argues in 'Reality', Christ in heaven is far greater, far more real than any reality we can know during this earthly existence. Therefore, the believer finds solace and delight in turning to the higher reality of Christ,

> From unreal words and unreal lives,
> Where truth with falsehood feebly strives;
> From the passings away, the chance and change,
> Flickerings, vanishings, swift and strange.

The 'infinite Reality' of Jesus, who is always 'far above' even our ideal, infinitely surpasses the reality of His earthly, historical symbols:

> Reality, reality,
> Lord Jesus Christ, is crowned in Thee.

> In Thee is every type fulfilled,
> In Thee is every yearning stilled
> For perfect beauty, truth, and love.

Of course, one might object that in this sense the historical Christ, who suffered on the cross, is – like His historical types– far less real than Christ in heaven.

John Keble's sermon, 'The True Riches', makes a similar point that heavenly things possess a greater reality than do earthly ones. Thus, the gold and riches mentioned in Revelation and other parts of the New Testament make us 'understand that the Holy of Holies in the tabernacle, and Solomon's temple, which were inlaid with gold, were but images, shadows, patterns of things in heaven, shewn to Moses in the mount, and to David by the spirit of God. The gold, and silver, and jewels, and other like things on earth, are but pictures and tokens of the real treasures; they *abide* in heaven far out of sight and beyond thought: they are the true riches, the others are but riches of unrighteousness' (*Sermons*, 1.277). When considered in the light of Old Testament history, the temple is a real, historically existing institution and building whose shape had been ordained by God; when considered, on the other hand, in the light of what will happen after time ceases to exist, it becomes relatively trivial and unimportant. As Keble makes clear, he believes that Christ wishes us to take the entire world and our own earthly existence as types of greater things:

> [Christ] would have us despise both the good and evil of this
> world, in comparison to that which is to come. He would have us
> firmly believe, that nothing is true and real which passes away so
> very soon: that it is all but a shadow, cast before, in the way which
> God knows best for us: a shadow of the true riches, the true glory,
> the true want, the true shame and reproach, which are to come.
> (*Sermons*, 1.279)

Of course, what Keble and others who make similar emphases have done is not to deny the reality of the type relative to its historical surroundings but only relative to an essentially non-historical, or meta-historical, antitype.

In contrast to placing a type thus within a heavenly perspective, which lessens the reality of the type only in so far as it lessens the reality of all earthly matters, the very act of interpretation often lessens our sense that a type possesses a reality of its own. As soon as one selects certain features of a thing in order to make an interpretation, one has begun to abstract that thing and hence lose its full reality. Carried too far, this process of selective interpretation deforms the type into an allegory, symbol, or mere static emblem – a process which, incidentally, seems to be more characteristic of High Church exegetes than those with Evangelical leanings.

Frequently interpreters so use the terms 'take the place of', 'impersonate', and 'are turned into' when relating type to antitype that they implicitly undercut the historical reality of the type. For instance, in 'The Beginning of Miracles', Keble's sermon on the miracle of transformed wine at Cana, he argues that the signifying function of this first miracle was to inform all that 'the Jewish law and ceremonies, the saints and commandments and histories of the Old Testament, were now to be made known to men in their full high meaning'. Each Old Testament type is now perceived to be something higher than itself, and its own original nature consequently becomes of less value:

> That which was glorious in Moses, hath no glory now, in comparison of the glory which excelleth. The Passover is turned into the Holy Communion, circumcision into Baptism, the brazen serpent into the Cross, the cleansing of the leper into the Absolution for remission of sins, Moses and the Prophets into Christ and His Apostles, the glory of the Lord over the Mercy-seat into the inward Presence of God the Holy Ghost. (*Sermons*, 2.426–7)

Closely related to this sapping of the individual, discrete historical reality of each type, which is implied by the use of such terminology, is the fundamental problem of how an individual, say, Moses or Jacob, can both be part of such a divinely instituted scheme and yet simultaneously possess his own individuality and free will. Typology, in other words, provides a sub-category or special case of the ancient problem of free will. How can a human being possess free will (and bear responsibility for his acts) if God has foreknowledge? How can Moses and other types participate in such an all-embracing scheme governing human history and yet have free will? For those Evangelicals who had calvinistic leanings, the specifically typological version of predestination – if one can justly term it that – would have presented no problems. Having already accepted the broader notion of predestination, the problems similar to it presented by typology would not have been particularly bothersome. One might have expected that other denominations might have confronted this problem, but in fact it does not seem to have occurred to most interpreters.

It is therefore of particular interest that John William Burgon, the incumbent of St Mary-le-Virgin, Oxford, the University church and once Newman's pulpit, raises the problem as part of the larger one, 'How can there really exist such a correspondence between type and its antitype; seeing that the two histories [that is, Old and New Testaments] are severed from each other by a full thousand years?'[25] Burgon broached this subject in his sermon on David and Goliath, which was part of a series intended for use in family worship and hence addressed to a general audience and not the theologically sophisticated. In arguing that typological correspondences are quite possible even when a type precedes the antitype by such long periods of time, Burgon asserts that there is

> nothing at all incredible, or even very hard to accept, in the supposition that God's Providence so overrules human events, so shapes the lives and actions of men, that, under certain circumstances, and for certain purposes, and in the hands of certain persons narrating them under the influence of God the Holy Ghost, – a kind of mysterious correspondence, (which we call 'typical',) shall be found to subsist between certain of Christ's ancestors and our Saviour Christ Himself.

Burgon here introduces, but does not actually explain, the problem of how it is that 'Providence so overrules human events' and yet men are free. According to him, God put 'no constraint' upon any of those human beings whom we later discover to be types of Christ and His dispensation. 'Each pursued the shapings of his private, unfettered, often wayward, will. But the result, – when an inspired historian refers to, or relates it, – is found nevertheless to possess this mysterious character which we freely claim for it. The loom in which the stuff was woven proves to be of Heaven, not of Earth; and the workmanship is in consequence Divine, not Human'. Burgon thus does not reconcile free will with the signifying function of the person who becomes a type. He simply asserts that there is no conflict between human free will and divine providence, and in a series of sermons such as these, which are intended for family devotions, his failure to confront and resolve the issue is hardly surprising. What is surprising, perhaps, is that Burgon provides one of the very rare examples of the interpreter who was even aware of the problem.

It is possible, however, that a characteristic emphasis of the more old-fashioned Victorian typologists originally came into being as a response to this theological crux. According to many seventeenth- and eighteenth-century typologists, the various Old Testament figures who served as types of Christ were granted special under-standings of both their status and the entire Gospel scheme for man's salvation, and many Victorians, particularly those with Evangelical leanings, continued to accept this notion. A related version of this idea of self-conscious types appears in the often unstated but implicit belief that the average Jewish believer in Old Testament times was more or less aware of the outlines of the coming Christian dispen-sation. As William Cowper phrased this idea in 'Old Testament Gospel', one of the Olney Hymns:

> Israel, in ancient days,
> Not only had a view
> Of Sinai in a blaze,
> But learn'd the Gospel too:
> The types and figures were a glass
> In which they saw a Saviour's face.

When Cowper writes of the paschal lamb and the blood-sprinkled lamb of the Passover, he does so only to point out that they 'Would teach the need of other blood,/ To reconcile an angry God', which might seem to be merely a general anticipation of Christian belief; but when in succeeding stanzas he mentions the lamb, dove, and scapegoat, he asserts that such communicated the more specifically Christian belief that anyone 'who can for sin atone,/ Must have no failings of his own'. By the close of his poem or hymn, he holds that the types in fact showed – as they can still usefully show – the Gospel itself.

Similarly, Melvill, we recall, held that God had instructed Abraham in the full significance of his acts, informing the patriarch both about 'the great truth of human redemption' and about 'the shinings of Christ's day'. Preachers were not always completely clear on precisely how detailed and exact were these privileged visions; and whereas some only assert that those participating in a typological scheme were granted a general notion that sacrifice alone could atone for breaking the moral law, others held that individual types in fact attained not only a full comprehension of Christian truths but also a full foreknowledge of Christ's coming sacrifice and its results. The less-educated preachers in the dissenting denominations probably accepted most fully these ideas, that were already becoming theologically unfashionable by the beginning of Victoria's reign.[26] Hymns and the dissenting tradition kept such views alive enough that Robert Browning could base 'Saul' upon them, and, clearly, Fairbairn found it necessary to caution his readers that 'in determining the existence and import of particular types, we must be guided, *not so much by any knowledge possessed, or supposed to be possessed, by the ancient worshippers concerning their prospective fulfillment, as from the light furnished by their realization in the great facts and revelations of the Gospel*' (1.145).

Fairbairn, who believes that the willingness of earlier typologists to accept this idea of a self-aware type constitutes a major failing, argues that they introduced irrelevant, distracting considerations. According to him, although 'all sincere and intelligent worshippers' may have comprehended the general bearing of types, these earlier believers 'did not necessarily perceive their further reference to the things of Christ's kingdom. Nor does the reality of the precise import of their typical character depend upon the correctness or the extent of the knowledge held respecting it by members of the Old Covenant' (1.146). Such a comprehension of the coming Gospel, Fairbairn believes, was simply unnecessary, since the most important parts of God's purpose may have been carried out without their understanding anything of His plan. Furthermore, he points out, since those making explicit prophecies of the Gospel in earlier times were not always granted an understanding of these visions, it is unlikely that types, which are generally less clear than prophecies, would have been understood. To make Joseph's, Melchizedek's, or the average Israelite's comprehension of his typological significance a standard of Christian interpretation is 'travelling in the wrong direction' (1.150), since 'it is the mind of God, not the discernment or faith of the ancient believer, that we have properly to do with' (1.146–7). In other words, to emphasize too much the self-understanding of any Old Testament type – or even the awareness of Old Testament people who lived among the types – is to place one's attention, not on the mind of God but rather on the mind of man; and to do so is also to lose sight of the fact that typological signification is a divinely instituted symbolic system.

Although many earlier typologists surely made outlandish and often outrageously naive assumptions about the Christian knowledge supposedly possessed by figures in the Old Testament, one can sympathize with the motives of these exegetes. Their attempts to reconcile a potential conflict between the free will of the individual who serves as a type and the controlling force of God's plan often led them to grant so much Christian knowledge to the ancient Israelites that the actual appearance of Christ seemed anticlimactic. In essence, this conflict occurs between the historical existence of the type and its function as signifying unity in God's extratemporal plan to redeem humanity. By making the participants in the typological scheme fully understand their purpose within it, older exegetes tried to preserve the historical status of the individuals who functioned as types. Fairbairn, who apparently sees no such conflict, answers these earlier writers on the grounds that they have neglected the all-important fact that the types are divinely instituted.

CHAPTER TWO

THE SMITTEN ROCK

When Israel's tribes were parch'd with thirst,
Forth from the rock the waters burst;
And all their future journey through
Yielded them drink, and gospel too!

In Moses' rod a type they saw
Of his severe and firy law;
The smitten rock prefigur'd Him
From whose pierc'd side all blessings stream.

   – John Newton, 'That Rock was Christ' (1772)

        Rivers of living waters
Broke from a thousand unsuspected springs;
And gushing cataracts, like that call'd forth
On Horeb by the rod of Amram's son,
Gladden'd the mountain slopes, and coursed adown
The startled defiles, till the crystal wealth,
Gather'd in what was once an arid vale,
A lake of azure and of silver shone,
A mirror for the sun and moon and stars.

      – Edward Henry Bickersteth, *Yesterday,*
      To-day, and For Ever (1866), 10.456–64

As a means of indicating the contributions which typology made to Victorian iconography, the following pages will examine the appearances in art and literature of a single commonplace type, that of Moses striking the rock. When the Israelites were desperate from thirst during their desert wanderings, the Lord instructed Moses: 'Behold, I will stand before thee there on the rock in Horeb; and thou shalt smite the rock, and there shall come water out of it, that the people may drink' (Exodus 17:6). Henry Melvill makes the standard interpretation of this incident when he holds that

> It is generally allowed that this rock in Horeb was typical of Christ; and that the circumstances of the rock yielding no water, until smitten by the rod of Moses, represented the important truth, that the Mediator must receive the blows of the law, before He could be the source of salvation to a parched and perishing world. It is to this that St Paul refers, when he says of the Jews, 'They did all drink of the same spiritual drink; for they drank of that spiritual rock that followed them, and that rock was Christ' [1 Corinthians 10:4].[1]

Because the Apostle himself had interpreted this incident typologically, virtually all interpreters accepted that it was an authenticated or innate type, and the very fact of such authentication made the stricken or smitten rock especially popular as a subject for such prefigurative exegesis, many examples of which are quite elaborate.[2]

Charles Haddon Spurgeon, probably the single most popular preacher in Victorian England, exemplifies this kind of Bible interpretation in its most complex, detailed form. When the Baptist Spurgeon delivers a sermon on that same text that Melvill cited from 1 Corinthians, he manages to uncover a series of complex parallels, all of which reveal how elaborately God uses the Old Testament to teach us our need of Christ. Spurgeon begins his reading by making the general claim that both the rock in Horeb and that smitten thirty-seven years afterwards in Kadesh 'were most eminent types of our blessed Lord Jesus Christ, who, being smitten, gives forth water for the refreshing of his people, and who follows them all the desert through with his refreshing floods'. Next, after reading aloud relevant passages from Exodus to provide the scriptural context for the first time the rock was struck, this famous Evangelical begins his detailed analysis by arguing that the very names of the rocks Moses struck in themselves bear a typological significance.[3] Thus, this first rock is called both 'Horeb', which means 'barrenness', and 'Rephidim', which means 'beds of rest', and both titles, says Spurgeon, refer to Christ Himself, who was obviously a bed of rest. Christ was also 'a rock in a barren and a dry land'. Citing the prophecy of Isaiah that the Messiah would 'be a "root out of a dry ground" ', the preacher urges that Christ similarly arose as an unexpected source of sustenance in a most unlikely place, for he 'came out of a family which, although once royal, was then almost extinct. His father and mother were but common people, of the tradesman class' (2.314), and to many of his contemporaries it seemed impossible that the Messiah could spring from such origins.

Having urged the prefigurative significance of the rock's two names, the preacher then begins to draw out the major parallels between the type and antitype, the first of which is that 'this rock, like our Saviour, GAVE FORTH NO WATER TILL IT WAS SMITTEN. Our Lord Jesus was no Saviour except as he was smitten; for he could not save man unless by his death' (2.315). Making a particularly Evangelical emphasis, Spurgeon adds: 'It is not Christ who is my salvation, unless I put it with his cross; it is Christ on Calvary who redeems my soul. . . . The rock yields no water until it is smitten, and so the Saviour yields no salvation until he is slain' (2.315).

Second, the rock must be struck in a particular manner: 'It must be SMITTEN WITH THE ROD OF THE LAWGIVER, or else no water will come forth. So our Saviour Jesus Christ was smitten with the sword of the lawgiver on earth, and by the rod of his great Father, the lawgiver in Heaven' (2.316). In making this point, Spurgeon places great emphasis upon the characteristic double vision produced by typological symbolism. According to him, 'it is true that the Roman nailed him to the tree; it is true the Jew dragged him to death; but it is equally true that it was *his Father* who did it all. It is a great fact that man slew the Saviour, but it is a great fact that *God* slew him too' (2.316).

Third, it was also necessary that the rock be struck publicly, for the Crucifixion which fulfills this event took place in the presence of both Jew and Gentile, men rich and poor, wise and ignorant, righteous and sinful. 'In fact, being near the time of the passover, there were gathered together Greeks, Parthians, and Medes, and

Elamites, and the dwellers in Mesopotamia. Persons out of all nations, standing as representatives of the whole earth, saw the Saviour die, even as the elders stood as the representatives of all the tribes of Israel' (2.318).

Fourth, 'this rock, which was smitten, and thus represented the humanity of our Saviour offered up for our sins, had DIVINITY ABOVE IT; for you will notice in the 6th verse, "Behold *I* will stand before thee upon the rock in Horeb." Although it was a barren rock, and so represented Christ's condition of dishonor; although it was a smitten rock, and so represented his suffering humanity; yet over that rock the bright light of the Shecinah shone. God, with out-stretched wings of cherubim, stood over the rock, and the people saw him; there was a manifestation of the deity upon Horeb. And so at Calvary' (2.318).

Fifth, another reason the rock prefigures Jesus is that 'WHEN SMITTEN THE WATER DID GUSH FORTH most freely, sufficient for all the children of Israel' (2.319). Having introduced this crucial idea that Christ's sacrifice was sufficient to save all men at all times, Spurgeon emotionally addresses his congregation: 'Christ smitten, my beloved, gives out water for all thirsty souls; affording enough for every child of Israel. Christ smitten gives forth a stream which does not flow to-day, nor to-morrow, but which flows forever' (2.319). In a characteristic Evangelical manner Spurgeon then attempts to place his listeners within the events of Old Testament history by using types as if they apply directly to the lives of all who hear him. If God's children, says Spurgeon, 'are brought to the wilderness of Zin, or the realms of Kadesh, Christ shall follow them; the efficacy of his blood, the light of his grace, the power of his gospel, shall attend them in all the ten thousand wanderings, however tortuous may be their paths, however winding the track in which the cloudy pillar shall lead them' (2.319). Next, after he has thus striven to move the members of his congregation from their everyday reality into the greater reality of God's Gospel scheme of redemption, Spurgeon addresses his Saviour in such a way as to demonstrate to his listeners – who 'overhear' this fervent prayer and confession – that he himself has been saved by having found himself within the world in which Moses strikes the rock:

O! blessed Jesus, thou art indeed a sweet antitype of the rock.

Once my thirsty soul clamoured for something to satisfy its wants; I hungered and I thirsted for righteousness; I looked to the heavens, but they were as brass, for an angry God seemed frowning on me; I looked to the earth, but it was as arid sand, and my good works failed me. . . . But well I remember when my thirsty soul fainted within me, and God said, 'Come hither, sinner, I will show thee where thou mayest drink,' and he showed me Christ on his cross, with his side pierced and his hands nailed. I thought I heard the expiring death shriek, 'It is finished,' and when I heard it, lo! I saw a stream of water, at which I slaked my burning thirst. . . . Had I not beheld that mighty stream flowing there, I had never washed away my thirst. . . . You see, then, beloved, that this rock is a type of Christ personally, it is a type of him dying, smitten for our sins. (2.319–20)

Spurgeon, who fervently believes that the Old Testament types can permit the prepared worshipper to experience the presence of Christ in both his own life and that of ancient believers, thus draws upon his own conversion as he moves from a merely explanatory to a dramatic, meditative mode. Evangelical preachers frequently recreated the scenes of Christ's passion and death because they believed it essential for their listeners to participate imaginatively in the mysteries of the atonement and thus bring it home to themselves. Spurgeon's procedure here reminds us that, having once become proficient at reading types with a spiritual or double vision, the preacher and believer did not require a specific Gospel event itself as the occasion for such a transcendental excursion. An Old Testament prefiguration, which God had ordained to lead men to Christ, could also prompt such powerful imaginative experience.

Spurgeon uses this emotional meditation to prepare for his next major point, which is that the second rock, the rock in Kadesh, prefigures the Church of Christ and hence all of those in his present audience. This famous preacher, who elsewhere confesses that he 'loves to be textual', opens his explanation by reading the passage in Numbers 20:1–13 which relates that Moses, while carried away by anger at his rebellious, ungrateful, unbelieving people, sins by striking the rock to bring forth water instead of praying as God had instructed him to do. According to Spurgeon, this second rock was not Christ personal but Christ mystical. 'The first rock was Christ himself, the Man–God, smitten for us; the second rock is Christ the church, Christ the head and all its members together; and out of the church, and out of the church only, must always flow all that the world requires' (2.322).

Once again, he claims a prefigurative significance for the names recorded in the Old Testament account of this event. Kadesh, for instance, signifies 'holiness', and that is 'just where Christ mystically dwells. We can tell Christ's church by its being separated from the world'. Furthermore, this rock was in the wilderness of Zin, 'which means "a buckler" and "a coldness" ', and in fact the church of God stands in 'a double position'– 'in coldness and indifference with regard to the world, and it stands also secure, as in a buckler, with regard to its blessed God' (2.322).

From the fact that God had instructed Moses to speak to, rather than smite, the rock, Spurgeon deduces that 'it is God's revealed will that Christ mystically should bless the world by speaking' (2.323). According to this Evangelical preacher, in other words, it is God's will that the Church and its individual members should spread God's blessings by preaching the Gospel. In contrast, High Churchmen, who characteristically wished to emphasize the importance of the sacraments, might be more likely to interpret the stricken rock as a type of communion.

From the fact that Moses sinfully smote the rock, Spurgeon deduces 'another significant parallel' between type and antitype – namely, that just as Moses wrongfully struck the rock, so also 'the wicked men of this world have smitten Christ again in his church; they have persecuted God's people'. Furthermore, 'although the smiting was a sinful act, THE WATER CAME FORTH, to show by persecution the church has been made a blessing to the world. . . . The smiting of God's gospel rock, the church, has scattered drops of precious water to lands where else it would never have flowed' (2.323). The immediate relevance of this last point to each believer is that by suffering on behalf of Christ, by suffering while attempting to preach His word, one imitates Christ.[4] Turning again to his own experience, as he had previously while setting forth the meaning of the rock in Horeb, Spurgeon relates how delighted he had been to realize that the rock in Kadesh, 'although smitten wrongly, was SMITTEN WITH THE ROD OF THE LAWGIVER', for this fact means that 'If I suffer for Christ, my sufferings are the sufferings of

Christ; and although they are occasioned by man as the second cause, yet they do really spring from God' (2.325).

Having thus far guided us through the complex web of meanings that apppear when one looks closely at a type, Spurgeon next points out that Moses was punished for his disobedience as have all been and will be who thus persecute God's church. In the course of explaining the typological meaning of these two smitten rocks, the preacher has related them to Old Testament prophecies, pointed out how even names and places bear unexpected significance, drawn upon his personal spiritual experience, and used a visual, meditative prose at times to show his listeners how they are to find Christ in their Old Testaments. He has done so in Evangelical fashion to emphasize Evangelical doctrines: the need to preach the Gospel, the terrible beauty of Christ's sacrifice, the centrality of this event to human history, the inevitability of suffering for Christ, and the crucial fact that God arranged sacred history as a semiotic or signifying system which the spiritual eye can read.

Turning to almost any popular nineteenth-century hymnal or collection of religious verse, one is certain to find numerous examples of this type. *The Book of Praise* (1863) compiled by Roundell Palmer, first Earl of Selborne, contains four uses of the image. The author draws heavily upon writers of the late eighteenth-century Evangelical revival as well as the earlier Watts, and the fact that as late as 1863 he chooses to print these earlier works and selects those which employ typology might suggest how important this mode of thought was to worshippers in England and America. Isaac Watts's 'Go, worship at Immanuel's feet' (1709) exemplifies one manner of incorporating typology into verse structure. Asking a series of questions which define the nature of Christ, the hymn inquires if He is a fountain, fire, door, temple, and so on. The tenth stanza thus asks:

> Is He a Rock? How firm He proves!
> The Rock of Ages never moves:
> Yet the sweet streams, that from Him flow,
> Attend us all the desert through.

Since the structure of this hymn is cumulative, heaping up more and more qualities of the Saviour, it never concentrates long on any particular analogy or type. Although this poetic structure prevents any satisfying aesthetic development of the initial idea, it compensates somewhat by making its main point effectively – that Christ is simultaneously many things to man, and that a listing of the various facts serves well to remind us how complex, how hard for the human to encompass, He is.

Other works in *The Book of Praise* develop this type differently. William Williams begins the brief 'Guide me, O Thou great Jehovah!' (1774) by emphasizing that he and all men are pilgrims in a 'barren land'. Here, as so frequently in Evangelical hymns, the image of man as a pilgrim in the desert of life brings to mind Moses guiding the children of God; and Moses leads one's thoughts to the type of the smitten rock:

> Open now the crystal Fountain,
>   Whence the healing streams do flow;
> Let the fiery cloudy pillar
>   Lead me all my journey through.

Similarly, in the course of John Newton's 'When Israel, by Divine command' (1799), we also learn our resemblance to those who accompanied Moses out of Egyptian bondage. Newton begins by focusing upon the wanderings of the Israelites:

> When Israel, by Divine command,
>   The pathless desert trod,
> They found, though 't was a barren land,
>   A sure resource in God.
>
> A cloudy pillar marked their road,
>   And screened them from the heat;
> From the hard rocks the water flowed,
>   And manna was their meat.

The hymn then points out that 'Like them, we pass a desert too', and then goes on to enforce the type, for 'We drink a wondrous stream from Heaven,/'Tis water, wine, and blood'. This last line makes the Old Testament passage serve as a type of several aspects of the Christian dispensation, for it figures forth the Crucifixion, the salvation purchased by it, the sacrament of communion, and possibly also the miraculous changing of water into wine, which is itself a type of communion. Rather than assemble a series of discrete symbols, as does Watts's 'Go, worship at Immanuel's feet', this hymn conflates various antitypes, all of which fulfill the Old Testament narrative differently. The effect is to emphasize the complexity and richness of the Gospel scheme by demonstrating how many of its strands come together at any one point in time. The type of the smitten rock therefore becomes a powerful meditative image, a window into the miraculous world of salvation.

Augustus Montague Toplady's 'Rock of Ages' (1776), perhaps the most famous application of this type in a hymn, conflates the rock in Horeb with that rock in which God placed Moses to protect him from the immanence of His glory.[5] Exodus 33:22–23 relates that after Moses asked to see the face of God, the Lord told him that no man could survive such a sight, but that 'I will put thee in a cleft of the rock, and will cover thee with mine hand while I pass by: And I will take away mine hand, and thou shalt see my back parts: but my face shall not be seen'. Toplady's hymn opens with the image of the Rock of Ages which has been cleft – and crucified– for the speaker:

> Rock of Ages, cleft for me,
> Let me hide myself in Thee!
> Let the water and the blood,
> From Thy riven side which flowed,
> Be of sin the double cure,
> Cleanse me from its guilt and power.

This poem develops this initial image by emphasizing that the worshipper remains helpless without Christ's aid, after which it ends with a repetition of the two opening lines. The extent to which this kind of hymn was immediately understood to use the commonplace type appears in an illustration the Dalziel brothers engraved more than a century after the poem's composition, apparently for a volume of Felicia Hemans's poems. The wood engraving, which depicts Moses striking water from the rock, bears the caption 'Rock of Ages cleft for me', words which immediately establish the Old Testament event in a Christian context.[6] Illustrations of Moses bringing forth water from the desert rock seem to have been fairly popular in the nineteenth century, perhaps suggesting the importance this type had for the average worshipper.

Of course, this type, whose first known appearance is on the tomb of Junius Bassus (d. AD 359), has had a long history in Christian art, but that history has not been very illustrious. Since the smitten rock was traditionally taken as a type of baptism, it appropriately appears on baptismal founts: a terracotta maquette for a font attributed to Pierre Francheville (1548?–1615), which was formerly in the collection of Bernard Black Gallery, New York, and the Fitzwilliam Museum's cast-lead plaquette by Peter Flötner (c. 1485–1546) exemplify sculpted versions of the subject with this particular application. Giulio and Polidoro painted this scene from Old Testament history as part of a series in the Vatican Logge, and Nicholaus Poussin painted it three times, once explicitly as a type of baptism. There also exist several monumental-size versions of the subject, including the Philadelphia *Moses striking the Rock* (c. 1660) and the Boston *Moses after striking the Rock* (1527) by Lucas van Leyden.[7] An interesting analogue to this subject appears in the York Art Gallery's *St Clement striking the Rock* by Bernardo Fungai (1460–1516), a painter of the Umbro-Sienese school.[8] The saint, who had refused to submit to Trajan and abandon his faith, was consequently sentenced to exile in the stone quarries, and Fungai's painting depicts him bringing forth water from a rock upon which stands the Lamb of God. In this way he, like Moses, relieved the people of God who were suffering from thirst, though he did so while they were still in a condition analogous to Egyptian slavery and not after they were freed.

Apart from this last, rather unusual work, the theme of the stricken rock served pre-nineteenth-century art as a type of baptism. But in Victorian religious art, as in Victorian sermons, this is no longer the standard – or even an especially common – interpretation. Apparently, more than half a century of Evangelical readings of the rock in Horeb as prefiguring the Crucifixion changed the significance of this type for most believers.[9] Even the Baptist Spurgeon, as we have already seen, does not take the smitten rock to adumbrate baptism.

During the Victorian period, then, representations of the smitten rock were both more commonly found and interpreted differently than in earlier art. At the lowest cultural levels, the theme appeared in chapbook Bibles, which depicted the event with crude woodcuts; and in more elegant illustrated Bibles, the subject was also common.[10] The Dalziel brothers, who were the leading Victorian wood engravers, made more than half a dozen versions of it. Both Moses striking the rock and the smitten rock alone occasionally appear in Victorian stained-glass decorations for churches. Water pouring from a cleft rock can be found, for instance, in William Holman Hunt's *Melchizedek* (1865), in which it probably stands as a type of the Crucifixion as sacrifice, and hence also as a type of Holy Communion. The complete type, with Moses smiting the rock, appears several decades later in the east window of the parish church in Burford, Oxfordshire, where its placement as the first of five paired panels depicting miraculous cures or rescues– Moses striking the rock is paired with 'Moses Prophet'– suggests that the event is taken as a type of both Christ's New Law of grace and also of His miracles, which themselves were types of His gift of eternal life.

As we have already observed in popular hymns, literary typology frequently parallels the organization of stained-glass programs in employing an additive structure to place one type in the presence of others. Other defining devices appear in 'The Cross' by Horatius Bonar (1808–90), a popular devotional poet. Bonar, who makes frequent use of typological symbolism, ends 'The Cross' with the recognition that

> Here the living water welleth,
> Here the rock, now smitten, telleth
> Of salvation freely given.
> This is the fount of love and pity,
> This is the pathway to the City;
> This is the very gate of Heaven.[11]

The previous four stanzas have emphasized the calm and peace that the Cross represents for the true believer, and, using a Tennysonian poetic structure, Bonar has them build towards a moment of vision or recognition. Appropriately, the type provides the core of this rhetorical and spiritual climax, to which the last three lines add the idea that the stricken rock, which prefigures the crucified Christ, is the source of the new dispensation's 'love and pity', the way to Heaven, and, finally, our entrance into it. The very mention of

'Heaven' signals the reader that the Old Testament event is being understood within a Christian context, since in the original narrative Moses saves the Israelites' bodies and not souls with his act. Furthermore, the poem's title, which also informs us immediately that the smitten rock must be understood typologically, directs the reader to the proper interpretation of the type – that is, as adumbrating the Cruxcifixion and not the sacraments of baptism or Holy Communion.

Although the literary examples at which we have thus far looked appear richer and more interesting once we recognize their use of prefigurative imagery, few of them have proved to possess any major poetic value, and most of them do not in fact release very much of the intrinsic imaginative power of typology. Since each type is a synecdoche for the entire Gospel scheme, it possesses the property of being able to generate the entire vision of time, causality, and salvation contained in that scheme. A typological image always has the potential to thrust the reader into another context, demonstrating in the process how everything and every man exists simultaneously in two realms of meaning.

In contrast to these rather pedestrian employments of this image, Gerard Manley Hopkins's 'Soliloquy of One of the Spies left in the Wilderness', which dates from about 1864, makes a particularly skillful use of it. The opening stanza forcefully presents the rebelliousness of a man who prefers the safety of Egyptian slavery to the dangers of the prophet's rule in the desert:

> Who is this Moses? who made him, we say,
> To be a judge and ruler over us?
> He slew the Egyptian yesterday. To-day
>   In hot sands perilous
> He hides our corpses dropping by the way
>   Wherein he makes us stray.

After two more stanzas that emphasize how much the speaker loathes both the discomforts of the journey and the manna which sustains him, he exclaims,

> Sicken'd and thicken'd by the glare and sand
> Who would drink water from a stony rock?

The reader, of course, is tempted to reply that in such a situation anyone would. Hopkins's use of this typological image – like that of the manna – effortlessly allows him to produce one of the important effects of the dramatic monologue, the creation of an ironic disparity between what the speaker intends to state and that additional meaning which the reader perceives. The commonplace type creates this essential disparity by setting the speaker simultaneously within two parallel contexts, which we may variously define as literal and metaphorical, historical and metahistorical, and Old Testament and New. Thus, on the literal level, the poem attempts to portray the rebelliousness and self-justifications of one of the Jews who preferred slavery in Egypt to the dangers of freedom with Moses. By the time the penultimate stanza presents his relishing the pleasures of slavery above the pains of liberty, we have also understood how much human weakness can do to corrupt itself:

> Give us the tale of bricks as heretofore;
> To plash with cool feet the clay juicy soil.
> Who tread the grapes are splay'd with stripes of gore,
>   And they who crush the oil
> Are spatter'd. We desire the yoke we bore,
>   The easy burden of yore.

Groping for excuses, for easy pleasures, the rebellious spy descends to a porcine or reptilean wallowing in cool Nile mud. On this level, then, the poem is analogous to those many Victorian paintings which attempt an archaeological reconstruction of scriptural or religious subjects. On this most basic level, it is also obvious that the speaker comes rather quickly to represent all men, or that element in human nature, which prefers enslavement, degradation, and ease to more bracing enterprises.

But the presence of the typological image of the smitten rock abruptly, economically, forcefully adds another dimension to the poem, for its presence suddenly makes us aware that the speaker exists in the Christian as well as the Judaic universe; or, perhaps more accurately, that he exists as part of the Gospel scheme of salvation as well as in his own purely human right. He represents, in other words, the sinner who refuses the atonement so dearly bought by the Crucifixion. He is the one for whom the rock is stricken in vain, the person who prefers the slavery of sin, the bondage of materiality, the imprisonment within time to the gifts offered by divine grace. As Keble urges in 'The hard service of sin', the ingratitude and rebelliousness of the ancient Jews is not something about which the Victorian believer can say, 'This is very aweful, but what is it to us Christians? Oh my brethren, it is every thing to us, in the way of the most solemn instruction and warning' (*Sermons*, 3.153). We also fail to appreciate our blessings, says Keble, 'or we refused to serve Him in joyfulness and gladness of heart, what little we did offer, was blemished with our own ill temper and discontent. In this as in many other respects, our fathers who came out of Egypt were too true a type and shadow of us Christians' (*Sermons*, 3.152).

Within Hopkins's poem, then, the appearance of the type thus establishes an entire additional set of meanings for all the details of the poem, and it also helps to explain certain details that might otherwise remain enigmatic. For example, at first the reader does not understand why the poet uses an upper-case 'H' when he wrote, 'He [Moses] feeds me with *His* manna every day' (emphasis added), if the speaker refers, as he clearly does, to the prophet. When we come upon the type of the stricken rock, however, we then recognize that the speaker takes his place in the Gospel scheme, referring unknowingly to Christ. (One might argue, of course, that the initial recognition occurs six lines earlier, where the speaker mentions the gift of manna, since manna was often interpreted figurally. It seems to me, however, that the poet's use of the food that miraculously sustained the tribes of Israel does not, like the smitten rock, at first demand interpretation as a type. After one perceives that the rock functions prefiguratively, one then makes the same recognition about the manna. But the important point here is that the manna does not possess the same drama – because it does not possess the movement – of the poem's central type.) The type functions as a sign, as an indication of the way we should react intellectually and emotionally to the words which surround its appearance.[12] In this way, Hopkins uses typological symbolism much as does Millais in *Christ in the House of His Parents*, to add another dimension of meaning which spiritually redeems the physical, the material, making it richer and more relevant. One must also note that the presence of the type has another effect, since it turns the reader back to the details of narrative and psychology. Because everything in the poem has gained new relevance from the presence of the symbol of Christ, that image demands that one devote close attention to the literal level to insure that we miss nothing of the speaker's manner and habit of thinking. In emphasizing the symbolic implications of the narrative, the typological image paradoxically also emphasizes the literal elements as well. This effect, one should notice, is parallel to that of Pre-Raphaelite painting, where the presence of complex symbolic statements forces the spectator back to the visual elements of the picture, thus insuring that he fully perceives the aesthetic surface.

A second, perhaps less strictly orthodox type occurs when poets use the image of Moses striking the desert rock to prefigure, not the Old Law bringing forth the New by means of the Crucifixion, but rather Christ Himself bringing forth tears of repentance from the stony heart of the individual worshipper. This second version of the type has had a long history in English verse. Henry Vaughan, for example, employed it as the author's 'emblem of himself', which opens the first part of *Silex Scintillans* (1650). In French Fogle's translation of this Latin emblem poem, which Vaughan wrote to accompany his visual emblem, the poet addressed God:

You launch your attack and shatter that boulder, my stony heart. What was stone, becomes flesh. Look at it, broken in pieces! Look, its fragments are flashing at last to heaven and you, and my cheeks are wet with tears wrung from flint. In the same way, ever provident for your people, you once commanded dry rocks to overflow and crags to gush with water. How marvelous your hand is![13]

In thus describing himself, Vaughan also describes his poetry, for we are henceforth to understand it as having been struck out of him by God, and the record or result of that smiting is to provide us with waters of grace. In other words, the image of divine intervention has simultaneously become an image of divine inspiration – just as it has in Donne and Milton.

This version of the type which refers to the individual believer appears in Book 6 of Wordsworth's *The Excursion*. Ellen, whose lover has betrayed her, tells her mother that God's grace has given

her strength to bear her pain, waking her at last from her deadened
state:

> There was a stony region in my heart;
> But He, at whose command the parchèd rock
> Was smitten, and poured forth a quenching stream,
> Hath softened that obduracy, and made
> Unlooked-for gladness in the desert place,
> To save the perishing. (918–23)

John Ruskin employs the same type in his poem 'The Broken
Chain', when (probably imitating Wordsworth, then his favorite
poet) he describes a character as a man who

> looked like one whom power or pain
> Had hardened, or had hewn, to rock
> That could not melt nor rend again,
> Unless the staff of God might shock,
> And burst the sacred waves to birth,
> That deck with bloom the Desert's dearth –
> That dearth that knows nor breeze, nor balm. (2.174)

Two points strike one about both Ruskin's and Wordsworth's use
of this type. In the first place, they both omit mention of Moses and
assume that since the reader recognizes Moses' prefiguration of
Christ, it is therefore legitimate to describe Moses' literal action as if
it were being performed by Christ Himself. Second, although the
omission of Moses requires a close knowledge of scripture – or at
least of the more popular passages in scripture – it also serves to make
the image fit more easily into the narrative context. Indeed, one does
not have to realize that this is a type to read the passage with some
basic understanding of what the author intends. None the less, a
recognition that both authors cite a commonplace type much
enriches the significance and emotional impact of the image: by
perceiving that Ellen received God's grace and that it will be necessary for Ruskin's hero to do so, the reader recognizes the essentially
Christian basis of both men's moral psychology. One might also
point out that for Evangelicalism, such typological imagery
economically demonstrates the essentially Christian conception of

sympathetic imagination shared by Romantic theory and Evangelical theology.

It is therefore not surprising that this image recurs frequently in nineteenth-century poetry. It appears, for instance, in John Keble's 'Sixth Sunday after Trinity', which attempts to comfort 'bitter thoughts, of conscience born' by showing their essential role in forgiveness and salvation. Employing as an epigraph David's confession of sin to Nathan and the prophet's assurance of divine mercy, the poem makes this Old Testament episode itself function as a type of confession of guilt and Christ's subsequent forgiveness. Explaining how 'Israel's crowned mourner felt/ The dull hard stone within him melt', the poem relates that when God saw 'the mighty grief ', He quickly eased the repentant, fearful sinner's pain. David's confession makes the angels in Heaven, who have turned from his music, welcome 'the broken heart to love's embrace'. At this juncture Keble enforces his point by making use of another typological image, a technique which demonstrates how interwoven are the acts and meanings of scriptural history:

> The rock is smitten, and to future years
> Springs ever fresh the tide of holy tears
> And holy music, whispering peace
> Till time and sin together cease.

This use of one type, here the smitten rock, to comment upon another, David's confession and forgiveness, shows how many layers of meaning the poet could employ because he had an audience that was both capable of following his use of typology and delighted to discover commonplace types in new contexts.

As one might expect from a poem which so skillfully employs the exegetical tradition, Keble's 'Sixth Sunday after Trinity' builds upon traditional readings. The poem's epigraph is taken from 2 Samuel 12:13 ('David said unto Nathan, I have sinned against the Lord. And Nathan said unto David, The Lord also hath put away thy sin; thou shalt not die') but the fifty-first Psalm and the traditional commentaries which have accrued to it are equally important. Keble himself cites this psalm as a footnote to his line 'Springs ever fresh the tide of holy tears', and he specifically refers to a single verse later in the poem. Psalm 51, whose title is 'A Psalm of David, when Nathan the

Prophet came unto him, after he had gone unto Bathsheba', refers in great detail to the Levitical sacrifices and makes what all interpreters saw as an obviously proto-Christian recognition that God

> desirest not sacrifice, else I would give it; thou delightest not in burnt-offerings.
> The sacrifices of God are a broken spirit; a broken and a contrite heart, O God, thou wilt not despise.
>
> (Psalm 51:16–17)

The psalm concludes with the assertion that God will be pleased with the various Levitical sacrifices when they are offered in the proper spirit, and Bishop George Horne, to whose commentary Keble refers in one of his notes to 'Sixth Sunday after Trinity', comments that David's statement that God will 'be pleased with the sacrifices of righteousness, with burnt-offering' was in fact literally fulfilled after David's son Solomon built the Temple in Jerusalem.

> It is spiritually true in the Christian church, where the substance of all Mosaic types and shadows is offered and presented to the Father, by the Prince of Peace, at the head of the Israel of God. And it will be eternally verified in the kingdom of heaven, where the sacrifices of righteousness and love, of praise and thanksgiving, will never cease to be offered to him that sitteth on the throne, by the church triumphant in glory.[14]

Keble, however, does not cite this aspect of the psalm at all and instead introduces another type, that of the smitten rock. Whereas an Evangelical would have emphasized that the legal types contained in the psalm prefigured Christ's sacrifice on the Cross, a High Churchman, as we have already observed, would have taken these to adumbrate the Eucharist – a meaning not particularly relevant to the subject of David's contrition. Therefore Keble introduces the smitten rock, a type commonly interpreted to symbolize the act of grace upon the sinner's heart.

Keble's 'Easter Eve', which also uses other types such as that of Joseph cast into the pit, again draws on the image of the stricken rock. After elucidating the significance of atonement, the speaker expresses his longing to be with God:

But stay, presumptuous – Christ with thee abides
   In the rock's dreary sides:
He from the stone will wring celestial dew
If but the prisoner's heart be faithful found and true.

When tears are spent, and thou art left alone
   With ghost of blessings gone,
Think thou art taken from the cross, and laid
   In JESUS' burial shade;
Take Moses' rod, the rod of prayer, and call
   Out of the rocky wall
The font of holy blood; and lift on high
Thy grovelling soul that feels so desolate and dry.

During the course of this passage Keble shifts emphasis from the actions of Christ which affect the worshipper to those of the worshipper himself. This movement is appropriate to the entire poem, since it begins with the fact of the Crucifixion and then proceeds to instruct us how we can secure the gifts it purchased. The movement, we observe, leads the poet to ring intricate changes on the basic figure. In the first place, Keble apparently conflates two uses of the type, so that the rock simultaneously symbolizes both the worshipper's heart and the crucified body of Christ. When we are told, 'Christ with thee abides', we wonder perhaps who then is going to strike the rock and thus bring forth the waters of life. Keble clarifies this point by making a variant, yet quite orthodox, application of the basic type: 'Moses' rod', it turns out, is 'the rod of prayer', and we must be the ones to produce the waters that will flow, simultaneously, from both Christ and our own hearts. The words 'Christ with thee abides' tell the reader both that He has elected to share our human nature and that He is always there to comfort us. Furthermore, there is another variation of the basic type here: whereas in Exodus God tells Moses to strike the rock, in Numbers He instructs him to speak to the rock. This second episode was intended to demonstrate, say some exegetes, that once Christ was crucified, prayer was enough to bring forth His grace, and Keble has apparently employed this second rock, that in Kadesh, as his type.

Tennyson's early 'Supposed Confessions of a Second-Rate Sensitive Mind not in Unity with Itself' (1830), which appeared three years after Keble's 'Easter Eve', seems a conscious attempt to write a dramatic monologue commenting upon the earlier poem from the fictional vantage point of one unable to believe. Both poems open with emphases upon the physical reality of the sacrificial suffering and death of Christ; both then mention the tranquil, happy state of those He has saved; and both employ the type of the smitten rock at a crucial point. We have already observed how Keble, the firm believer, recognizes that it is presumptuous to say that he will be with Christ only in death since He is already with him in 'the rock's dreary sides' ready to spring forth when called by the 'rod of prayer'. In contrast, Tennyson's speaker, who is too proud of his despair and doubt to believe, first claims that he is cut off from the joys of Christian belief and then apparently blames God for his painful state. Next, in the poem's second movement, which begins at line 68, the speaker turns to address his dead mother, claiming that her faith had not served to protect him from doubts. He knows, of course, that if his mother were still alive she would tell him:

> I must brook the rod
> And chastisement of human pride;
> That pride, the sin of devils, stood
> Betwixt me and the light of God!
> That hitherto I had defied
> And had rejected God – that grace
> Would drop from his o'er-brimming love,
> As manna on my wilderness,
> If I would pray – that God would move
> And strike the hard, hard rock, and thence
> Sweet in their utmost bitterness
> Would issue tears of penitence
> Which would keep green hope's life. (107–19)

Well aware of his dismal spiritual condition but unable to do anything about it, Tennyson's speaker, who is an embodiment of Sartrean 'bad faith', refuses to see that he is in fact so proud of his doubt and failure that he has cut himself off from God. In the characteristic manner of the dramatic monologue Tennyson's 'Confessions' allows the speaker to say more than he realizes, for we soon perceive that his attempt to anticipate and refute what his mother would say if she were still alive in fact convicts him of this intellectual and spiritual pride.

In the third movement of the poem, which begins at line 139, when the speaker again addresses God, he presents his youthful doubts as if they were purely a matter of high intellectual courage. In the poem's closing lines he first throws himself on God's mercy and then, at the very end, pulls back and bemoans his 'damned vacillating state'. The lines which dramatize his admission of a desperate need for God seem again to owe much to Keble's poem. The last stanza of 'Easter Eve', which immediately follows those that employ the type of the smitten rock, alludes to Zechariah 9:12 in addressing Keble himself as a 'Prisoner of Hope' and commanding him to 'look up and sing/ In hope of promised spring'. Just as Joseph when cast by his brothers into the pit knew

> his God would save [him] . . . from that living grave,
> So, buried with our Lord, we'll close our eyes
> To the decaying world, till Angels bid us rise.

In sharp contrast, Tennyson's speaker finds himself a prisoner of despair, not hope, and thinks not of promised spring but of the decay of his own 'morn of youth' and the fate of spring lambs. Desperate, not so much for belief as for an escape from the pains of unbelief, he implores God:

> Let Thy Dove
> Shadow me over, and my sins
> Be unremembered, and Thy love
> Enlighten me. Oh teach me yet
> Somewhat before the heavy clod
> Weighs on me, and the busy fret
> Of that sharp-headed worm begins
> In the gross blackness underneath. (180–7)

These lines apparently comprise a passionately eloquent prayer to something outside himself, but the three final lines of the poem reveal they are fundamentally insincere. The speaker passionately desires relief from his spiritual malaise, knows the forms of belief, but is finally unable to cast away pride and independence enough to have true faith in something other than himself. Consequently, he remains unlike Keble, who is one of those who can 'close our eyes to the decaying world', and indeed the last fifty lines of the poem show how much this decaying world obsesses him. Unable to turn his thoughts away from himself enough to believe in his Lord, he imagines the weight of 'the heavy clod' upon him and terrified awaits the touch of the worm in 'the gross blackness underneath'.

Although Tennyson's poem parallels Keble's 'Easter Eve' so closely that it appears a parody of its predecessor, it in fact uses similar argument and scriptural allusion, not to mock religious poetry, but to dramatize – and satirize – the peculiarly modern, Arnoldian state of unbelief mixed with a desire for faith in which Tennyson apparently found himself occasionally, even before the death of Hallam. As at times in Browning's poetry, a speaker's knowledge of typological symbolism demonstrates, not that he is particularly spiritually minded, but rather that he uses religious forms without appropriate feeling and belief. Such deployments of typology, a form of symbolism well suited to produce the dramatic monologue's characteristic irony, are particularly useful in portraying how the imaginative worlds of belief and unbelief collide in the Victorian world.

Christina Rossetti's 'Good Friday' (1862), which also uses this type, differs from the poems of Tennyson and Keble at which we have looked because its play upon the stricken rock generates the structure of the entire poem: here the figure of the rock is not merely a forceful image employed by the poet but rather a conceit which contains the germ of all sixteen lines of the poem. Her initial opposition of stone and sheep, which she may have derived from one of the Olney Hymns, sets the conceit in motion:[15]

> Am I a stone and not a sheep,
> That I can stand, O Christ, beneath Thy cross,
> To number drop by drop Thy blood's slow loss
> And yet not weep?

The opening line establishes the contrasts that provide the axis of the poem: she calls herself a stone, one who does not react deeply enough, humanly enough, to the reality of Christ's sacrifice, and yet she wants to make herself one of the shepherd's flock, one of those whom He will save. The next two stanzas emphasize the other people and even things that grieved: Mary and the other women, Peter, the thief, even the sun and moon. After confessing at the end of the third stanza that 'I, only I', remain a stone, she turns to God in lines which brilliantly resolve the spiritual – and poetic – problem introduced by her initial contrast:

> Yet give not o'er,
> But seek Thy sheep, true Shepherd of the flock
> Greater than Moses, turn and look once more,
> And smite a rock.

The entire poem moves toward this last action and culminates in it. She manages a brevity, force, and wit not found in Keble's more diffuse poems, and unlike her fellow High Church poet she can purposefully blend her symbols with greater effect. Most important, her poem, like Hopkins's, employs the typological image as an essential part of its structure. It is clearly the core of the poem, its generating conceit, and when we arrive at the carefully prepared-for type of the smitten rock, it detonates, releasing us into a new universe and a New Law of hope.

Yet another use of this figure appears in Section 131 of *In Memoriam*, which closes the main portion of the poem:

> O living will that shalt endure
>   When all that seems shall suffer shock,
>   Rise in the spiritual rock,
> Flow through our deeds and make them pure,
>
> That we may lift from out of dust
>   A voice as unto him that hears
>   A cry above the conquered years
> To one that with us works, and trust,
>
> With faith that comes of self-control,
>   The truths that never can be proved
>   Until we close with all we loved,
> And all we flow from, soul in soul.

The image of the smitten rock works with that complexity we have come to expect from Tennyson. First of all, the 'living will', which Tennyson himself glossed as man's free will, is also the will of God.[16] To appreciate the full meaning of the type, then, we must perceive that the living will is that of the speaker, Christ, and Hallam, or at least an embodiment, like him, of the highest element in mankind. After the shock that the poet has suffered, he now confidently expects the living will (which here essentially replaces grace or merges with it) to rise in his heart, in his life, guiding him out of the desert of this life to union with Hallam. At the same time, it is also Christ himself who is to rise in the spiritual rock, providing salvation. And, finally, it is also Hallam who is to be the guide. Hallam, who becomes analogous to both Beatrice and Christ in the course of *In Memoriam*, here also gains a resemblance to Moses. That mystical union of God, Hallam, and the poet which takes place in the ninety-fifth section of the poem is here recapitulated in the lines which close it.[17]

Once the type of the stricken rock becomes a commonplace of nineteenth-century poetry, it begins to appear in what we may term a secularized or extended form. Poetry can employ types in at least four different ways: first of all, hymns and devotional verse can simply remind the audience of the existence of types, providing standard interpretations of them and perhaps juxtaposing several to enforce points of doctrine. Here the poet does little more than assist the preacher to educate people to read the Bible in terms of types and figures of Christ. Second, at a level of somewhat greater complexity, the writer applies types to his own spiritual situation in verse of personal devotion. The dividing line between this and the first use of types is often difficult to locate, particularly in the case of minor poetry, but the distinguishing characteristic of the mode is its personal, even idiosyncratic, application and development of this form of symbolism. A third use of typological imagery occurs when the poet applies it in a fictional narrative. Such transference of biblical symbolism – which God Himself had supposedly placed in the scriptures – to secular fiction requires the poet to make a slight leap. None the less, the poetry which results still uses typological imagery to convey straightforward, orthodox Christian doctrine. Thus, when Ruskin and Wordsworth refer to the rock in Horeb, they still intend it to convey an essentially Christian point about the way God vivifies the human heart. In contrast, Robert Calder Campbell and Emily Dickinson, at whom we shall next look, exemplify various secularized forms of this type, precisely because they employ it in the modernist manner to create poetic emphasis rather than to communicate ideas about salvation and grace.

For instance, Campbell's untitled love sonnet in *The Germ* (1850), the short-lived publication of the Pre-Raphaelite Brotherhood, uses the commonplace type as the basis of a witty conceit. The linked images of manna and smitten rock define the positions of speaker and listener, lover and beloved, rather than conveying Christian doctrine. The sonnet opens with a description of the lovers at play, and a gamesome, light tone characterizes this not very inspired poetic effort. The speaker tells his beloved that when she pulls

> Pink scented apples from the garden trees
> To fling at me, I catch them, on my knees,
> Like those who gather'd manna.

This whimsical introduction of the miraculous food in the wilderness prepares here, as it does so often in hymns and devotional verse, for the associated type of the smitten rock. Pointing out that when he is with her he can speak his love, the poet confesses:

> but when thou'rt gone
> I have no speech, – no magic that beguiles,
> The stream of utterance from the harden'd rock.

In the manner of many love poets, Campbell sets his beloved at the center of his imaginative world, thus displacing God, for her presence produced the desired vitalization of the heart – her presence, her grace replaces that of God. Of course, the tone is light here, and this playful poem makes no attempt to be either blasphemously ardent or critical of the original text.

To what extent, one wonders, does this obviously secular poem require that the reader perceive the existence both of biblical allusion and typological symbolism? To begin with, it seems clear that unless one recognizes the allusions to the Old Testament one cannot follow the poem very well. On the other hand, although the image of the manna seems rather strained if one does not perceive a prefigurative significance, it still remains intelligible. None the less, the reference to the miraculous food in the desert makes far more poetic sense when the reader recognizes that it functions to prepare for the rock in Horeb. This second image, which provides the poetic climax for the sonnet, demands that we understand the allusion to the common-place type, because the line 'The stream of utterance from the harden'd rock' refers, not to the Old Testament passage, but to Christian interpretations of it as a figure of Christ; that is, not to the literal water that came forth from the rock but to its typological interpretation as the effect of grace upon the heart.

Glancing briefly across the Atlantic, we can observe Emily Dickinson's far less light-hearted use of the image in a poem that obviously owes much to Protestant hymnody:

> A *Wounded* Deer – leaps highest –
> I've heard the Hunter tell –
> 'Tis but the Ecstasy of *death* –
> And then the Brake is still!
>
> The *Smitten* Rock that gushes!
> The *trampled* Steel that springs!
> A Cheek is always redder
> Just where the Hectic stings!
>
> Mirth is the Mail of Anguish –
> In which it Cautious Arm,
> Lest anybody spy the blood
> And 'you're hurt' exclaim! (*c.* 1860)

Like many hymns of old and New England, this poem proceeds by assembling a list of analogies, and to some extent the poet's italiciz-ing serves to make the parallels she perceives clearer and more convincing. After the opening image of the stricken deer's leap, the poem provides three similar examples of the way a force impinging upon objects, whether animate or inanimate, produces a powerful – she proposes the most powerful– reaction. The last stanza then effects a turn, indeed a resolution, by offering the 'solution' that mirth can protect one from such troublesome capacity for pain.

What role in the poem, then, does the line 'The *Smitten* Rock that gushes!' have, and how essential is it for the reader to perceive its commonplace typological significance – whether as prefiguration of the Crucifixion or the action of grace upon the heart? To begin with, unless we recognize the allusion, this line makes little sense, for it does not seem to refer to drilling wells or any such enterprise. In fact, only by recognizing the original importance of the image as a type of Christ does the reader allow it full impact. Although originally an image of major Christian significance, Dickinson has here emptied it of its christological meaning, using it only for powerful emphasis. None the less, in what is an apparent paradox, unless we recognize the original Christian import of the symbol, it will not function in its new role.[18]

Browning, perhaps the Victorian poet most devoted to typological allusions, provides another secularized version of this stock image. In 'One Word More', the poem which dedicates *Men and Women* (1855) to Elizabeth Barrett Browning, the poet explicitly makes Moses a symbol for himself and all artists – as had Donne, Vaughan, and Milton before him.[19] Complaining that the artist sorrows because of the way the 'earth'– here largely the poet's audience– lessens and even negates the heavenly gift of poetry, Browning tells his fellow poet:

> He who smites the rock and spreads the water,
> Bidding drink and live a crowd beneath
> Even he, the minute makes immortal,
> Proves, perchance, but mortal in the minute,
> Desecrates, belike, the deed in doing.
> While he smites, how can he but remember,
> So he smote before, in such a peril,
> When they stood and mocked – 'Shall smiting help us?'
> When they drank and sneered – 'A stroke is easy!'
> When they wiped their mouths and went their journey,
> Throwing him for thanks – 'But drought was pleasant.'
> Thus old memories mar the actual triumph. . . .
> For he bears an ancient wrong about him,
> Sees and knows again those phalanxed faces,
> Hears, yet one time more, the 'customed prelude –
> 'How shouldst thou, of all men, smite, and save us?'

Guesses what is like to prove the sequel –
'Egypt's flesh-pots – nay, the drought was better.'

Clearly, this purely personal application of the old figure places its
major emphasis upon the beleaguered, unappreciated Moses, since
his actions and position in relation to his people receive more attention than does the water he brought forth from the rock. None the
less, this use of the commonplace (which, incidentally, is very
probably the direct source of Hopkins's more orthodox employ-
ment of the type)[20] receives additional impact if we recognize its
figural sense. The poet, in other words, sees himself, like Moses and
Christ, bringing the water of life – of truth, feeling, and spiritual
strength – to the hostile crowd. Of course, this image works fairly
effectively even if one does not perceive a typological dimension, a
dimension which here serves largely to provide emphasis. Moreover, one major emphasis of Browning's allusion – that he, like
Moses, sinned in bringing forth water from the rock a second time –
does not accept a typological reading.

One finds it difficult to demonstrate that Browning intended us to
find a typological significance here, although one somewhat ambiguous bit of evidence might be cited in favor of such a thesis:
The line 'Even he, the minute makes immortal' can be taken to
indicate that in bringing water from the rock, Moses becomes
'immortal' for a brief instant because he then (and only then)
partakes of the type. Moses himself would not be seen as immortal in
performing this act if it referred only to himself and not to the Gospel
scheme. None the less, one is reduced, finally, to accept merely a
probability: Browning draws extensively upon typology for the
complex imagery of *Paracelsus*, 'Saul', and *The Ring and the Book*; he
several times uses this same image typologically; and he probably
therefore, made conscious use of the typological sense of the image
of the smitten rock.[21]

This brief examination of Victorian poetry's use of a single
commonplace type suggests how varied such applications can be.
Typology furnished a large fund of intrinsically powerful stock
images. Second, both secular and religious poetry drew upon this
fund of types in such a way as to suggest that many authors who
were not conventional believers in Christianity, much less Evangelicals or High Churchmen, also made use of it. Third, the rather

anachronistic notions of time and existence implicit in typological symbolism were capable, on occasion, of producing an entire world-view, an entire imaginative universe. Finally, this kind of symbolism was used in ways which varied from thus generating an imaginative world to providing mere points of emphasis. Such evidence suggests that typology played an important, if little noticed, role in Victorian literature. To inform ourselves about its influence upon non-fiction, the novel, narrative poetry, and dramatic monologue, we shall next examine its appearance in these literary forms.

CHAPTER THREE

TYPOLOGY IN FICTION AND NON-FICTION

Alas, where now are the Hengsts and Alarics . . . who, when their home is grown too narrow, will enlist and, like fire-pillars, guide onwards those superfluous masses of indomitable living Valour. . . ? Where are they? – Preserving their Game!

– Thomas Carlyle, 'Chartism' (1839)

Typology, which thus provides Victorian poetry with imagery and theme, also has other important literary applications. Prose fiction, narrative poetry, and related forms, such as the dramatic monologue, frequently employ this form of symbolism as a device for creating and defining character. Charlotte Brontë's *Jane Eyre* (1847) provides examples of two contrasting uses of scriptural types to describe the moral and spiritual condition of a character. Immediately after Jane has fled from Rochester upon discovering the existence of his insane wife, she shuts herself in her room and discovers herself bereft of hope and faith. Describing herself to the reader in the third person, she confesses:

> Jane Eyre, who had been an ardent, expectant woman – almost a bride – was a cold, solitary girl again. . . . My hopes were all dead – struck with a subtle doom, such as, in one night, fell on all the first-born in the land of Egypt. I looked on my cherished wishes, yesterday so blooming and glowing; they lay stark, chill, livid corpses, that could never revive. I looked at my love: that feeling which was my master's – which he had created; it shivered in my heart, like a suffering child in a cold cradle. (ch. 26)

In comparing her love to the dead first-born of the Egyptians who had perished in the tenth plague, Jane places that love within an existing spiritual context. She recognizes that she is being punished for not obeying the precepts of the true God, and she also realizes that she is guilty of the sin of the Egyptians – of believing both that God's powers are limited and that they could evade his law.

Brontë has prepared for this scriptural allusion several chapters earlier. At the close of the twenty-fourth chapter, Jane admits, 'My future husband was becoming to me my whole world; and more than the world: almost my hope of heaven. He stood between me and every thought of religion, as an eclipse intervenes between man and the broad sun. I could not, in those days, see God for his creature of whom I had made an idol.' Jane worshipped a man instead of God, and she made an idol of Rochester, worshipping a false god and, as it turned out, a false man as well. After discovering Bertha's existence, she finds her 'faith death-struck', and her citation of the type of the first-born makes us aware that this faith was not merely a confidence of one mature woman in her beloved but faith raised to the level of religious belief.[1] She soon enough learns that such faith is false religion; but when she loses it, a merciful and forgiving God sustains her: 'One idea only still throbbed life-like within me – a remembrance of God: it begot a muttered prayer.' Having found that the love and faith fathered upon her by Rochester have been blighted, she is sustained by God when a remembrance of Him 'begot' a prayer.[2]

Jane's citation of this Exodus type to describe her own spiritual weakness and consequent punishment serves two ends. First, it places her character and actions within a clearly defined scheme of values; and, second, because she self-consciously and accurately applies this type to herself, it serves to dramatize her new self-awareness and her admission of guilt. Rochester, we soon discover, has made no such recognition of his own guilt. Whereas her application of the death of the first-born children makes an explicit judgment on her own romantic idolatry, Rochester's citation of scripture demonstrates a complete lack of self-awareness. After Jane leaves her room convinced that she has disobeyed God's commandments, he tries to convince her to go away with him, and he tells her that he does not 'mean to torment you with the hideous associations and recollections of Thornfield Hall – this accursed place – this tent of Achan . . . – this narrow stone hell, with its one real fiend, worse than a legion of such as we imagine' (ch. 27).

In mentioning Achan's tent, Rochester condemns himself by admitting more than he realizes, for Achan was the Israelite who, disobeying God's command that no Jew should take spoil from conquered Jericho, brought disaster upon his people. When Joshua prostrates himself in the dust before God's ark, the Lord informs him that He will no longer 'be with you any more, except ye destroy the accursed among you' (Joshua 7:12). When Joshua urges Achan to glorify the Lord with his confession of guilt, he admits that he has hidden gold, silver, and 'a goodly Babylonish garment' beneath his tent. Thereupon, the Israelites punish the source of their alienation from God and consequent military disaster by stoning Achan and his family to death and then burning their bodies. Rochester, who still refuses to see that he has done anything wrong in trying to marry Jane while his first wife still lives, believes that Thornfield Hall is a 'tent of Achan' only in so far as it contains the evidence of crime.

Furthermore, Rochester, who has failed to learn from the story of Achan that God punishes severely, still believes he can evade all consequences of his acts. Thus, in a manner quite common in works whose characters misapply types to themselves and their situations, *Jane Eyre* uses such symbolism to convict Rochester of both sin and lack of self-knowledge. By placing these contrasting citations of types within a few pages of each other, Brontë manages to define the spiritual condition of her two main characters at a crucial point in the narrative. Moreover, by having Rochester describe Thornfield in terms of stone and fire– that is, as 'a narrow stone hell'– she reminds her reader of Achan's fate and, as it turns out, also makes that fate a partial type of Rochester's.

Applications of orthodox types to judge oneself sternly, such as Jane makes, are found more often in spiritual autobiographies and sermons than in novels, and the fact that *Jane Eyre* takes the form of an autobiography explains in part how such types can there be used so effectively. Rochester's misapplication of scriptural texts exemplifies a far more common use in fiction of prefigurative symbolism. A third use of types for purposes of characterization is the purely mimetic one by which their appearance in dialogue identifies someone as belonging to a particular Church party or dissenting sect. Since Evangelicals habitually salted their conversation with scriptural quotation and paraphrase, writers sometimes include types merely for realistic effect. Similarly, when imitating or describing Evangelical sermons, writers also naturally cite types because Evangelical preachers so frequently employed them.

For instance, Browning's 'Christmas Eve' (1850) in part uses such citation of typology for purposes of verisimilitude, and so does George Eliot's 'The Sad Fortunes of the Reverend Amos Barton' from *Scenes of Clerical Life* (1858). Eliot relates how poor Barton tried without much success to instruct the paupers in the local workhouse about the mysteries of typological exegesis:

> He talked of Israel and its sins, of chosen vessels, of the Paschal lamb, of blood as a medium of reconciliation; and he strove in this way to convey religious truth within reach of the Fodge and Fitchett mind. This very morning, the first lesson was the twelfth chapter of Exodus, and Mr Barton's exposition turned on unleavened bread. Nothing in the world more suited to the simple

understanding than instruction through types and symbols! But
there is always this danger attending it, that the interest or
comprehension of your hearers may stop short precisely at the
point where your spiritual interpretation begins. And Mr Barton
this morning succeeded in carrying the pauper imagination to the
dough-tub, but unfortunately was not able to carry it upwards
from that well-known object to the unknown truths which it was
intended to shadow forth. (ch. 2)

Unlike Brontë's use of types, the applications made in this delightful
passage serve almost entirely the purely mimetic function of
representing a character engaged in a daily activity. Of course,
Eliot's citation of typology does not take the form of dialogue, but it
differs most from Brontë's by not containing explicit or implicit
judgments of the character who states them in typological terms.
After reading Eliot's description of this Evangelical's complete
inability to 'bring home the gospel', we realize that Barton is sadly
unsuited to the practice of his profession. But our recognition does
not receive the additional assistance of Barton's misinterpretation of
particular types, for we are told only that he failed to convey any
gospel truths by means of the dough-tub.

However, since all types bear a heavy burden of meaning, they do
not often appear in dialogue or indirect discourse without releasing
some of it, and, therefore, they rarely play such a neutral role in
creating character. The typological image or event readily generates
multiple meanings because, by definition, it exists in at least two
contexts, times, and senses: that of the literal historical type and that
to which the type refers. The ability to perceive such meanings
serves as a handy gauge of a character's general discernment, since a
type provides author and audience with something whose meanings
have been established by convention. Types, therefore, provide the
author with a means of dramatizing a character's understanding or
misunderstanding of commonplace, if also often complex,
materials. The reader observes a character interpreting a known type
and bases his judgment of that character upon the result.

For example, we first meet Amos Barton as he walks home alone
after dinner with the local squire and his family. The threadbare
parson, whose inadequate stipend does not permit him to purchase a
coat that will keep off the chill, strolls along, 'meditating fresh

pastoral exertions on the morrow', the most important of which is to set going

> his lending library; in which he had introduced some books that would be a pretty sharp blow to the Dissenters – one especially, purporting to be written by a working man, who, out of pure zeal for the welfare of his class, took the trouble to warn them in this way against those hypocritical thieves, the Dissenting preachers. The Rev. Amos Barton profoundly believed in the existence of that working man, and had thoughts of writing to him. Dissent, he considered, would have its head bruised in Shepperton, for did he not attack it in two ways? He preached Low-Church doctrine – as evangelical as anything to be heard in the independent Chapel; and he made a High-Church assertion of ecclesiastical powers and functions. Clearly, the Dissenters would feel that 'the parson' was too many for them. Nothing like a man who combines shrewdness with energy. The wisdom of the serpent, Mr. Barton considered, was one of his strong points. (ch. 2)

Barton, a disciple of the Evangelical greats Venn, Newton, and Simeon, has come under the influence of Tractarian thought, and however his belief has developed since his days at Cambridge, he remains a fierce partisan of the established Church. Unlike many Evangelical Anglicans, he does not try to build bridges to similar dissenting denominations and clearly considers them agents of the Evil One. His judgment in these matters is characterized by his application of the passage from Genesis 3:15 about bruising the serpent's head to his attempts to conquer the dissenters in Shepperton. Like preachers of all parties, he accepts that the Christian bruises the serpent's head by advancing spiritual doctrine, and also like preachers of all parties, he defines spiritual doctrine, naturally enough, as that in which he believes. Keble, we recall, pronounced fasting to be a Christian's means of bruising the serpent's head, whereas the Cambridge Evangelical Clayton found it to lie in preaching the Gospel.[3] Barton, on the other hand, makes not just the general battle against dissent, but his particular use of tracts directed at the labourer the fulfillment of this prophetic type. The reader's recognition that Barton and his opponents share a great many basic tenets immediately casts into doubt his judgment here, for the reader soon realizes that the minister's interpretation of this central biblical type is as ill-founded as his belief that a working man wrote his favorite tract or his confidence that he has the wisdom of the serpent.

Although Eliot's use of Genesis 3:15 within a passage of indirect discourse serves the obvious mimetic purpose of showing her audience how such a man thinks and feels, it also effectively satirizes the man for his comical self-aggrandizement. In the process, this former Evangelical also suggests some of the obvious shortcomings of applying types to the individual. Granted, it was a devotional commonplace that the individual worshipper, who was part of the Church or Christ Mystical, found types fulfilled in his own life, but what, implies Eliot, is the result of thus permitting Everyman to see himself in these grandiose terms? However stirring it might seem in the abstract to apply types to the lives of all believers – if only because such applications provided powerful stimuli to act in a Christian manner – this procedure appears foolish when followed by a specific, very fallible person like Amos Barton. In Eliot's hands this humorous application of types becomes a sub-category of the mock-heroic; and whereas this form usually mocks, not the heroic itself, but that to which it is juxtaposed, here the irony cuts both ways. Not only does Barton fall far short of the standard created by the type, but the very notion that typology could involve individuals seems called into question.

Eliot gives her gentle satire another twist several chapters later when she informs the reader that his 'notable plan of introducing anti-Dissenting books into his Lending Library did not in the least appear to have bruised the head of Dissent, though it had certainly made Dissent strongly inclined to bite the Rev. Amos's heel' (ch. 5). Whereas the first part of Genesis 3:15 was taken to prefigure the ultimate triumph of good over evil in the person of Christ and His Church; the second was interpreted to signify the fact that to have such a victory, Christ and the Church would have to be bruised – or crucified. When applied to the individual worshipper, such bruising took the form of any of his sufferings for Christ or, in practice, any which he chose to believe were on behalf of his Saviour. The wit of this second application of the bruising passage arises from the fact that the relatively mild discomfort Barton endures because of his ill-conceived plan in no way matches the bruising of martyrdom or

Crucifixion. Eliot applies this phrase to her character directly, for this second use of it occurs, not in indirect discourse representing his interior monologue, but in the author's commentary. The gap between the seriousness of the metaphorical bruising which Barton suffers at the hand of the dissenters of Shepperton and that suffered by Christ further mocks him and his inability to interpret or apply properly the things of God to the things of man.

The almost inevitable disparities between type and fulfillment in the life of a fictional character, like a character's misapplication or misinterpretation of such symbolism, produces a range of ironic commentary on fictional personages. Since the time the Wife of Bath argued for female superiority with wonderfully twisted allusions to scripture, English authors have long employed such subjective distortions of interpretive procedures as a means of creating and occasionally satirizing figures in their own works. As Barton demonstrates, such uses of commonplace types can produce gentle, if far-reaching, satire. They can also induce the reader to make far harsher judgments of a fictional character, and Rochester's misapplication and misreading of Achan's tent exemplifies such an earnest condemnation.

The double perspective or context provided by typology makes it particularly useful to the writer of dramatic monologues, since the disparity between literal and symbolical (or type and antitype) provides him with an effective means of allowing his character to convey more than he intends. Robert Browning, who is the great typologist among Victorian poets, frequently employs types for this purpose. For instance, 'The Bishop Orders His Tomb at Saint Praxed's Church. Rome, 15—' (1845) uses a number of types to emphasize the precise nature of the prelate's characterizing attitudes towards life and death, matter and spirit. The Bishop, whom Ruskin took to be a brilliantly achieved emblem of the Renaissance, persistently confuses matter and spirit in a most blasphemous manner, for having no true belief in Christian immortality, he yet tries to secure himself a kind of bizarre life after death. Browning's many citations of types in the poem reveal his speaker continually misinterpreting heavenly spiritual matters which he appropriates and misapplies to his passionate yearning to make himself immortal. As George Monteiro has pointed out, 'in ordering his tomb – and the entire poem is organized around this piece of business – the Bishop in effect parodies the Lord's command to Moses to build him a sanctuary: "According to all that I show thee, after the pattern of the tabernacle" (Exodus xxv.9)'.[4] The Bishop, who sees himself as 'an object worthy of worship', wishes his tomb to be constructed of stones from the Tabernacle, moreover, which were types of Heaven. Furthermore, the very details, such as the nine pillars supporting his tomb, turn out to be allusions to passages in Exodus which were commonly read as prefigurative images of Heaven as well. 'Without hope for personal salvation and with no faith in the Christian Resurrection, the Bishop reduces references to John the Baptist and the Madonna to nothing more than aesthetic comparisons for his beloved *lapis lazuli*. At the same time, taking over metaphors which emblematize salvation, he attempts to remake them into the letter of an earthbound immortality of sorts'.[5]

We may add that the Bishop's many blasphemies find their center in his complete inability to comprehend the nature of matter, spirit, and the relationship between them. In particular, he cannot interpret the literal expression of spiritual matters properly. Augustine's *Confessions* tell that during his earlier Manichaean stage when he accepted the sect's belief in philosophical materialism, he could not conceive symbolic interpretation, and that as he came to believe in a world of the spirit, he also came to accept and understand symbolic reading of texts. In fact, the connection of the two remains so close for Augustine that he terms 'spiritual' what we today would subsume under the broad category 'symbolical'.[6] Browning's Bishop finds himself in the predicament of a Manichaean who can only accept the material and yet passionately desires immortality, which requires a belief in spirituality. As a result, he collapses matter and spirit into each other, now calling upon the capacities of the one and now the other. This fusion and confusion of states of being, which his passionate desire for immortality produces, is well suited to the psychological state of a dying man, and perhaps this suitability provides another reason why Browning chose to set this character portrait within the context of a death-bed scene.

The dying prelate provides only the most extreme example from Browning's work of a character who can neither interpret nor apply types properly, but the preacher in 'Christmas Eve' (1850), like many in *The Ring and the Book* (1868–9), embodies an equally effective use of this method of character definition. His long poems also depict characters by means both of these figures' self-conscious distortion of types for dishonest ends and of their apparently unconscious citation of such biblical images. For example, in *The Ring and the Book* the villainous Count Guido Francheschini represents himself as an innocent, selfless man by dramatizing himself as Christ-like.[7] But when he refers to 'God's decree,/ In which I, bowing bruised head, acquiesce' (4.1410–11), he reminds us that he is, in fact, far more like Satan than like Christ. Guido's Satanic nature is recognized by other characters in the poem, including Caponsacchi, who, realizing his adversary's dangerous scheming, had thought to himself: 'No mother nor brother Viper of the [Francheschini] brood/ Shall scuttle off without the instructive bruise' (6.677–8). The authoritative statement of Guido's nature in terms of this image is made, of course, by the old Pope, who sees Pompilia acting analogously to Christ when she treads this Satan-figure into hell– and, the reader adds, is herself 'bruised'. Browning uses the same typological allusions in *The Inn Album* (1875). When the evil nobleman mentions in passing that 'Head and feet/ Are vulnerable both, and I, foot-sure,/ Forgot that ducking down saves brow from bruise', the reader might not perceive this as an allusion to Genesis 3:15. But when his former mistress describes him more elaborately, we cannot miss the allusion:

> Let him slink hence till some subtler Eve
> Than I, anticipate the snake – bruise head
> Ere he bruise heel – or, warier than the first,
> Some Adam purge earth's garden of its pest
> Before the slaver spoil the Tree of Life.[8]

Two points demand mention here. First, Browning has his characters employ typological allusions to locate his villain for the reader, thus providing a means of authorial commentary even in the midst of forms modeled on dramatic monologue in which he cannot speak in his own person. Wayne C. Booth's *The Rhetoric of Fiction* (1961) demonstrates the intrinsic difficulties that first-person narration has in identifying the author's point of view, and recent debates about the correct reading of dramatic monologues by Tennyson and Browning suggest that such problems are intrinsic to this poetic form.[9] Typology, however, offers one solution to such interpretive problems. Even though no single character's application of a type may be entirely correct, the fact that several speakers employ the same type identifies for us the terms in which Browning wants defined the issues in question.[10] In some cases, such as that exemplified by the Pope, one character has sufficient moral, spiritual, and intellectual authority that his interpretation compels our assent. In others, the authority exists, as it were, in the correct, usually the traditional, readings of the type. Of course, when Browning uses a typological image which traditionally possesses several antitypes or interpretations, then he puts the reader, like his characters, to the test.

In addition to using this detailed typological reference for several related modes of character definition, Victorian novels employ other, far more secularized versions of typology, some of which are so distantly related to this kind of biblical symbolism that they are most profitably considered as secular analogues or offspring. Building upon the work of Paul J. Korshin and other scholars of seventeenth- and eighteenth-century literature, John R. Reed has well described

a tradition of secularized and immediate typology in English literature which persists into the nineteenth century. Consequently, it is not surprising to find Charles Dickens utilizing the model of *The Pilgrim's Progress* in *The Old Curiosity Shop*, or entitling his first novel *The Adventures of Oliver Twist: or, The Parish Boy's Progress*. Nor is it remarkable when Thackeray entitles one of his novels *The Adventures of Philip on His Way Through the World Showing Who Robbed Him, Who Helped Him and Who Passed Him By*, and continues the Samaritan motif throughout the novel in allusion as well as illustration. . . . Charles Aubrey, enduring his ordeal in *Ten Thousand A-Year*, is likened to Job in his suffering (See vol. 2, ch. 7; vol. 3, ch. 5). The story of Jacob's experience with Leah and Rachel serves as a rough parallel to Stephen Blackpool's situation in *Hard Times* (see vol. 1, ch. 13). He has married a wife who is no pleasure to him, while he dreams of the unattainable Rachel who is his true love. The friendship of John Halifax and Phineas Fletcher in Miss Mulock's *John Halifax, Gentleman* is sanctified by its resemblance to the scriptural model of Jonathan and David. These scriptural associations may be incidental or central to the stories concerned; they may be merely verbal or have a more stylized pictorial quality.[11]

Hugh Witemeyer's *George Eliot and the Visual Arts* (1979) discusses this kind of scriptural association in the novelist's work. After demonstrating her knowledge of both scriptural typology and the history of art, Professor Witemeyer convincingly demonstrates how she based her literary characterizations upon a wide variety of pictorial techniques, themes, and models. For example, in explaining Eliot's 'pictorial and overtly typological' idealization of Mordecai in *Daniel Deronda* (1876), he remarks that 'Daniel's first impression of the consumptive scholar is that "such a physiognomy as that might possibly have been seen in a prophet of the Exile, or in some New Hebrew poet of the medieval time" (33: 165). Later Daniel sees Mordecai as "an illuminated type of bodily emaciation and spiritual eagerness" (40:327)'.[12] Although the novelist's first mention of prophets of the Babylonian exile suggests that her allusive description might function somewhat like a scriptural type, the comparison with a mediaeval poet which immediately follows demonstrates that she has abandoned most of the defining characteristics of this symbolic mode. Professor Witemeyer points out that Victorians often used 'type' to mean 'any exemplary moral or religious norm which finds successive incarnations in history', and we may add that they also used it to denote a species or class, an exemplary or defining instance, a distinctive mark or sign, a symbol, and a wood or metal block used in printing.[13] Each of these meanings obviously relates to both the Greek and Roman root words from which 'type' derives and also to the use of the term in biblical interpretation. Professor Witemeyer also uses the term to apply to characteristic and occasionally idealizing pictorial forms created by great painters, such as Titian, Rembrandt, and Reynolds, for he concerns himself with showing that Eliot bases her characters upon these pictorial examples.

Typology and the habits of mind it encourages certainly support this kind of allusive literary iconography by habituating writers to think in terms of prior models. Such techniques, however they may derive from orthodox typology, have little in common with it, and we must be careful not to confuse the two. In fact, one of the most important literary applications of the term, which is to describe something very like a humor character, is only very distantly related to this form of biblical symbolism. John R. Reed convincingly argues that both Victorian and modern fiction retains 'conventions of character' analogous to earlier ones:

> Our stylizations are largely Freudian, as Victorians' were moral and physiognomical, and earlier centuries' were humorous or canonical. . . . In Victorian literature, what we would call realistic motivation is often incorporate with type fulfillment. Characters do not act according to a system of humors or ruling passions, nor are they moved by the complexes and neuroses of the twentieth-century man; instead, they exhibit predictable combinations of attributes which result in conventional types.[14]

Within this kind of typology (which, incidentally, is not a symbolic mode) a character is said to fulfill a type when he or she completes a recognized pattern; say, the lonely maiden or the orphan child; and such completing of a pre-established pattern bears resemblances to the operations of scriptural typology.

Although there exists a minor temporal element in this secular typology– the character does match the pattern created by a stylization or an historical character of the past– even this element receives significantly different emphases. Whereas the christological type, which plays an essential role in a scheme of progressive revelation, points towards the future, such secular typology, which shares much with classical thought, looks back at the past. Although Christian typology does include fulfillment of the the prefiguration within the life of the individual, it places major emphasis upon the way earlier figures from the Old Testament lead towards their completion in Christ. In keeping with this emphasis, this form of biblical symbolism has the lesser anticipate the greater. In contrast, secular notions of typology pattern a later character upon– literally 'after'– some greater figure who precedes him.

Far more important, of course, is the fact that such canonical images and idealizations have none of christological typology's most interesting features – namely, its connection of two times, one of which fulfills the other; its juxtaposition of the temporal and the eternal within an historical fact; its ability to generate the entire

Gospel scheme and history; its emphasis upon the reality of both poles of the symbolic relation; its privileged status as a divinely instituted signifying system; and its long tradition as both a hermeneutic and iconographic repository which makes it an additionally powerful influence upon the Victorians.

If biblical typology had almost no major influence in the Victorian period, one could justifiably use its terminology in loose applications without ill effect. But, as we have already observed, this form of scriptural symbolism had pervasive major influence upon Victorian literature, and, therefore, at this early stage of the investigation of Victorian typology, we should be particularly careful to apply our teminology as precisely as possible. Unfortunately, the terms 'type' and 'typology' have widely accepted, non-theological meanings, and one cannot resort to using 'figure' and 'figuralism', which are common theological synonyms, since they possess a technical application in the study of art. When Professor Reed, who is well aware of the difference between biblical and characteriological typology, uses the term 'type', he thus makes a common, acceptable application of the word. These potentially troublesome termino-logical difficulties require the student of Victorian typology and its cultural effects to exercise extreme caution. In particular, we must remain aware of the differences that exist between this form of biblical symbolism and other modes of thought which are discussed in confusingly similar vocabularies. If scholars do not take proper care to distinguish between various forms of thought in character-ization and other areas, they will inevitably apply the attributes of typology to subjects in which these attributes have no place. Similarly, if scholars wish to determine the precise manner in which secularization proceeds during the course of the nineteenth century, they must begin with fairly clear ideas of what constituted religious thought. Returning to the subject of literary characterization and its relation to biblical typology, we realize that we cannot determine how the creation of literary character evolves under the influence of this symbolic mode unless we have a well-defined notion of its most orthodox applications. As soon as one considers orthodox types and their very distant analogues to be much the same thing, one loses an important opportunity for understanding the past.

In addition to contributing to poetry and the novel, typology also had an influence upon what is probably the most characteristic

109

Victorian literary form, that kind of non-fiction best described as the creation of the Victorian Sage.[15] This genre, which variously combines the attributes of the sermon, Jeremiad, and neo-classical satire, attempts to interpret contemporary phenomena in much the same way that the sermons of Spurgeon, Melvill, and Newman interpret scriptural fact and event. The nature of this enterprise demands that both the sage and his audience conceive of his role as a special one – as one, in fact, that is distinguished by his superior comprehension of the significance of transitory phenomena and their relation to eternal laws or principles. Clearly, the eighteenth-century familiar essay in which a writer addresses himself to his equals is not suited for such purposes; but the sermon, particularly the Evangelical sermon, establishes precisely the desired position of sage in relation to his readers and offers other necessary elements as well.

For example, the sage must convince his audience not only that he possesses superior vision but also that his subjects and examples are indeed significant. The Victorian preacher, who confronted the same problems, often attracted his audience's attention by identifying an interpretive crux which he presented as being especially important, intriguing, or paradoxical. In showing his congregation how unexpected truths often lay hidden in the most unexpected places – particularly in types – this preacher convinced his listeners that he could provide them with something of value. One important technique in this procedure takes the form of defining or redefining major terms, such as 'Christian', 'type', and 'sacrifice'. This practice effectively demonstrates that the preacher's congregation does not properly understand crucial matters: at best its members are ignorant and uninformed, at worst they find their sinful state preventing them from seeing with clear eyes. This procedure consequently demonstrates to his listeners that they need his leadership. Having established his definitions, the preacher frequently points to the literal meaning of his text and sets forth whatever lessons or problems it may contain. Then, if he concerns himself with setting forth types and shadows of Christ, the preacher again leads and entertains his audience by revealing his ability to perceive important truths in unexpected places. Some Evangelical preachers, such as Spurgeon, would also relate their personal experiences as models for their congregations, and again such a practice confirms the audience's dependent relationship. All of these matters of procedure mark the writings of the Victorian Sage, many of which bear the obvious impress of the homiletic tradition.

In particular, Ruskin's *Modern Painters* (1843–60), *The Seven Lamps of Architecture* (1848), and *The Stones of Venice* (1851–2), which employ a number of typologically supported arguments, often read like sermons about the relation of aesthetic concerns to Bible fact. When Ruskin opposes conservative notions that color is relatively unimportant in great art, he advances this aspect of his romantic art theory with a sermon on the typological significance of the rainbow. Thus, in the second volume of *The Stones of Venice,* when he wishes to demonstrate 'the connection of of pure colour with profound and noble thought' (10.174), he sounds much like any other art critic, historian, or theorist in his citations of Venetian painting and Gothic cathedrals. However, he sounds a rather different note when he sets forth 'a noble reason for this universal law':

> In that heavenly circle which binds the statutes of colour upon the front of the sky, when it became the sign of the covenant of peace, the pure hues of divided light were sanctified to the human heart for ever; nor this, it would seem, by mere arbitrary appointment, but in consequence of the fore-ordained and marvellous constitution of those hues into a sevenfold, or, more strictly still, a threefold order, typical of the Divine nature itself. Observe also, the name Shem, or Splendour, given to that son of Noah in whom this covenant with mankind was to be fulfilled, and see how that name was justified by every one of the Asiatic races which descended from him. Not without meaning was the love of Israel to his chosen son expressed by the coat 'of many colours'; not without deep sense of the sacredness of that symbol of purity did the lost daughter of David tear it from her breast: – 'With such robes were the king's daughters that were virgins apparelled.' We know it to have been by Divine command that the Israelite, rescued from servitude, veiled the tabernacle with its rain of purple and scarlet, while the under sunshine flashed through the fall of the colour from its tenons of gold. (10.174–5)

Similarly, when Ruskin argues in the concluding volume of *Modern Painters* (1860) that color 'is the purifying or sanctifying element of material beauty' (7.417n), he again cites biblical types as evidence. In order to defend his assertion about the spiritual value of color, he explains that in one sense form is prior to color, because 'on form depends existence; on colour, only purity. Under the Levitical law, neither scarlet nor hyssop could purify the deformed. So, under all natural law, there must be rightly shaped members first; then sanctifying colour and fire in them' (7.417n). Despite the fact that Ruskin had already abandoned his childhood faith two years before writing this fifth volume of *Modern Painters*, he still persists in citing the scriptures as though every word they contain were literally true.[16] Therefore, if the Bible contains certain incidental facts about the Levitical sacrifices, such as the way color was to be applied to them by the priest, then he draws upon such facts as if they were divinely authenticated ones. Moreover, like Keble and other Tractarians, Ruskin also accepts that the physical world bears a divine impress which the sensitive eye can read in terms of type and symbol.

The major support for his defense of color in art and nature comes again from the ninth chapter of Genesis, which relates that God made the rainbow, a natural phenomenon, as the sign of this covenant never again to destroy man by a flood:

> The cloud, or firmament, . . . signifies the ministration of the heavens to man. That ministration may be in judgment or mercy— in the lightning, or the dew. But the bow, or colour of the cloud, signifies always mercy, the sparing of life; such ministry of the heaven as shall feed and prolong life. And as the sunlight, undivided, is the type of the wisdom and righteousness of God, so divided, and softened into colour by means of the firmamental ministry, fitted to every need of man, as to every delight, and becoming one chief source of human beauty, by being made part of the flesh of man;– thus divided, the sunlight is the type of the wisdom of God, becoming sanctification and redemption.
> Various in work– various in beauty – various in power. (7.418)

The rainbow, a sign of God's covenant with man, was interpreted by Christian exegetes as a type of Christ, who both brought the new covenant of grace and was Himself its sign.[17] What distinguishes the rainbow from almost all other types is that it is a natural phenomenon, not a unique event or person, which prefigures Christ.

Strictly speaking, one might claim that only the rainbow that appeared to Noah after leaving the ark could serve as a true type, since only that particular occurrence of this natural phenomenon possesses the unique situational parallel intrinsic to a true type. Victorian interpreters, however, do not thus limit the typological significance of the rainbow to its appearance in Genesis, and therefore it serves them as a major example of something which functions typologically in both of God's books – the Bible and the Book of Nature. Unlike most exegetes, Ruskin does not rest his interpretation solely upon the fact that God placed a covenant-sign (or contract) in the heavens and then Himself explained its significance for man. Assuming that anything which bears the impress of divine nature can be read for information about God and His laws, Ruskin here draws an elaborate analogy between natural phenomena and theological fact: bright sunlight thus turns out to be an emblem of God the Father's wisdom and righteousness, while the rainbow stands for Christ's 'sanctification and redemption'.

In citing the rainbow in support of his belief that color is a central, not a peripheral, element in the arts, Ruskin draws upon orthodox interpretations of this natural phenomenon. But in addition to employing straightforward applications of commonplace types, he includes evidence based on his characteristic extension of biblical typology to include looser forms of symbolism.[18] Most obviously, whereas the rainbow serves as an orthodox type of Christ, since in Noah's time it prefigured His later appearance, the sun does not prefigure God at all; rather, it symbolizes Him. Similarly, Ruskin's summoning of the tabernacle and the sacrificial hyssop, both Levitical types, uses material associated with this form of exegesis, rather than the primary type, as support for his argument. Ruskin, in other words, does not concern himself primarily with the fact that the Levitical animal sacrifice prefigures Christ's, for he employs a more elegant argument which involves analyzing facts associated with the original type. Although such procedure is quite orthodox, it does move out of clearly defined areas that receive the authentication of the New Testament. Thus, when he mentions Joseph's coat of many colors to support his contention that these bright hues symbolize divine love, he applies details associated with a type of Christ to his argument. In this case, Ruskin's point seems to be that since Jacob gave his son a brightly colored garment because he so loved Joseph, the interpreter, knowing that Joseph is a type of Christ, can take Jacob analogously as God the Father. Therefore, since both God and Jacob bestowed bright color upon those they loved – Jacob with Joseph's robe, God with the rainbow (which is also Christ) – color means the sanctifying element of divine love. Even in this extended chain of assumptions that Ruskin bases on a type, his main evidence still comes from the orthodox type of the rainbow. Both less central qualities or attributes associated with types, such as Joseph's coat, and facts associated with figures who do not act as types, such as the violated Tamar, function only to provide additional support in the form of analogy.

These two passages from *The Stones of Venice* and *Modern Painters*, which exemplify Ruskin's skilled application of orthodox typology in his early career, take the form of citing scriptural evidence in the midst of an apparently secular discourse. Such procedure served several rhetorical purposes, not the least of which was to shift the terms of a discussion or place it in a universal context. Such use of typologically supported arguments further provided Ruskin with a means of appealing to many present or former Evangelicals in his audience, since such argument not only used terms and reasoning known to many in his audience but also immediately demonstrated that aesthetic questions bore major spiritual importance. For Ruskin, who was trying to open the eyes of Evangelical Englishmen to the glories of art and architecture, this kind of argumentation possessed the ability to speak to Evangelicals in their own terms and thereby convince them that Gothic architecture, religious painting, and other sources of beauty, contaminated for them by a long connection with Roman Catholicism, had true religious value. The major example of this kind of typological argument in the service of the arts is 'The Lamp of Sacrifice', the opening chapter in Ruskin's *The Seven Lamps of Architecture* (1849), which, unlike most of his other uses of types, takes the form of a full Evangelical sermon about typology and not just the application of it to a wider argument. [19]

Such transfer of the arguments, imagery, and manner of proceeding of the typological sermon to art criticism represents one way in which a Victorian sage employed types. Another influence of this form of symbolism upon the writings of the sage appears in those works which interpret contemporary events much as preachers interpret ancient biblical ones. Ruskin's later writings on political-economics exemplify this second effect of typology upon Victorian non-fiction, but since Thomas Carlyle, whom he accepted as his 'Master', first developed this literary form, we shall briefly examine his works to observe what happens when certain habits of thought associated with typology appear in other contexts.[20]

According to *Past and Present* (1843), all history, and not just that detailed in the Bible, is informed by divine revelation: 'Men believe in Bibles, and disbelieve in them: but of all Bibles the frightfulest to disbelieve in is this "Bible of Universal History". This is the Eternal Bible and God's-Book, "in which every born man", till once the soul and eyesight are extinguished in him, "can and must, with his own eyes, see the God's-Finger writing"! To discredit this, is an *infidelity* like no other' (10.240). Two events, in particular, demand that men read them for their bits of divine revelation: the French Revolution and the Peterloo Massacre. Indeed, *Past and Present*'s third chapter reminds his readers that in 'all hearts that witnessed Peterloo, stands written, as in fire-characters, or smoke-characters prompt to become fire again, a legible balance-account of grim vengeance; very unjustly balanced, much exaggerated, as is the way with such accounts: but payable readily at sight, in full compound interest! Such things should be avoided as the very pestilence!' (10.16–17). The one way a society can avoid having to make such a fearful settlement in blood and suffering, says Carlyle, is to understand what God has written in the book of history before warnings become judgments. As he points out in 'Chartism' (1839), the history of revolutionary France contains multiple scripture lessons for the English reader: 'France is a pregnant example in all ways. Aristocracies that do not govern, Priesthoods that do not teach; the misery of that, and the misery of altering that, – are written in Belshazzar fire-letters on the history of France' (29.161–2). The fifth chapter of the Book of Daniel relates that God's finger wrote a judgment upon Belshazzar, son of Nebuchadnezzar, in fire-letters on the walls of his palace, and Carlyle, who finds himself cast into the role of Daniel and Jeremiah, tries to warn his contemporaries so that they will not have to suffer for their sins.

The distinguishing claim of Carlyle and Ruskin as sages is that they can read the Belshazzar fire-letters of past and contemporary events. Whereas Ruskin's applications of orthodox types follow the model of the Victorian preacher, these uses of extended forms of this symbolism self-consciously rely upon that of the Old Testament prophets. Like them, Carlyle and Ruskin try to make their contemporaries realize that they have abandoned the ways of God and Nature; and that unless they return to them, they will suffer terrible punishments. To convince their audience that they have a valid message, they must first demonstrate that they can perceive meaningful signs where others do not, after which they must convince them that their interpretations are correct. Therefore, a prime technique of the Victorian sage lies in his discoveries of moral, political, and spiritual law in the most apparently trivial phenomena of contemporary life. For like both preacher and prophet, the sage must convince his listeners that he has access to the grammar and dictionary of reality and hence can read the lessons of contemporary events.

Typology furnishes the Victorian sage with three kinds of assistance. First, as Ruskin's earlier writings demonstrate, he can apply orthodox types to some contemporary question, such as the value of the arts in human life. Second, as we shall observe in Chapter Five when we examine Carlylean application of political types, the sage can manipulate orthodox typology for satirical and other effects. Third, as *Past and Present* reveals, the sage can treat some contemporary fact or event as material for interpretation – as a Belshazzar fire-letter. Although these events bear a serious meaning, the secular prophet who finds spiritual significance in actual historical events often adopts the tone and methods of the satirist. 'Phenomena', the opening chapter of the third book of *Past and Present*, thus presents a series of contemporary facts as wonderfully grotesque emblems of what is wrong with the modern world. First, Carlyle presents us with the fact of an 'amphibious Pope':

the old Pope of Rome, finding it laborious to kneel so long while they cart him through the streets to bless the people on *Corpus-Christi* Day, complains of rheumatism; whereupon his Cardinals consult;– construct him, after some study, a stuffed cloaked figure, of iron and wood, with wool or baked hair; and place it in a kneeling posture. Stuffed figure, or rump of a figure; to this stuffed rump he, sitting at his ease on a lower level, joins, by the aid of cloaks and drapery, his living head and outspread hands: the rump with its cloaks kneels, the Pope looks, and holds his hands spread; and so the two in concert bless the Roman population on *Corpus-Christi* Day, as well they can. . . . Here is a Supreme Priest who believes . . . that all worship of God is a scenic phantasmagory of wax-candles, organ-blasts, Gregorian chants, massbrayings, purple monsignori, wool-and-iron rumps, artistically spread out, – to save the ignorant from worse. . . . There is in this poor Pope, and his practice of the Scenic Theory of Worship, a frankness which I rather honour. (10.138–9)

For Carlyle, a rather trivial fact, such as the way a Pope's infirmities were accommodated one feast day, becomes a message written in Belshazzar fire-letters warning his contemporaries that they cannot survive by using an obsolete religion to prop up obsolete political systems.

But, 'alas, why go to Rome for Phantasms walking the streets?' (10.140), asks Carlyle, who then proceeds to find them in his England. Taking 'that great Hat seven-feet high, which now perambulates London Streets' (10.141), as such a grotesque emblem of England's spiritual malaise, he demonstrates that the underlying principle of modern business is, not to make better products, but to convince one's potential customers by puffery that one has done so. Both Carlyle's amphibious Pope and his seven-foot Hat represent the sage's common technique of taking some trivial event as an emblem of spiritual laws, and these contemporary examples often receive a heavy dose of satire at his hands. Other exemplary facts, such as the population of England's workhouses and the Irish widow who only convinced the inhabitants of Edinburgh of her fellow humanity by giving them typhus, are presented more somberly, though they also have satiric functions. A third form of such analogies appears in the invented fables Carlyle and Ruskin employ, which may be as grandiose as the entire story of Diogenes Teufelsdröckh or as brief as Ruskin's Goddess-of-Getting-On or his parody of the armaments race in 'Traffic' (1864). Like much of what is most characteristic in the writings of Ruskin and Carlyle, such satiric fables and emblems represent an effect of scriptural typology, of course, and not that mode of symbolism itself. As many of their works demonstrate, the Victorian sage defines himself by his superior ability to make interpretations – interpretations, readings, of all kinds of things, events, and people.

117

Trained in techniques of Bible reading that encouraged them to take everything in the scriptures, even the most trivial detail, as bearing the impress of God, they became accustomed to finding such meanings outside the Bible as well, and this habit of mind was in complete accord with Evangelical rules of interpretation that found types reaching fulfillment in the life of the individual worshipper. What Ruskin, Carlyle, and so many other Victorians acquired from years of meditating upon the Bible was a habit of mind, an assurance that everything possessed significant meaning if only one knew how to discover it. The scriptures released their many truths once the reader understood that Christ hovered beneath the literal facts and events of the Old Testament. Even after Ruskin and Carlyle (and many other of their contemporaries) abandoned the faith which shaped these basic attitudes towards the world of man and nature, these attitudes remained. Typology, which taught so many Victorians how to interpret biblical events and those of contemporary life, often persisted after a belief in Christianity disappeared from the lives of many men and women.

CHAPTER FOUR

TYPOLOGY IN THE VISUAL ARTS

In encountering the many appearances of typology in the visual arts of the period, the student of Victorian culture confronts three questions. First, how does Victorian art use typological symbolism? Second, what is the nature of visual uses of typology – or, put differently, what is the nature of typological images that appear in the visual arts? Third, what particular relation exists between visual and verbal applications of typology? Before attempting to answer these last two questions, which lead us into problems of aesthetics and semiotics, I should like to examine some of the important ways in which typology influenced Victorian art and art theory.

Probably the single most interesting influence of typology upon the art of the period appears in the way it provided the basis for theories of symbolic realism. Ruskin, Hunt, Millais, and many artists in the Pre-Raphaelite circle advocated realistic technique, not because they were interested in painterly realism for its own sake, but because they wished to have the artist, particularly the beginning artist, move beyond conventional modes of representation and thus discover new sources of beauty and truth.[1] Building upon the work of Maclise, Mulready, Dyce, and others, the young Pre-Raphaelites rather quickly created a fashion for what has come to be termed 'hard-edge realism'. Although an emphasis upon preserving the details of visual fact certainly informed the congeries of attitudes which constitute the 'program' of the Pre-Raphaelite Brotherhood, it was only a single factor in the young painters' testing of received academic conventions. The members of the Brotherhood also concerned themselves with reanimating painterly iconography and symbolic conventions, since they accepted that a pure realism, such as that practiced in France, produced an unimaginative, materialistic, ultimately demoralizing art. As Hunt emphasized to the painter-poet William Bell Scott, the reason for 'the dead-alive poetry and art of the day' lay in 'the totally material nature of the views cultivated in modern schools[.] Trying to limit speculation within the bounds of sense only must produce poor sculpture, feeble painting, dilettante poetry'.[2] Therefore, drawing upon the work of Hogarth, Northern Renaissance masters, and contemporary writers, such as Dickens and Tennyson, the young men and their associates sought to find means of endowing visual images with imaginative and moral power.[3]

The chief inspiration for such attempts, according to Hunt, came from John Ruskin. After a fellow student had given Hunt the second volume of *Modern Painters* (1846), under the very mistaken belief that its author had converted to Roman Catholicism, the young painter found himself deeply moved by Ruskin's high conceptions of the art, but one passage in particular, to which he recurs several times in his autobiography, provided him with a specific artistic program. While explaining the penetrative imagination of the great artist, Ruskin drew upon Tintoretto's painting of *The Annunciation* in the Scuola di San Rocco, Venice (Plate 1), for an example which turned out to have far greater effect upon himself and his contemporaries than he could ever have expected.

The critic first explains that the painting represents the Virgin sitting beneath a ruined palace vestibule. 'The spectator turns away at first, revolted, from the central object of the picture forced painfully and coarsely forward, a mass of shattered brickwork, with the plaster mildewed away from it, and the mortar mouldering from its seams'. Explanations for such coarse realism exist, say Ruskin, in the fact that Tintoretto, who draws upon the conditions of contemporary Venice, is trying to suggest Joseph's occupation as well. But as the spectator examines this image of earthly desolation, he realizes suddenly that these realistically presented visual facts bear far more important significance. In fact, the entire composition of the picture leads the viewer's eye to 'an object at the top of the brickwork, a white stone, four square, the corner-stone of the old edifice, the base of its supporting column'. This cornerstone, a visual allusion to Psalms 118, is a type, and when the spectator recognizes its meaning, he finds himself released into a world of Christian meanings: 'The ruined house is the Jewish dispensation; that obscurely arising in the dawning of the sky is the Christian; but the corner-stone of the old building remains, though the builders' tools lie idle beside it, and the stone which the builders refused is become the Headstone of the Corner' (4.264–5). That passage from Psalms 118 about the cornerstone refused by the builders is a commonplace prophetical type of Christ, and, as Ruskin has demonstrated, Tintoretto has employed it in a most traditional way to reinforce the central meaning of the annunciation theme.

William Holman Hunt, who found himself extremely excited by the artistic possibilities of such symbolism, immediately visited John Everett Millais, to whom he explained how Ruskin made the great

Venetian seem a 'sublime Hogarth' – a painter, that is, who created works rich in meaning but not dependent, as were Hogarth's, upon satire for their prime impetus. The intrinsic capacity of the typological image to combine realistic detail and complex spiritual reference offered the young artists a means of solving some of the problems they had encountered when they turned to a realistic style of painting. As long as they chose subjects that permitted either orthodox or extended applications of such symbolism, they could demonstrate that their abandoning received pictorial conventions propounded by the Academy schools and periodical critics led to a richer humanistic art – and not one that had its ideal in technological processes for reproducing images, such as the daguerreotype.[4] At the same time, these self-proclaimed 'art revolutionaries' could use types to create both new iconographies and new subjects for high art.

Millais's *Christ in the House of His Parents* (1850, Plate 2) and Hunt's *The Finding of the Saviour in the Temple* (1854–60, Plate 3) exemplify the early Pre-Raphaelite use of typology as a basis for symbolic realism. Millais, who was inspired by a High Anglican sermon in Oxford to paint his picture, provides an instance of Tractarian use of such symbolism, for his representation of an imagined event from the life of Jesus serves as an image of Christ as priest and sacrifice. The painter has represented the boy Christ immediately after He has wounded Himself trying to remove a nail from a board with pincers, and this event, like the cornerstone in Tintoretto's *Annunciation*, turns the coarse details of genre painting into spiritual fact. Jesus, whom Mary comforts, holds up His hand so that both Joseph and the spectator can see His wound. The blood on His wounded palm and that which has dropped upon His foot presents a prefigurative image of both the Crucifixion and the resurrected Christ presenting Himself to the eye of faith in the form of the Man of Sorrows.[5] Many of the details in *Christ in the House of His Parents* also prefigure the passion and death of Christ and thus reinforce the meaning of the picture's central image. The pincers and nail toward which Anne extends her hand are emblems of the Crucifixion, and the carpenter's tools and ladder on the wall behind Jesus also remind us of this event. Similarly, John's coming to Christ with a bowl of water probably serves as loose types of Christ's baptism and also of the vinegar and gall offered to Him when He was dying on the Cross. It is even possible that it could allude to the water and blood which poured forth from Christ's side when pierced by a spear – but here the possibility seems rather distant indeed. The partially woven basket on the painting's extreme left suggests both that the total scheme of Christ's atonement is not yet complete and that these reeds prefigure those mockingly thrust on Christ as King of the Jews. The bird perched on the ladder symbolizes the Holy Ghost, the sheep outside all human beings, and the workbench the communion table.

Whereas one set of types and symbols prefigures this imagined event's significance as a type of the passion and death of Jesus, another makes the specifically High Church interpretation of them in terms of an ordained priesthood.[6] The Tractarian notion of 'reserve', which is based on the belief that sacred truths must be protected from profanation by the uninitiated, finds one of its embodiments in this party's emphasis upon devices separating laity and priesthood.[7] Tractarian reserve, which colors High Church sermons, devotional poetry, and church design, here takes the visual form of a composition that separates the sacred interior inhabited by the Holy Family from that exterior space containing the sheep. Drawing upon older Northern Renaissance compositional schemes which derive from depicting the Virgin and child against a Cloth of Honour, Millais sets this event from the childhood of Jesus against a central panel surrounded by two openings into the distance. He then sets his image of the wounded Jesus close to the picture plane against the picture's central panel. Like Hunt's *The Finding of the Saviour in the Temple*, Millais's painting partially surrounds the young Jesus by a group of symbolic figures, and although Mary stands closest to her son in both pictures, she takes on a different meaning in each. In *Christ in the House of His Parents*, Mary joins her son as an object of veneration, for her sorrow at the young boy's wound prefigures greater sorrow in the same way that the wound serves as a type of the Crucifixion. In fact, Mary, who does not even embrace her son, appears to adopt a prayerful, reverent attitude as if she understands the full significance of this apparently everyday event – as she does in similar matters in James Collinson's 'The Child Jesus. A Record Typical of the Five Sorrowful Mysteries' (1848–50), an almost exactly contemporaneous poem written by another member of the Brotherhood.[8] If Mary's attitude or pose is thus taken as one of sorrowful prayer, it may also be understood to prefigure her conduct at the foot of the Cross. In contrast, Hunt's portrayal of Mary and her son makes it clear that, however well-intentioned a mother she is, she takes her place with those in the temple who do not understand her son's message or significance.

Whereas *Christ in the House of His Parents* makes Tractarian emphases upon separation of priest and laity and upon the high spiritual status of Mary, Hunt's *The Finding of the Saviour in the Temple*, which obviously does not support Mariolatry, presents an Evangelical rendering of scriptural events. First of all, like the Evangelical preacher who emphasizes the importance of meditating upon the Bible's literal meaning or narrative, Hunt devotes much more personal energy and pictorial emphasis than does Millais to elaborate archeological reconstructions of dress, custom, architecture, and facial type. Moreover, because Hunt accepts that the literal significance of a biblical event includes the mental experiences of those who participate in it, he includes an entire gallery of psychological portraits, and these also serve to prefigure the ways in which men continue to resist Christ's message.[9] Whereas Millais relies upon an assemblage of types within Christ's life to prefigure the Saviour's death and passion, Hunt uses a similar gathering of images to present a more original interpretation of the person and message of Christ. In presenting that moment when Christ suddenly recognizes who He is – and that He has come to fulfill type and prophecy – he presents a specifically Evangelical interpretation of older pictorial themes. Like most Evangelicals, Hunt markedly de-emphasizes the role and importance of Mary, and so *The Finding of the Saviour in the Temple*, which presents what is essentially Christ's 'conversion', provides an image of God's appearance in history. In other words, in a characteristically daring manner Hunt reinterprets the traditional theme of the dispute with the doctors and thus produces an Evangelical analogue to the Annunciation to Mary. Furthermore, Hunt's painting not only in this way reshapes and reapplies an older pictorial convention, but it also emphasizes another Evangelical doctrine, the importance of preaching the Gospel, for Christ is shown in the midst of reinterpreting the Law when His parents arrive.

Like Northern Renaissance images of the Annunciation or Adoration which use types to transform these earthly scenes into emblems of the Eternal Mass in Heaven, Hunt employs a wide range of types to turn this historical moment into a privileged instant during which the temporal and eternal coincide.[10] As one who placed little emphasis upon the sacraments, Holman Hunt was unable to devote himself, like Millais, to types which could create images of the Mass in this traditional manner, and so he dedicated much of his efforts in religious painting to finding modern equivalents for older themes. None the less, he still employs typology, much as had Van Eyck and Memling, to surround a central image with scriptural symbols that serve to place it in a privileged, sacred time and space. For example, in *The Finding*, which combines Evangelical emphases upon preaching and conversion, Hunt includes types that comment upon the central encounter. Thus, the cornerstone originally rejected by the builders appears in the courtyard at the right side of the painting, and one is meant to perceive that the completion of the old dispensation which takes place in physical form outside the temple is also taking place in spiritual form within. Similarly, just as someone tries to drive out a dove, which represents the Holy Ghost, the Rabbis are trying to drive out Christ's new spiritualization of the Law. The blind beggar outside the door advances the picture's meaning in two ways: first, he serves as an emblem of the blind ignorance within and, second, he is a type of the blind given sight by Christ. The lamb brought to slaughter over the objections of its mother offers another double significance: it parallels the relation of Christ and Mary and it shows Christ, the true sacrifice, coming to complete and abrogate the Levitical law. Even the cross on Christ's belt, which had been an ornamental design since ancient times, becomes endowed with new significance in this context.

Typology, which has the intrinsic capacity to bridge pictorial realism and complex iconography, also serves to endow the scene represented with imaginative grandeur. Both Millais and Hunt produce realistically conceived representations of events from Christ's youth. Although only Hunt's subject receives the sanction of scripture, both use types to make the events they depict seem central moments in human history. Furthermore, both *Christ in the House of His Parents* and *The Finding of the Saviour in the Temple* use typological images to set their major actions in several temporal contexts. Millais's painting of the young Christ thus participates in several times: in that of the tormenting and Crucifixion of Jesus, His resurrection, and His presence in the sacrament of the Eucharist. Hunt's painting, which, unlike that of his friend, employs traditional Old Testament types, similarly participates in several times, since the images of lamb, cornerstone, and blind man set these events unfolding before our eyes within the context of Christ's later ministry and death as well as within that provided by the Church's later preaching of the Gospel. Furthermore, Hunt, who often tends to conceive himself as an artistic Messiah, also probably intends his image of Christ's discovery of His nature to apply to the self-recognitions of all those who would bring new truths to unwilling listeners.

Having glanced briefly at the effects of typological imagery upon two major works of Victorian painting in a realistic style, we can now turn to consider the broader question of the nature of such imagery in the visual arts of the period. How do painting, sculpture, metalwork, book illustration, stained glass, mosaic, and work in other media convey the fact to the spectator that any individual image or entire scene is a type, and, once having conveyed that crucial fact, how do they guide the spectator to make a proper reading of it? A type, which is a divinely instituted adumbration or reference to some future thing, contains within itself the juxta-position of present and future, type and antitype, literal and spiritual. The artistic effect of the typological image arises in the fact that it thus exists simultaneously in several locations, times, and senses. The artistic difficulty of the type arises in the same fact, for unless the work contains some sort of a signal, the spectator will frequently be unable to determine whether an individual image should be read as a type. He will be unable to determine, for instance, if a representation of Moses should be taken as Moses-as-type-of-Christ or just as Moses himself. One device artists use to identify the way they wish their scenes understood appears in the Dalziel brothers' wood engraving mentioned earlier. This illustration depicts Moses striking the rock; beneath the main image the artist has included as a caption the text, 'Rock of Ages cleft for me', which immediately places it in a Christian context. Toplady's hymn, which combines a typological reading of the smitten rock with a second event taken similarly, establishes how the image must be understood. This humble example reminds us that the artist must place near his image either a text or some other non-linguistic device that prompts the

127

viewer to seek the juxtapositions in the original image. In other words, juxtaposition, which is the essential or defining characteristic of the type itself, is also required to inform the spectator that he should consider any individual image a type.

Without such juxtaposition in the form of a text or defining context, the viewer cannot be sure how to evaluate a representation of scriptural events that are often read typologically. A particularly intriguing example of a Victorian work that lacks such devices is Joseph Durham's *Striking the Rock* (1866, Plate 4), a bronze high-relief panel for an elaborate gothic-canopied drinking fountain erected in Guildhall Yard, London, as a memorial to the ancient benefactors of the parish. Since a contemporary account suggests that the entire enterprise was intended to be an instance of Art for the Masses, one would like to be able to determine precisely how its intended audience was expected to understand the subject. The 1869 *Art-Journal,* which accompanied its friendly review of 'this great work' with an engraved reproduction, quotes relevant passages from Exodus but does not provide any explicit typological reading of the subject. The reviewer, who claims that Durham's work has successfully instructed the common people, does not, however, tell us in what way they have been instructed:

> It is well when artists engaged on any work which must attract the masses seek to invest it with what is instructive as much as with, if not more than, the qualities of good art. In this *alto-relievo* Mr. Durham has striven after and attained both, so that the wayfarer who would slake his thirst with the refreshing water may at the same time have his attention drawn to the lesson taught by what he sees represented.[11]

Oddly enough, the reviewer's remaining comments make no attempt to explain just what this 'lesson' might be, and his one interpretive remark tells us only that Moses 'stands in seeming reverential awe . . . apparently wondering at the miracle God had given him the power to accomplish'.

This inability to comprehend even the most commonplace iconography which characterizes this influential periodical does not prevent us from perceiving that an implicit typological allusion was intended by whoever chose the subject for the fountain – almost certainly the church authorities mentioned in the review. The depiction of Moses bringing forth water from the rock reminded those who used the fountain that they existed within the bounds of the scriptural narrative. Although there seems to be no christological type intended here – either of baptism or of the Crucifixion – the fountain clearly asserts both that God sustains man and that whatever power man has derives from God. Furthermore, since the *Art-Journal* reviewer so emphasizes the political fact that this fountain was intended to sustain the 'masses', one is tempted to see a political type at work here. The Durham plaque, which depicts Moses bringing forth water to sustain the Israelites, establishes an obvious analogy between these earlier children of God and those who will use the fountain. But, as preachers frequently pointed out, the Israelites to whom these modern-day common people are being compared were unbelieving, ungrateful, and rebellious; and they were at last punished for their sins by snakes and other hardships during their desert wandering. Therefore, in this instance the image of the smitten rock may have taken on the following series of related political meanings: the 'masses' are warned, first of all, that power comes from God; second, precisely because power thus comes from God, those who do not have it should not question those who do; third, that they should be grateful to those, such as Moses or his antitype, the parish authorities and others like them, who have sustained them; and, finally, that they should neither ask for better conditions, as did the rebellious Jews, nor display ingratitude and rebelliousness against divinely constituted authority.

The idea that such a public commission might communicate this kind of pointed political message by means of types strikes us today as rather far-fetched, and yet ample evidence exists to demonstrate that political application of typological imagery did not cease with the seventeenth-century Puritans or eighteenth-century satirists. In fact, the use of typology derived from Exodus was a commonplace of nineteenth-century political discourse, and one encounters such political applications of types not only in Carlyle and Kingsley but also in working-class poets, such as Gerald Massey, and in the speeches of strikers imploring their fellows not to return to 'Egyptian slavery'.[12] Had the parish authorities chosen thus to make a political statement, they would not have been making an arcane theological point unintelligible to many working men and women.

Rather, they would have been employing a favorite convention of contemporary political discourse, particularly among workers. Moreover, since Durham's *Striking the Rock* was executed during a period of renewed political agitation for the extension of the franchise, such a conservative statement in the worker's own idiom might have seemed especially timely.

However attractive this political interpretation of *Striking the Rock* might appear, without firmer evidence, such as written commentary by artist, patrons or working-class audience, it can only remain a possibility. This fact tells us something about Victorian typology in general and about its use in the visual arts as well. This particular type of the smitten rock was more popular in Victorian than in earlier religious art, and its increased popularity owed much to the appeal it had for Evangelicals within and without the Church of England. Moreover, in painting as in literature Victorian applications are far more varied – even downright idiosyncratic – compared with earlier uses in the visual arts, when it most frequently follows the Pauline interpretation as a type of baptism. The presence of numerous religious parties each with its own doctrinal emphasis accounts for the greater range of applicable meanings that this scene offers during the Victorian period. But, as we have already observed in the case of Durham's work, one of the results of such varied and often peculiarly original applications of types is that, without external evidence, proving how either artist or audience interpreted them is difficult. William Holman Hunt made the interpretation of his major works relatively easy by furnishing his audience with detailed exhibition pamphlets explaining his intentions. He thus sets forth the meaning of *The Finding of the Saviour* in both a key plate and a book his friend Stephens wrote under his direction.[13]

Such juxtapositions of text and image take many forms, and Hunt, who was obviously intrigued by such devices, employs almost every kind of them. In addition to providing epigraphs, key plates, and detailed written explanations of his work, the artist also employed other means of reinforcing the typological significance of his paintings. In *The Shadow of Death* (Plate 5), for example, the title directs the viewer to the picture's central typological image. In this painting, which is Hunt's recapitulation and reinterpretation of Millais's *Christ in the House of His Parents*, the adult Christ extends His hands in prayer after a day's labor as a carpenter and thus casts a prefiguring shadow of the Crucifixion upon the workshop wall. Hunt also includes typological and prefigurative texts upon the frames of his paintings, and he frequently includes images of commonplace types, such as the brazen serpent, as well. Borrowing the technique from William Hogarth, he also includes written texts within the picture itself. Thus, *The Finding of the Saviour in the Temple* includes a large circular disk immediately behind the Holy Family, and on this golden disk appear Hebrew and Latin versions of Malachi 3:1: 'And the Lord, whom ye seek, shall suddenly come to his Temple'. Like the types within the picture, this text, which is appropriately inscribed on the entrance to the Temple, points to the meaning of the painting's main action.

Dante Gabriel Rossetti, not Hunt, exemplifies another means of placing a typological image within a linguistic context when he creates a poem, a separate and yet conjoined work, to achieve this effect. For example, 'The Passover in the Holy Family' (1870, Plate 6), which he wrote for his watercolor with the same title painted for Ruskin in 1856, both guides the viewer through his picture and makes a characteristically Rossettian emphasis upon typology's ability to provide privileged moments. The sonnet opens 'Here meet together the prefiguring day/And day prefigured', as Rossetti, like his Pre-Raphaelite brethren, takes an imagined event from the life of Christ and transforms it into a meditative image that contains the entire Gospel scheme of salvation. After the introduction, which thus emphasizes that the picture represents a Rossettian significant moment, his sonnet proceeds by setting forth the details – the types– that prefigure Christ's ultimate self-sacrifice. First, Rossetti invokes not just the celebration of the Passover but all the events of the Exodus it celebrates. Christ, who is a second Moses, is assisting His family in the commemoration of the events which serve as types of Himself and His coming actions, so that the picture *The Passover in the Holy Family* simultaneously commemorates and fulfills an ancient event that functions as a type, represents the literal events of one Passover during the childhood of Jesus, and prefigures Christ's own sacrifice that will enable Him to lead all believers from the Egyptian slavery of sin and death. Thus, after relating the details of the Exodus and its celebration in the Passover ritual, the poet emphasizes that 'now' in the time of Jesus, this reenactment of the ancient celebration of deliverance brings together Old Law and

131

New: 'The slain lamb confronts the Lamb to slay'. In ancient times it was the blood of the lamb that kept death away from the Egyptians; Jesus and His family commemorate that event in their celebration of the holiday; later, after the passion and death of Christ it will be His blood which will conquer death.

The sestet therefore moves to the actual sacrifice, itself another type of the Crucifixion, as the poet turns our attention from the present to the future:

> What shadow of Death the Boy's fair brow subdues
> Who holds that blood wherewith the porch is stained
> By Zachary the Priest?

Just as the blood of the paschal lamb kept the Angel of Death from the houses of the enslaved Jews, so shall the blood of Christ in future years enable man to triumph over death. At this point, Rossetti refers to both type and prophecy when he has John bind the shoes 'He deemed himself not worthy to unloose'. Like Millais's *Christ in the House of His Parents*, Rossetti's watercolor includes John the Baptist as a means of pointing toward the future of the boy Saviour. The poem closes with Mary gathering the bitter herbs, which in the Passover ritual symbolize the past sufferings of the enslaved Israelites. Here they also prefigure the suffering of Jesus and his mother, for, again like Millais, Rossetti has created a High Church interpretation of this imagined event.

In addition to setting forth the proper interpretation of individual typological images within his watercolor, Rossetti's sonnet, as we have seen, places a realistically conceived scene within several temporal contexts. Ever since Lessing had pointed out certain basic differences between visual and literary art, artists had accepted that paintings were limited to the depiction of single moments. Consequently, artists strove to capture dramatically climactic moments, such as Millais does in *Isabella* (1849) and Hunt in *Rienzi* (1849). But typology offers a means of enriching a picture's effect by locating it simultaneously in several different times.

Dante Gabriel Rossetti's use of language for such purposes appears with particular clarity in poems he wrote about other artists' paintings, for in these cases he adds the typological dimensions on his own authority. His characteristic fascination with the role of time in the arts thus informs 'The Holy Family', a sonnet written for a painting in the National Gallery, London, once thought to be by Michelangelo, Rossetti's sonnet opens with Mary begging her son not to look at the 'prophet's page, o son! He knew/ All that thou has to suffer,' and his note informs the reader: 'In this picture the Virgin Mother is seen withholding from the Child Saviour the prophetic writings in which his sufferings are foretold'. Mary, who then withholds the darker portions of her child's fate from Him, inspires Him with prophecies of man's coming salvation:

> Still before Eden waves the fiery sword, –
> > Her Tree of Life unransomed: whose sad Tree
> > Of knowledge yet to growth of Calvary
> > Must yield its Tempter, – Hell the earliest dead
> Of Earth resign, – and yet, o Son and Lord,
> > The Seed o' the woman bruise the serpent's head.

Mary, who the poet supposes has a full knowledge of the future, thus draws her son's attention to His great victory over sin and death. These six lines become prophecy as she ranges over all human time from the Fall to the unnamed Crucifixion and Harrowing of Hell, but she always stops short of telling Christ about His sacrifice. The poem ends with a fine use of a commonplace type: Mary, who has avoided telling her son of His impending doom, again leads up to an allusion to it and again refuses to present the entire truth. Repeating God's words in the Garden, Jesus's mother tells Him that 'the Seed o' the woman [will] bruise the serpent's head', thus defeating sin and death. What she does not tell him is that the serpent will, in turn, bruise the heel of man – a prophecy usually taken to indicate the Crucifixion.

By providing only the first portion of the commonplace text, Rossetti skillfully reinforces the poignant interpretation he has given the painting. Essentially, he uses the partial statement of Genesis 3:15 much as Browning, Hopkins, and Tennyson employ typological citation in many of their dramatic monologues: to permit the speaker to state more than at first appears. Usually such typological imagery serves to permit the author a way of having the speaker unknowingly convict himself of some flaw, but Rossetti's 'The Holy Family' instead uses it as a means of preventing the self-conscious speaker from divulging too much information to one not ready for it. Rossetti, in other words, employs the Tractarian doctrine of reserve as a model for Mary's relation to her son.[14]

Although the original painting for which Rossetti wrote this companion poem contains scrolls that supposedly contain a prophecy, he added the specific types of the tree and bruising the serpent. Since prophetic passages such as those in Isaiah referred to the coming Messiah, Rossetti's poem does not violate the spirit of the painting by employing prefigurative symbolism. By adding additional types and by using them as the means for resolving his poem, Rossetti gives the painting a new meaning. Like Ruskin, who creates works of literature to comment upon paintings, Rossetti creates an essentially new work of verbal art to explain a visual one.[15] Of course, now we have moved from the question of how painters use linguistic texts to define their own images to something quite different: the way language and the poet who uses it can create a new work of art by endowing paintings with meanings they may not originally have possessed.

Rossetti's citation of the prophetical type from Genesis 3:15 in 'The Holy Family' leads to another question concerning the relation of visual and verbal arts. When he makes the passage from Genesis 3:15 the organizing conceit of his poem, he employs a type which does not appear in the painting by the Manchester Master. Such a procedure is particularly appropriate to this type, because, although it is frequently echoed in literature, it does not enjoy the same popularity in the visual arts, and it does not enjoy equal popularity because it is difficult to illustrate. Certain problems arise in making representations of Genesis 3:15 since it comprises a prophetic, rather than an historic or legal, type. Unlike other kinds of types, a prophetic type does not necessarily offer a visual image. The problem is essentially that whereas other forms of typological symbolism possess two poles, both of which provide images, this prophetic type collapses the biblical text into its antitype: one cannot literally illustrate the type of bruising the serpent's head except by illustrating its antitype, the Crucifixion, which is an image in its own right. The ways in which artists have created images that embody this commonplace type provide important information about the relations between visual and verbal arts.

One common solution is to combine two realistically depicted images in a realistic – that is, non-historical – manner. For example, mediaeval carvings of the Madonna which show her with one foot upon a serpent take Mary as the seed of the woman. These carved Madonnas offer visual images of a symbolic or spiritual act, since Mary nowhere in the Bible treads upon a snake. The artist therefore has juxtaposed two realistic images, one of Mary and one of a serpent. Whereas the pictorial representation of a legal or historical type depicts only those elements present in the type itself, this portrayal of a prophetic type conflates two times, for it includes the serpent from the Fall and Mary, mother of Jesus, in the same image. A second instance of such conflation of two times appears in those mediaeval Crucifixions that include a snake curled around the Cross. The snake rarely gives the impression of having been bruised, and only the viewer's knowledge of Genesis 3:15 explains its presence. Another much rarer representation of this text that takes Jesus as the seed of the woman appears in the late seventeenth-century *Resurrected Christ* now in the Hospital of St John, Bruges. Christ rests one foot upon a skull, perhaps representing the old Adam, behind which curls a serpent with a human face – a familiar rendering of the serpent at the Fall. Christ's other foot rests on an orb that would seem to symbolize His dominion over the world. The juxtaposition of the risen Christ and the serpent from the Garden of Eden creates another assemblage of things which exist in separate times.

In addition to applying the words 'the seed of the woman' to Mary and Christ, Bible commentators also took them to refer to the Church and its members, Isaac Watts's hymn 'Captain and Conqueror' (1709) prays, for example, 'Now let my soul arise/ And tread the tempter down', thus making the individual as a member of the mystical body of Christ fulfill a type applied to Him. Such applications of this type do not, however, appear in the visual arts during the last century, though the parallel applications to the Church are common.[16] For example, a bishop's pastoral staff (1890) by J. D. Sedding (1838–91) in St Asaph's Cathedral depicts Christ's charge to St Peter within a crook terminating in a serpent's head. The positions relative to each other of the serpent and the scene representing the institution of the Church communicate the fact that after Christ bruises the serpent Evil by giving Himself to be crucified, he continues this battle with it by means of His Church.[17] Rossetti's central panel from his Llandaff Cathedral triptych, *The Seed of David*

(1860–4, Plate 7), offers another version of this theme. One of the shepherds come to adore the infant Jesus extends his shepherd's crook in homage, and in so doing he appears to drive forth a worm from an apple. This figure, who is both an antitype of David and a type of Christ's bishops, again exemplifies the principle of juxtaposition necessary to illustrate a prophetic type. Like the other examples we have observed, Rossetti's proceeds by juxtaposing either real events from different times or physically existing ones and symbols.

Far more popular than such attempts to illustrate Genesis 3:15 with this kind of device is using various analogues that embody good defeating evil. According to the Christian interpretation of this so-called first prophecy, Christ conquers Satan only by suffering on behalf of others. Unfortunately, this interpretation is impossible to illustrate literally with a single image, since the actual Crucifixion, that event which bruises both Satan and Christ, shows only His suffering. Visual analogues, such as SS Michael and George defeating a dragon, create effective images of victory, but to do so they sacrifice the major spiritual truth contained in the Christian reading of the original text. Unlike attempts to represent Genesis 3:15 by combining literally true events from different times, such analogues take two different forms. The battle of St Michael with the dragon, for instance, takes place outside historical time, and by illustrating it, the artist can make a statement about the universality of the battle of good and evil. William Burgess (1827–81), who possessed an extraordinarily detailed knowledge of Christian iconography, uses this conflict for the dominant image in his 1878 design for an altar and reredos for Truro Cathedral, Cornwall.[18] Burgess places a sculpted St Michael standing upon a dragon and thrusting his spear into this embodiment of satanic evil. Since this large central panel of the design was meant to appear behind the high altar on which would stand a crucifix, the worshipper would encounter a juxtaposition of cross and conquest.[19]

Like such representations of St Michael and his dragon, purely allegorical images of such essential and universal conflict take place or exist in a spiritual realm outside time. Faith, hope, and charity are the three chief Christian virtues, and their representations frequently occur in church art. Drawing upon mediaeval iconographic tradition, Edward Burne-Jones (1833–98) transforms such representations of the virtues into images of their conquest of the appropriate sins in the stained glass he designed for Jesus College Chapel, Cambridge, in 1873. Thus, Hope stands on Despair, Faith on Unbelief, and Charity on Hate.[20] The theme seems to have been a relatively popular one, for the artist repeated it in three lights designed for the Cathedral of St Mary the Virgin in Blackburn, Lancs (c. 1874–87). Another purely symbolical or allegorical presentation of spiritual conflict appears on the brass lectern (1862), now in Gloucester Cathedral, which John Francis Bentley (1839–1902) designed for Hart and Son. Bentley, who converted to the Roman Church the same year he produced the design for this lectern, represented the Gospel triumphing over infidelity in the form of a magnificent eagle surmounting a dragon.[21]

Unlike these allegorical representations, essentially secular analogues, such as Perseus and the sea-serpent, St George and the dragon, and Apollo and Python, supposedly depict historical facts, though of course they may be treated either as myth or as a repository of conventional symbols. Many Victorian versions of these subjects, particularly those by Burne-Jones, concentrate more upon the man's rescue of the helpless maiden than upon any religious significance, but there are a few that have religious overtones as well. For example, when William Holman Hunt replaced a representation of a bas-relief of the Crucifixion which he had employed in an earlier version of *The Lady of Shalott*, he chose a well-known mythic analogue to Genesis 3:15. His final version (1896) embellishes the Lady's chamber with a bas-relief of Hercules obtaining the golden apples of the Hesperides from the dragon-guarded tree, a subject which Ruskin had discussed at considerable length in the last volume of *Modern Painters* (1860) in precisely these terms.[22] Like Browning, who follows Milton in making elaborate use of classical materials for types, Hunt occasionally uses them as specific types and not just as partial analogues.[23]

Our reading of Hunt's Hercules in *The Lady of Shalott* depends upon a particular form of the principle of juxtaposition, since in tracing the picture's development through many extant sketches, Hunt's illustration for the Moxon Tennyson (1857), and the Manchester and Hartford versions of the painting, we receive clues to its meaning.[24] As this rather special case suggests, the principle of juxtaposition necessary to identify an image as a type does not require that the image be accompanied by a linguistic text. Its position next to other typological images, or in a context created by their presence, also serves to indicate how such pictorial forms should be interpreted. Triptychs and other forms of image seriation exemplify that kind of juxtaposition created by placing complete scenes or pictures, rather than separate details, next to each other. Such means of organization inform Victorian religious painting, stained-glass programs, mosaics, eucharistic vessels, and other church art.

For instance, William Butterfield's elaborate mosaic program (finished 1876) for the walls of Keble College Chapel, defines the significance of individual types by juxtaposing them to others. The designer, who arranged the Old Testament prefigurations in groups of three, included Moses striking the rock. This type, which can accept various interpretations, appears within such a triad, the central and largest scene of which depicts the miracle of the brazen serpent, a type of the Crucifixion. Moses bringing forth water from the rock appears on the right of the brazen serpent, while to the left of it – and closer to the high altar – appear both Moses holding the tablets of the Law and Aaron as priest. This combination of typological scenes suggests that the designer of the program, in the manner of Victorian preachers such as Keble himself, intended the image of Moses striking the rock to bear several meanings simultaneously. Within the context of surrounding objects, it appears both as type of the Crucifixion and the New Law of grace; and, compared to Aaron, priest of the Old Law of ritual sacrifice, it also appears as a type of the new sacrifice, the sacrament of Holy Communion.

Another means of establishing typological relations appears in the stained-glass program in Jesus College Chapel, Oxford, a program dating from 1852 (Plate 8).[25] Here, rather than defining the individual scenes by placing them next to others from the Old Testament, each type is paired with its antitype. Thus, God creating Adam appears beneath the Nativity, in which God created the New Adam; either Moses striking the rock or sweetening the waters of Marah prefigures John baptizing Christ, and, taking the paired scenes from left to right, the following typological relations are made: the Passover and the Last Supper, the brazen serpent and the Crucifixion, Jonah being disgorged by Leviathan and the Resurrection, either God giving the law to Moses or Moses and Aaron passing on the priesthood and Christ preaching in the Temple, and Elijah's chariot and Christ's ascension in the presence of the Apostles.

Like this traditional pairing of type and antitype, Rossetti's altarpiece for Llandaff Cathedral, *The Seed of David* (1860–4), defines its typological imagery by juxtaposition of old and new. The work flanks a Nativity by two representations of David, that on the left as a boy ready to slay Goliath, that on the opposite wing as a crowned king singing praises to the Lord. Rossetti explained in a letter that he intended the side panels to present 'the ancestor of Christ embodying in his own person the shepherd and king who are seen worshipping in the Nativity'.[26] David the shepherd thus prefigures the shepherds at the Nativity, but he also serves as a complex type of Christ, since he is the hero who slew Goliath. Furthermore, as shepherd he prefigures not only Christ but also the Church hierarchy. Similarly, David the king is not only a type of Christ but of all rulers who must give praise and allegiance to God. Moreover, just as David the shepherd prefigures the humble men present at the Nativity, so his portrayal as ruler symbolizes the three kings. Finally, following Keble, Browning, Woolner, and others, Rossetti makes David into a type of the true poet and artist. Again, the juxtaposition of images, say, David as shepherd and the shepherds at the Nativity, leads the viewer to read these congeries of typological images in the intended manner.

Church furnishings and items related directly to the Eucharist, such as chalices, monstrances, and pyxes, set the individual type within one or more defining contexts and hence do not present problems of interpretation. None the less, such ecclesiastical vessels frequently bear a series of juxtaposed types, not primarily to indicate the presence of typological imagery but to remind the celebrant that all Old Testament history leads to Christ's past and continuing sacrifice. Since elaborately decorated eucharistic vessels would be purchased or commissioned only by Roman Catholic and High Anglican churches, the types found upon such ecclesiastical metalwork are naturally those that appealed to these kinds of worshipper. Like the sermons of Keble and Newman, such eucharistic vessels employ types to prefigure this sacrament and not just the Crucifixion. For example, a silver flagon designed by Burgess (1862) contains images of David, Meichizedek, Abel, and Noah, while a chalice (1868) by John Hardman Powell (1827–95) similarly employs the sacrifice of Isaac and other types.[27] One also encounters monstrances, chalices, and other vessels bearing the Tree of Life or depictions of the Expulsion from the Garden.[28]

Such ecclesiastical vessels that contain representations of separate typological scenes as part of another work fall in between two basic forms of juxtaposition. The first, exemplified by polyptychs, places complete scenes side by side or in series; and the second, at which we shall now look, includes types within realistically depicted scenes. The lamb and cornerstone in Hunt's *The Finding*, like many of the details of Millais's *Christ in the House of His Parents*, exemplify this form: juxtaposition that provides realistically conceived religious painting with a means of indicating the presence of types. Such devices are extremely valuable to the artist who wishes to employ types within a realistic setting, for without them he produces an ambiguous image. One indication that Millais intends the spectator to interpret *The Blind Girl* (1856) in terms of Christian symbolism is that he includes at least two obvious symbols. First, he includes a rainbow, which is a type of Christ and His promise of heavenly life, and, second, he places a butterfly, an emblem of the soul, on the poor girl's clothing.[29] Paintings of the life of Christ, on the other hand, do not require such juxtaposition of two or more typological images to suggest their meaning, and, therefore, when William Gale depicts the boy Jesus in *Nazareth* (1869) holding a plough in the carpenter's shop, he makes an allusion to the many scriptural passages which describe the Saviour's career in terms of the ploughman.[30]

In addition to including types on a picture's frame, as Hunt does in *The Finding* when he there presents an image of the brazen serpent, the artist can also include such imagery on the walls of a depicted scene. Thus, Charles Collins, who wishes to point a parallel between Joseph and Richard the Lionhearted, includes a portrayal of the Joseph story in *The Pedlar* (1850). Such applications, which are common in Victorian painting, represent extensions of biblical typology to other subjects. Whereas Hunt includes pomegranates, or passion fruit, in *The Shadow of Death* (1873) to allude to Christ's passion, Millais employs one in *Isabella* (1849) to prefigure the lover's murder by the jealous family.

Occasionally, purely religious applications of typology follow the Northern Renaissance example and employ visual puns. For example, the shadow cast upon the wall of the carpenter's shop in *The Shadow of Death* is essentially a visual pun, and so is the way a shadow of one of the tools appears to be the spear about to pierce Christ's side. Similarly, the curved window behind Christ's head, like the firescreen in the Master of Flemalle's *Virgin and Child* in the National Gallery, London, creates the image of a halo. The use of the workbench in *Christ in the House of His Parents* to prefigure the high altar and Hunt's placement of his missionary in the pose of a Deposition in *Early Christians Rescuing a Missionary from the Persecution of the Druids* (1850) further exemplify such visual puns. Ever since Jacques Louis David painted *The Death of Marat* (1793) in the guise of a secular martyrdom, British and European painters occasionally borrowed the compositional schemes of religious art for secular applications. Henry Wallis creates such a secular martyrdom in *The Death of Chatterton* (1856) and Hunt does the same thing in *Rienzi* (1848–9).

A completely secular prefiguration, which owes little to typology, often appears in Victorian narrative painting. For example, in Robert Martineau's *The Last Day in the Old Home* (1862) the wastrel father's destruction of his son is prefigured by his sharing with the boy a champagne toast. The ancient family home is being auctioned to pay the father's debts, and, characteristically, one of the few objects the father has chosen to set apart from those being sold is a picture of a favorite race horse. The mother's anxious glance at the two suggests she fears that wine and horses will lead the father to bring his family even lower. Such narrative elements even occur in religious paintings employing typology, but they still do not represent an influence of this form of symbolism. For example, the skeleton of an animal which perished on the shores of the Dead Sea informs the viewer of Hunt's *The Scapegoat* (1856) just what this goat's fate will be. This grisly indication of the scapegoat's death, however, does not function as a typological image and we here have an analogue, and not an example, of this form of symbolism.

Like Victorian literature, Victorian painting and other kinds of visual art make many interesting applications of biblical typology. Ruskin and the Pre-Raphaelites base a theory of symbolic realism upon it, and designers of stained glass, mosaic, and other church art use it both as a source of iconography and as a means of organizing entire decorative programs. Like literary applications of prefigur-

141

ative imagery, pictorial ones also appear in secular art, thus providing yet another instance of typology's effect upon Victorian culture.

CHAPTER FIVE

POLITICAL TYPES

The Puritans, asserting their liberty to restrain tyrants, found the Hebrew history closely symbolical of their feelings and purpose; and it can hardly be correct to cast the blame of their less laudable doings on the writings they invoked, since their opponents made use of the same writings for different ends, finding there a strong warrant for the divine right of kings and denunciation of those who, like Korah, Dathan, and Abiram, took on themselves the office of priesthood, which belonged of right solely to Aaron and his sons, or, in other words, to men ordained by the English bishops.

– George Eliot, 'The Modern Hep! Hep! Hep!'

Political applications of religious typology exemplify an area of Victorian thought in which authors commonly extend or secularize this form of symbolism. We may properly speak of a 'secularized' or 'extended' typology when any of the defining elements of the orthodox form of this kind of biblical symbolism have been modified. Perhaps the most common change observed in political typology involves the christological reference, which authors frequently redefine in terms of something they wish to aggrandize, such as Tudor England, contemporary Italy, or the Victorian working classes. Such secularizations of typology do not depend upon the religious belief of the author who employs them, and they occur both in the works of Swinburne, who was an atheist, and Mrs Browning, who was a believing Christian. Furthermore, although, as we shall observe, such secularized figuralism generally characterizes Victorian use of types for political purposes, certain applications do take strictly orthodox forms. After examining a few instances of orthodox political types, we shall be better able to discern what occurs when authors transform them into secularized or extended versions.

Since the Church of England is an established or state church, in a certain sense it serves as an arm of government: the reigning monarch is the official head of the Church, some of its prelates sit in the House of Lords, and it is subject to Parliamentary legislation. Certain past and present affairs of state inevitably had effects upon the Church, and since Victorian commentators accepted that many things referring to Christ also referred to His Church, such matters of state which influenced the Church could be understood by orthodox observers as serving as part of a typological scheme ordained by God.

Several of the poems which close John Keble's *The Christian Year* employ types to comment upon political matters. 'King Charles the Martyr', a poem written to commemorate Charles I's death, which was celebrated in the Church calendar, presents him as an antitype of Christ, one who, like Christ Himself, fulfills earlier types and one who also fulfills a type created by Christ. Keble can make such an interpretation, because Charles I, as head of the established church, was commonly taken by Tories and High Churchmen to have died a religious martyr to Puritan political and religious oppression. The poet begins his aggrandizement of Charles I by admitting that

145

although the skies no longer 'thunder' with prophecy, and although the Apostles no longer defeat the powers of darkness 'in our sight', England still possesses the 'Martyrs' noble army', which is composed not only of the humble and obscure but also of a king. Part of the glory of England and its Church is that 'a monarch from his throne/ Springs to his Cross and finds his glory there'. In conventional terms Charles I stands as both a martyr and an antitype: he is a martyr because he died as a witness to Christ, and he is an antitype because his sufferings as a member of His Church make him a part of Christ Mystical – and the types can be fulfilled in both the person (Christ Personal) and Church (Christ Mystical) of Christ.

Keble's note to this poem suggests that he accepted fully the notion that Charles acted as part of a divinely instituted typological scheme or structure, for he quotes a section of *Herbert's Memoirs* which relates that Bishop Juxon, who was with the king immediately before his death, read 'the 27th chapter of the Gospel of St. Matthew, which relateth the passion of our Blessed Saviour. The King, after the service was done, asked the Bishop, if he had made choice of that chapter, being so applicable to his present condition? The Bishop replied, "May it please your Gracious Majesty, it is the proper lesson for the day, as appears by the Kalendar." ' In other words, Keble's note makes clear that precisely the kind of signifying or meaningful event which characterizes a type has taken place when the Church calendar and Charles I's execution coincided.

'Gunpowder Treason', another poem celebrating a political event mentioned in the Church calendar, avoids relating any details of the Roman Catholic inspired plot to destroy the English government, and instead contrasts the Churches of England and Rome. According to Keble, at the Crucifixion the 'widow'd Church' stood by weeping while others scorned; and even today the same pattern pertains, for still

> We know the lonely Spouse
> By the dear mark her Saviour bore
> Trac'd on her patient brows.

The Crown of Thorns thus prefigures those many wounds suffered by Christ's spouse, the Church. The poet then mentions the specific sorrows occasioned by the Roman Catholic error of turning from

1 Jacopo Tintoretto. *The Annunciation. c.* 1582–7. Oil on canvas, 116 × 214½ in. (Scuola di San Rocco, Venice)

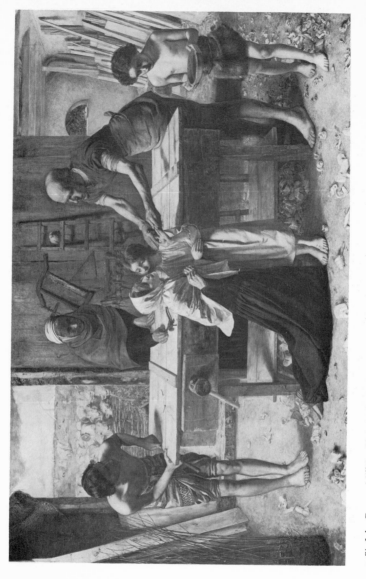

2 Sir John Everett Millais. *Christ in the House of His Parents*. 1849–50. Oil on canvas, 34 × 55 in. (Tate Gallery, London)

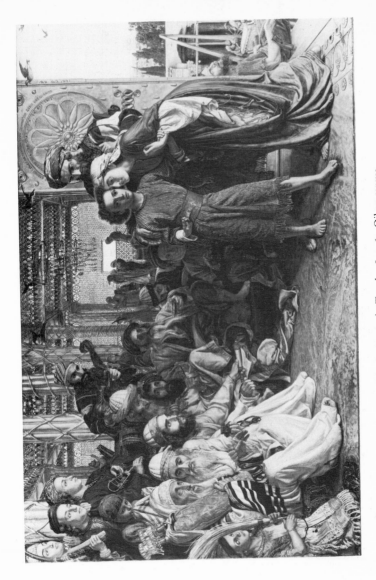

3 William Holman Hunt. *The Finding of the Saviour in the Temple.* 1854–60. Oil on canvas, 33¾ × 55½ in. (Birmingham City Museums and Art Gallery)

4 Joseph Durham. *Striking the Rock.* 1866. Bronze alto relievo. (Illustration from *The Art-Journal*, 31 (1869), 59)

5 William Holman Hunt. *The Shadow of Death*. 1869–73. Oil on canvas, $83\frac{1}{2} \times 65\frac{1}{2}$ in. (Manchester City Art Gallery)

6 Dante Gabriel Rossetti. *The Passover in the Holy Family: Gathering Bitter Herbs.* 1855–6. Watercolour, 16 × 17 in. (Tate Gallery, London)

7 Dante Gabriel Rossetti. *The Seed of David*. 1858–64. Oil on canvas, arched top, central portion 90 × 60 in., wings each 73 × 24½ in. (Llandaff Cathedral)

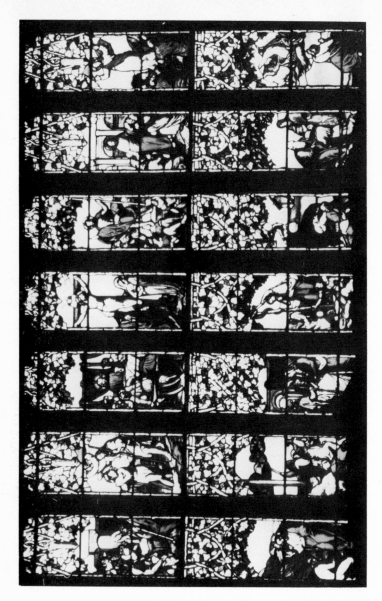

8 Stained glass, Jesus College, Oxford. 1852.

Christ to worship the lesser parts of His dispensation: Mary and the saints. Hence the 'lonely Spouse'

> mourns that tender hearts should bend
> Before a meaner shrine,
> And upon Saint or Angel spend
> The love that should be thine.

Then, in a surprisingly gentle close, Keble requests that we 'speak gently of our sister's fall' in hopes that patient love might win the Roman church back to God's ways. Except for the title's allusion to a specific political fact, the poem concerns itself entirely with doctrinal contrasts and so its citation of a type hardly seems particularly political.[1]

In contrast, 'The Accession', which employs Old Testament history to prefigure the way a new monarch comes to the English throne, more obviously places contemporary political events within a religious context. Keble claims that:

> The voice that from the glory came
> To tell how Moses died unseen,
> And waken Joshua's spear of flame
> To victory on the mountains green,
> Its trumpet tones are sounding still,
> When Kings or Parents pass away,
> They greet us with a cheering thrill
> Of power and comfort in decay.

Although Keble makes the divinely prompted transition of power from Moses to Joshua both a type and archetype of all such transitions, he characteristically turns away from the political import such a typological relation might possess to find consolation for all mourners. In fact, despite its title, the poem focuses upon the death of parents and monarchs and not upon the accession to their role in society of those who must take up their functions.

In contrast to these three poems of Keble which seem to avoid making specific reference to contemporary politics, Newman's 'Uzzah and Obed-Edom' (1833) employs types to comment upon specific political issues involving the Church of England. Newman, who steadfastly opposed any attempts by secular authorities to reform the Church of Ireland or make the income of bishops more equitable, employs the story of the ill-fated Uzzah to warn those who would meddle in sacred affairs. The poem begins with the warning that God's ark, which is a type of the Church, has hidden power which earthly eyes cannot judge:

> The ark of God has hidden strength;
>> Who reverence or profane,
> They, or their seed, shall find at length
>> The penalty or gain.

Having thus set forth his chief principle, that we mere humans cannot judge the true condition of either ark or Church, Newman then draws a lesson from the fate of Uzzah, who sought with his hand to support the falling ark:

> There was one, outstripping all
> The holy-vestured band,
> Who laid on it, to save its fall,
> A rude corrective hand.

> Read, who the Church would cleanse, and mark
> How stern the warning runs;
> There are two ways to aid her ark
> As patrons, and as sons.

The second Book of Samuel 6:6–7 tells that when those transporting the ark 'came to Nachon's threshing floor, Uzzah put forth his hand to the ark of God, and took hold of it; for the oxen shook it. And the anger of the Lord was kindled against Uzzah; and God smote him there for his error; and there he died by the ark of God.' Scriptural commentators such as Thomas Scott see Uzzah's action as an example of irreverence and presumption and his punishment as a divinely intended warning to David, the priests, and the entire nation of Israel. Newman, who takes the history of Uzzah and the ark as a type of the way in which contemporary liberalism misguidedly attempts to help the Church of England, tries to warn all believers how blasphemous must be such attempts to act as her 'patrons' and not 'sons'.

Newman inscribed his poem 'At Sea. June 24th, 1833', and so it anticipates by three weeks John Keble's famous Assize Sermon on 'National Apostasy', which he preached in the University pulpit and which Newman and others took as the beginning of the Oxford Movement. Newman had returned from his travels to hear Keble urge that, since England was a Christian nation bound by the laws of the Church, it was committing national Apostasy when its Parliament suppressed Anglican sees in Ireland in a sacrilegious attempt to assist and 'cleanse' the Church. Uzzah, it appears, was both type and symbol of liberalism, which Newman defines in his *Apologia* as 'false liberty of thought, or the exercise of thought upon matters, in which, from the constitution of the human mind, thought cannot be brought to any successful issue, and therefore is out of place'. According to him, such matters include all sorts of 'first principles' and all 'truths of Revelation'. Liberalism then 'is the mistake of subjecting to human judgment those revealed doctrines which are in their nature beyond and independent of it, and of claiming to determine on rational grounds the truth and value of propositions which rest for their reception simply on the external authority of the Divine Word'.[2]

Newman, ever a superb polemicist, has chosen a wonderfully appropriate episode from Old Testament history to use as a type. Certainly, the eye of common sense – the eye of liberalism, that is, which is not informed by faith – finds it difficult to perceive how Uzzah could have sinned sufficiently to deserve such punishment. Although divinely revealed law instructed man that anyone who touched the ark of God must die for such sacrilege, common sense argues that perhaps God did not literally mean the ark could not be touched, and that, anyway, Uzzah meant well. Similarly, the sin and error of liberalism, according to Newman, is that it attempts to apply human standards to matters already decided by the 'external authority of the Divine Word'. In essence, the sin of liberalism, like the sin of Uzzah, is that irreverent presumption which arises in a lack of faith: Political liberals, like this ill-fated figure from ancient times, do not believe that God really meant what He said in the scriptures.

Elizabeth Barrett Browning's *Casa Guidi Windows* (1851), which also attacks irreverence and presumption, offers the example of a

Low Church application of types and typological argument to the contemporary political scene. Like Ruskin's *Notes Towards the Construction of Sheepfolds* (1851), Mrs Browning makes the usual Evangelical point that Christ's incarnation removed the need for all human priesthoods. Citing the typologically significant garments of the Levitical priesthood, she argues that since Christ has fulfilled all these types in Himself, earthly 'priests' no longer exist:

> Through heaven's lifted gate
> The priestly ephod in sole glory swept
> When Christ ascended, entered in, and sate . . .
> At Deity's right hand, to mediate
> He alone, He for ever. On His breast
> The Urim and the Thummim, fed with fire
> From the full Godhead, flicker with the unrest
> Of human pitiful heartbeats. Come up higher,
> All Christians! Levi's tribe is dispossest.

She therefore claims that all Christians should admire, 'but not cast lots for', the solitary alb of Christ's priesthood. In fact, she holds that the last time consecrated oil ever anointed anyone authentically was when it was used at Christ's burial:

> The last chrism, poured right,
> Was on that Head, and poured for burial
> And not for domination in men's sight.

Therefore, she looks critically at both High Church Anglican and Roman Catholic 'juggling with the sleight/ Of surplice, candlestick and altar-pall', and suggests that both parties abandon their sinful, irreverent presumption.

> And make concordats 'twixt their soul and mouth,
> Succeed St. Paul by working at the tent,
> Become infallible guides by speaking truth,
> And excommunicate their pride that bent
> And cramped the souls of men.

All believers accepted that Christ's incarnation abrogated the Old

Testament priesthood, which had prefigured Him. Whereas the Low Church then proceeded to argue that Christ, who was our only priest, removed need for any other, the High Church claimed in contrast that these Old Testament figures prefigured both Christ and a new priesthood of His Church. Ruskin had urged that Christ was the only true priest as a means of promoting tolerance and co-operation among the English clergy, but his friend Elizabeth Barrett Browning does so largely as a means of attacking the Papacy. Although both Ruskin and Mrs Browning write with an eye upon the recent reinstitution of Roman Catholic dioceses in England, Ruskin concerns himself primarily with internal English religious politics while she concerns herself with the secular politics of Italy during the Risorgimento.

Mrs Browning introduces her views of Christian priesthood into *Casa Guidi Windows* as a means of attacking Pius IX, the Pope whose repressive policies had so harmed both Italian reunification and Italian liberty. Pio Nono, as he was commonly known, had begun his rule with liberal intentions, but the stirrings of revolution had so troubled him that he quickly exchanged his early liberal politics for reactionary ones which made him infamous to an entire generation of political poets. Referring to his earlier attitudes, Mrs Browning, who believes that 'Priestcraft burns out', claims that his later actions have unintentionally aided Italy, which will never again believe a pope.

> Why, almost, through this Pius, we believed
> The priesthood could be an honest thing, he smiled
> So saintly while our corn was being sheaved
> For his own granaries! Showing now defiled
> His hireling hands, a better help's achieved
> Than if they blessed us shepherd–like and mild.
> False doctrine, strangled by its own amen,
> Dies in the throat of all this nation. Who
> Will speak a pope's name as they rise again?
> What woman or what child will count him true?

Although this passage attacking Pio Nono, which owes much to Milton's 'Lycidas' and an entire tradition of satires against false pastors, does not itself employ types, it follows from Mrs

Browning's typological argument against the existence of any Christian priesthood.

All of the political applications of types we have thus far observed in *Casa Guidi Windows* have been strictly orthodox ones. On the other hand, when she takes the oppressed people of a disunited, conquered Italy as equivalent to Christ, she introduces us to secularized or extended versions of this form of religious symbolism. According to *Casa Guidi Windows*, the ruling members of the Church

> take the advantage, agonizing Christ
> By rustier nails than those of Cedron's brook,
> I' the people's body very cheaply priced, –
> And quote high priesthood out of Holy Book,
> While buying death-fields with the sacrificed.

This passage represents secularized typology because it abandons orthodox religious typological relations in making the people equivalent to Christ Himself. Although members of the Church of Christ can be taken to be antitypes both of those things which prefigure Christ and of Christ Himself, one cannot take the people of Italy in the same manner. First of all, being a member of a nation is not at all the same thing as being a member of the Church of Christ. Moreover, one suspects that an Evangelical, such as Mrs Browning, would not literally accept that most Italians, as Roman Catholics, belonged to a church which enabled them to be considered part of Christ Mystical.

Such secularized types, which can only be employed when many in one's audience have a knowledge of biblical typology, have several valuable effects for the political writer and polemicist. To begin with, they permit the Victorian writer to communicate with his audience in terms of a recognizable, culturally acceptable narrative or structure which has many powerful associations attached to it. Types, which have the power to generate the entire Gospel scheme, also provide a particularly economical way of assigning moral and spiritual value to various political figures, conditions, or events. Once one has employed a type which suggests the people have the virtues and greatness of Christ, one has already implicitly charged any of their opponents with possessing satanic natures. One

152

important result of such economical assignment of moral value with typological imagery is that it is often used to particular effect as a device of political invective.

Swinburne, a master of such invective, frequently employs secularized versions of commonplace types for both praise and blame. 'The Armada' (1888), which he wrote to commemorate the three-hundredth anniversary of England's great victory over Spain, exemplifies both uses. When he addresses Pope Sixtus and Philip of Spain, telling them that 'England's heel is upon you', one might not be certain that he is alluding to Genesis 3:15; but when he later applies the second half of this prophetic type to England, he makes sure that one recognizes his allusion to the commonplace type that was always taken to announce a universal battle between good and evil which would eventually end in the complete triumph of Christ over Satan. Swinburne tells England:

> Freedom lives by the grace she gives thee, born again
>   from thy deathless youth:
> Faith should fail, and the world turn pale, wert thou
>   the prey of the serpent's tooth.
> Greed and fraud, unabashed, unawed, may strive to
>   sting thee at heel in vain.

Christ was to bruise the head of the serpent, who in turn would bruise the heel of the seed of woman – a prophecy commonly understood to refer to the Crucifixion.

Swinburne, who has made England take the place of Christ in this version of the type, further modifies it by omitting the expected suffering of the world saviour. His strategy, in other words, is to introduce the subject of the bruised heel to make certain his audience recognizes the allusion to Genesis 3:15, but he manipulates and modifies the type for his own purposes, which do not include advancing the notion of sacrificial atonement. Swinburne's replacement of Christ by England as saviour makes the triumph of the English fleet over the Armada one of those centers to human history analogous to that provided for Christians by the appearance, earthly ministry, and sacrificial death of Jesus. At the same time, his use of this typological allusion defines the greatness of England for his audience.

153

Swinburne again uses Genesis 3:15 to praise a nation that fought to be free in 'A Song of Italy' (1867) when he praises

> Milan, whose imperial tread
> Bruised once the German head;
> Whose might, by northern swords left desolate,
> Set foot on fear and fate.

Like Swinburne's poetic celebration of England's defeat of the Armada, his poem on the liberation of Italy makes a nation's battles appear to play a major role in a universal struggle of good with evil. Again, part of his procedure in secularizing this commonplace type is to leave out a crucial portion of its significance. He makes a somewhat different modification of it in 'A Counsel', one of the 'Dirae' (1869) written in imitation of Hugo's poems of political invective. There he sets the initial conceit in motion and then does not complete it, for he instructs the 'strong Republic' that he hopes will come into being:

> When thy foot's tread hath crushed their crowns and creeds,
> Care thou not then to crush the beast that bleeds,
>   The snake whose belly cleaveth to the sod,
> Nor set thine heel on men as on their deeds;
>   But let the worm Napoleon crawl untrod,
>   Nor grant Mastai the gallows of his God.

The implication is that, greater than the Christian saviour, a republican Italy is so far above these evil men that it need not crush them physically. A truly free nation, it appears, is greater and more gracious than Christ. Literature from Dante to Swift shows that writers have long used types to attack political opponents, and like his predecessors Swinburne uses typological allusion to aggrandize parties he favors and savage those he opposes. What is new, however, is that this Victorian political poet who often makes effective use of typology does not believe in Christianity.

None the less, he can use types because he reinterprets his major terms and makes, for example, England, Italy, Garibaldi, or the people take the place of Christ. Purporting to discover the same moral principles in the political situations he interprets as are contained in Gospel events, he can effectively apply the interpretive modes of what was for him a despised religion – and he can do so with effect and without alienating his Victorian contemporaries. Like Ruskin after he lost his early Evangelical belief, Swinburne frequently employs vocabulary, rhetoric, and iconography which appeal to many in the contemporary audience. In 'Super Flumina Babylonis' (1871), he presents Christ's passion, death, and resurrection as simultaneously the antitype of Israel's Babylonian captivity and deliverance and also a type of Italy's enslavement and coming freedom. Resurrection becomes equivalent to the Risorgimento. Rather than beginning with his usual equivalence of Christ and Italy, he opens the poem with an allusion to Psalm 137, which begins: 'By the rivers of Babylon, there we sat down; yet, we wept when we remembered Zion. We hanged our harps upon the willows, in the midst thereof. For there they that carried us away captive, required of us a song.' Swinburne gives these lines his own intonation and characteristically omits important elements irrelevant to his purpose, for he begins 'Super Flumina Babylonis':

> By the waters of Babylon we sat down and wept,
>> Remembering thee,
> That for ages of agony hast endured, and slept,
>> And wouldst not see.

Swinburne, who does not choose to take advantage of the original psalm's statements about a poetry of exile, also establishes a moral and spiritual distance between his speaker and Zion which does not exist in the original psalm. He moves from a position 'By the waters of Babylon' to one 'By the waters of Italy' and finally to those 'By the hillside of Calvary' and 'By the stone of the Sepulchre'.

Although the poet obviously expects his reader to perceive the standard prefigurative relation between the sufferings of Israel and those of Christ, he does not use them primarily to serve as types of Italy.[3] Rather, when Swinburne mentions Israel or Christ he really means Italy: in other words, he is not so much employing types as he is using both parts of a typological relation for a political allegory. Like so many Victorian political writers, he uses the events of Christ's passion and death for an elaborate analogy whose moral and spiritual values are conveniently known to his audience. Comparing

155

Italy to Christ endows this then oppressed nation with a spiritual status and grants its people's sufferings a quasi-religious value. Although Swinburne usually alludes to types as a means of emphasizing and aggrandizing the sufferings of an oppressed people, he here employs a somewhat different strategy, using them to suggest the hope of secular 'resurrection'. Although in his conceit Risorgimento becomes equal to Resurrection, he does not make any fuller equation of Christ and Italy. The nation's sufferings do not, for example, atone to a higher power for anything. Another way of stating Swinburne's modifications of a typological scheme is to observe that since he believes that suffering is essentially without meaning or purpose, he can use types only to emphasize the fact of such suffering and the hope of its end; he cannot really use them to provide a higher, spiritual meaning for earthly pain.

This characteristic Swinburnean use of Christ's passion and death appears in poems which present, not Italy, but its common people in terms of the Saviour Himself. 'Christmas Antiphones' (1871) thus presents the oppressed poor crucified on the tree of life, and 'The Litany of Nations' (1871), which presents an image of 'the blood-sweat of the people in the garden/ Inwalled of kings', makes the condition of the masses equivalent to Christ's agony in the garden. None the less, despite the poet's skillful manipulation of such aspects of the Gospel narrative, he does not use them, as a believer might, to suggest any full equivalence between the people and Christ, since he cannot accept any of its emphases other than that upon innocent suffering. This same approach to Christian belief and the typology which that belief created appears in 'Before a Crucifix' (1871), which is one of Swinburne's most effective political poems. The poem begins as a meditation upon a weather-scarred roadside crucifix, presumably in Italy, to which the poor bring their sorrows. After admitting that he has neither 'tongue nor knee/ For prayer', Swinburne addresses the shrine as if it were Christ and demands if His coming had produced only a suffering race of men praying to a suffering image of man.

Swinburne's chief point, however, is not that Christianity has done so little good but that it has done so much harm, and so he continues his interrogation by asking:

156

It was for this then, that thy speech
   Was blown about the world in flame
And men's souls shot up out of reach
   Of fear or lust or thwarting shame –
That thy faith over souls should pass
As sea-winds burning the grey grass? . . .

It was for this, that men should make
   Thy name a fetter on men's necks,
Poor men's made poorer for thy sake,
   And women's withered out of sex?
It was for this, that slaves should be,
Thy word was passed to set men free?

The nineteenth wave of the ages rolls
   Now deathward since thy death and birth.
Hast thou fed full men's starved-out souls?
   Hast thou brought freedom upon earth?
Or are there less oppressions done
In this wild world under the sun?

Having thus bitterly interrogated Christ, Swinburne turns to his
actual target, the Roman Catholic Church. He explains to Christ
that His supposed priests have used His suffering to establish their
tyrannical dominion over men. Heaping up satirical analogies,
types, and parodied types, the poet charges that priests and prelates
have enslaved the people while enriching themselves:

The thirst that made thy dry throat shrink
To their moist mouths commends the drink.

The toothèd thorns that bit thy brows
   Lighten the weight of gold on theirs;
Thy nakedness enrobes thy spouse
   With the soft sanguine stuff she wears
Whose old limbs use for ointment yet
Thine agony and bloody sweat.

After thus attacking the Roman Church in lines which echo and in part parody Keble's 'Gunpowder Treason', Swinburne makes his chief indictment: that Christ's priests, who exploit the suffering of Jesus as a means of enriching themselves, crucify the people and force them continually to reenact the agonies of their supposed Saviour.

> With iron for thy linen bands
>   And unclean cloths for winding-sheet
> They bind the people's nail-pierced hands,
>   They hide the people's nail-pierced feet;
> And what man or what angel known
> Shall roll back the sepulchral stone?

The poet expects us to answer that he and the heroes of Italian liberty and reunification will be the men who will issue in that nation's true Risorgimento, which has now fully become a true, not a priestly, resurrection. Like preachers contrasting the true, complete law of the Gospel with the relatively false and incomplete Old Testament law, Swinburne finds some hint of a higher gospel of freedom, and its chief cornerstone must be that the people abandon a false, enslaving religion with its 'phantom of a Christless cross/ Shadowing the sheltered heads of kings'. Democracy must be an entirely new movement independent of the false priests of a false religion. Swinburne, who cannot accept that the people's centuries of suffering atoned for any sin or produced any spiritual development, commands those who would be free:

> Set not thine hand unto their cross.
>   Give not thy soul up sacrificed.
> Change not the gold of faith for dross
>   Of Christian creeds that spit on Christ.
> Let not thy tree of freedom be
> Regrafted from that rotting tree.

Swinburne, much like Puritan and Evangelical tractwriters attacking the Roman Church, soon makes it clear that 'the gold of faith' of which he writes is no purified Christianity or even one almost completely redefined in the manner of some extreme Broad Church sympathizers. His faith is faith in man and representative democracy. Swinburne, who despises both the theory and practice of Christianity, has produced a *tour de force* of polemical virtuosity in 'Before a Crucifix' by employing the trick of setting up the ideas and images of this religion to attack itself. After charging Christ with having failed to bring anything but oppression to the world, Swinburne condemns His supposed priests, first for having enriched themselves and second for having crushed the people beneath tyranny, poverty, and ignorance.

At this point he uses the passion and crucifixion of Christ as a powerful device of invective, for he holds that the Church has, in essence, crucified the people. Having set forth the corruptions of Christianity, Swinburne can now urge the masses to free themselves from its bonds. He then closes 'Before a Crucifix' with a final necessary twist, attacking the notion that Christ could be a God and thereby preventing any reader from believing that a purified Christianity could exist. According to Swinburne, who is still meditating upon the battered, sun- and rain-bleached crucifix, 'This dead God here against my face/ Hath help for no man'. He has never done any good, nor can he, says Swinburne, and in the penultimate stanza he asks what high nature could possibly exist in a God who sees the worship of His satanic priests, 'and is dumb?' Therefore, 'No soul that lived, loved, wrought, and died,/ Is this their carrion crucified'. In other words, having employed Christ to bludgeon the enemies of man, Swinburne then easily tosses away his weapon when no longer needed.

As will be obvious, such a use of the Christian mythos and its associated types can arise only at a particular moment in the history of Christianity. To employ secular, extended, or parodied types, an author only has to have acquired some knowledge of biblical typology, but if he wishes to communicate effectively with his audience, its members must also share that knowledge. Although secularized extensions of typology appear any time when readers have been taught to study their Bibles for prefigurations of Christ, Swinburnean uses of types to attack the religion of which they are a part can only appear very frequently at a particular cultural moment. They require a point in the spiritual and religious history of an age characterized by the fact that many in the writer's intended audience possess a thorough knowledge of Christian typology but no longer accept its authenticity. Before then such secularized types would immediately alienate the writer's audience, and afterwards, say, in the second half of the twentieth century, most in his audience would fail to understand these allusions. As Swinburne's scriptural allusions in 'Dolores' (1866) demonstrate, he was often willing to risk alienating many of his readers; but when he came to see himself as the bard of Italian freedom, he began to take more care to prevent such possible alienation. Like so many other Victorians, this atheistic poet found scriptural typology an effective means of communicating with an audience many of whose members possessed a knowledge of scriptural exegetics. Matthew Arnold well realized that his century was a time of transition, and such a time grants unexpected privileges to its artists and writers who work close enough to older traditions and structures of meaning (such as Christian typology) to enjoy the comforts they provide and yet are distant enough from them to feel free to handle them ironically.

Before closing our examination of Swinburne's manipulation of political types, we would do well to emphasize how detailed, how expert such manipulations could be during the reign of Victoria. For our purposes two examples will suffice. The first, a passage from 'A Song of Italy' (1867), exemplifies Swinburne's employing types to aggrandize political martyrs and victims as he urges the coming 'priestless Rome that shalt be' to treasure the memories of all who died to make her thus free.

> Be the least
> To thee indeed a priest,
> Priest and burnt-offering and blood-sacrifice
> Given without prayer or price,
> A holier immolation than men wist,
> A costlier eucharist,
> A sacrament more saving.

Swinburne's skillful citation of the Old Testament prefigurations of Christ, priesthood, and the Eucharist is blasphemous finally only because it makes man more important and higher than God, and he is close enough to a High Church reading of martyrdom that it is possible to conceive a similar conceit by Keble or Newman. In fact, Hopkins's 'The Wreck of the Deutschland' (1876), the work of a

High Church convert to Roman Catholicism, employs a similar extravagant conceit to effect the poem's elegiac resolution. Hopkins claims that the chief of the exiled German nuns was an antitype of the Blessed Virgin, since in calling for Christ she supposedly brought Him forth to a waiting world; and while the poet does not claim, like Swinburne, that this victim of political oppression is greater than Mary, his citation of a typological relation does have much the same extravagance.

Swinburne's own extravagance, which can both create the impression of great energy and also ultimately weary his reader, appears more characteristically when he applies the image of the Eucharist to attack the enemies of freedom. His 'Birthday Ode' (1880) for Victor Hugo tells his master that empire had defiled freedom while murder, empire's servant, 'plies lust' with hideous human sacrifice:

> With offering of an old man and a child,
> With holy body and blood, inexpiable
> Communion in the sacrament of hell,
> Till, reeking from their monstrous eucharist,
> The lips wax cold that murdered where they kissed.

This passage, unlike Swinburne's use of eucharistic imagery in 'A Song of Italy', exists on the vaguely defined border between extended typology and parodic inversion of Christian ideas and symbols. Properly speaking, the poet does not cite either a type of Christ or something from His life which is fulfilled in the lives of believers. If one takes the murdering kiss to be the antitype of Judas's kiss, however, one could legitimately interpret the entire passage as an elaborate system of inverted types and antitypes – or at least an extension of them. Patrick Fairbairn, we recall, allowed that 'the form of evil which from time to time confronted the type' could serve 'as itself the type of something similar, which should afterwards arise as a counter-form of evil to the antitype. Antichrist, therefore, may be said to have had his types as well as Christ' (1.145). Although Swinburne obviously does not believe in Christ, he takes great delight in making His Church and the states aligned with it appear in the guise of Antichrist.

Despite the frequent savagery of Swinburne's invective, which bristles with energetic denunciation and coarse analogy, he seems far more conservative and far less violent than a working-class poet like Gerald Massey. Although this product of Eton, Oxford, and a High Anglican family sincerely despises those who have deprived Italy of unity and freedom, he seems largely unaware of the condition of the working classes at home. Similarly, although Swinburne obviously delights in hurling invective at Pio Nono, Napoleon III, and others who have both oppressed the poor and deprived them of freedom, his is a purely verbal violence – something, one must admit, which is particularly appropriate to a poet. Gerald Massey, on the other hand, who is far less skillful a writer, makes it clear that he longs for real physical violence, probably because he has more experience of class injustice, dangerous working conditions, and the effects of being unable to find work than does Swinburne.[4]

Massey's characteristic use of extended and secularized types appears in his frequent citation of Exodus typology. The biblical account of how God freed His people from Egyptian slavery, prepared them to live as free men by their desert wanderings, and brought them at last to the promised land found ready application wherever people conceived of themselves as oppressed, and hence often appears in descriptions of the worker's lot. In the final pages of Charles Kingsley's *Alton Locke* (1850), for example, the dying hero, who has heard the happy voices of his fellow emigrants to the New World 'welcoming their future home', explains: 'Laugh on, happy ones! – come out of Egypt and the house of bondage, and the waste and howling wilderness of slavery and competition, workhouses and prisons, into a good land and large, a land flowing with milk and honey'.[5]

Massey's 'New Year's Eve in Exile' makes this usual application of such imagery drawn from the Exodus narrative when an aged fighter for freedom, whom the poet implicitly compares to Moses, prays: 'Come, great Deliverer, call the peoples up, – / Up from the Egypt of their slavery!/ Ring out the death-knell of old Tyranny'. This passage, which calls for a 'great Deliverer', is somewhat unusual in his poems, since it appears a completely orthodox application of political types. In contrast, his 'Song of the Red Republican' uses the same type, not to call upon God for deliverance, but solely to summon workers with 'hands labour-brown' to battle for their own freedom:

> Up, up from the Slave-land; who stirreth to stay us,
> Shall fall, as of old, in the Red Sea of wrath.

Here, as in so many of his poems, Massey's main interests are to awaken the lower classes to the possibility of freedom and to suggest to his fellow workers that their enemies will receive deserved vengeance.

His mention of the 'Blood of Christ', a 'promise-portal', and a 'glorious Crown' reveals that, like so many working-class radicals, Massey drew heavily upon Evangelical hymns and sermons for his images, rhetoric, and manner of proceeding. Similarly, 'Down in Australia', which again cites the familiar Exodus type, combines it with allusions to Genesis, Isaiah, and Revelation, much as Evangelical hymns often proceed by juxtaposing types. According to Massey,

> Fair Freedom's wandered Bird
> Shall wing back with leaf of promise from the Old Land!
>   And the Peoples shall come out
> From their slavery

into the freedom of Australia. Later, 'when the smoke of Battle rises' after the revolution comes to Europe and England, tyrants shall fall and freedom, which Massey describes in terms applied to the Messiah in Isaiah and Revelation, 'shall thrash her foes like corn'. 'The Exile to His Country' again alludes to this image of the winepress which was frequently interpreted as an analogue to the passage from Genesis 3:15 on bruising the serpent's head:

> And many are the tears must fall, and prayers go up to God,
> But swift the vintage ripens, and the winepress shall be trod!
> The Harvest reddens rich for death![6]

The pervasive influence of Evangelicalism upon the British working classes accounts for the presence of such characteristically Evangelical rhetoric, tone, and imagery in the political poetry of Massey and other working-class writers. In particular, his zeal and certainty that vengeance would ultimately destroy the forces of evil has an Evangelical ring to it.

As the nineteenth century unfolded, the relationship of the various Evangelical denominations to the working classes became increasingly complex. After the enclosure of village lands, creation of factory towns, and growth of urban areas had begun to reshape the face of the nation, the established Church long failed to minister to the new working-class populations. During the late-eighteenth-century religious revival, Evangelicals within and without the Church of England stepped into the spiritual vacuum created by the Church hierarchy's indifference and inefficiency. Tabernacles, chapels, and open-air prayer meetings brought religion to many in the lower orders, and Evangelical emphasis upon the centrality of the scriptures directly created an important increase in literacy.

Although the Evangelicals were sincerely concerned with the spiritual welfare of the working classes, the extreme political and economic conservatism of many believers alienated many workers.[7] Although the Evangelicals led the battle to stamp out Negro slavery at home and abroad, they resisted legislation to outlaw child labor, protect the worker from unsafe conditions, or otherwise interfere between master and worker. Therefore, the charge became common that Evangelicals cared more about black slaves than about English workers who often endured worse physical deprivation than the explicitly enslaved.[8] Similarly, opponents, of whom Dickens was one of the fiercest, argued that the Evangelicals, who were devoted to foreign missionary work, spent too much time and energy caring for natives of Africa and the East when many British poor had great need for such assistance. Furthermore, the Evangelical emphasis upon a strict observance of the Sabbath led these denominations to support stringent Sunday blue laws which effectively took away innocent pastimes from the workers while leaving such diversions readily available to those with the time and money to enjoy them during the week.[9]

Since the Evangelicals sought to raise the moral tone of the country by making blatant vice unfashionable, they often pursued policies which struck neutral observers as hypocritical. For example, their attempts to win over the rich, titled, and fashionable often suggested to many that the Evangelical Anglicans, who made so much of their emotional experience of Christ, were in fact toadying social climbers. Similarly, the Evangelical attempts to make vice

unfashionable occasionally led them to bizarre policies: As I have
pointed out elsewhere,

> Evangelical organizers of societies to save 'fallen women' thought
> nothing amiss in making well-known rakes, if titled, their patrons
> and honorary presidents, since such action would in the long run,
> they believed, serve the interests of morality. Thus, we have the
> grotesque situation in which those who helped women fall, and
> delighted when they did, presided over movements to stamp out
> their favorite pleasures.[10]

As the nineteenth century went on, an increasingly large number
of factors drove members of the working classes, as they drove
members of all classes, away from orthodox religious belief. The
Evangelicals, whose intellectual conservatism left them particularly
vulnerable to the challenges of geology, biology, and comparative
religion, lost the dominance of British religion which they had
enjoyed during the first four decades of the century. Furthermore, as
one might expect from the way they alienated many workers, they
also lost ground with members of the lower classes. Broad Church
Christian Socialism, High Church missionaries to the urban poor,
and various secular movements, such as Marxism, also competed
with them for adherents.

Nevertheless, in certain areas and under certain conditions, the
laboring classes long remained loyal to Evangelical belief. In the
slate-quarrying regions of North Wales, for example, nonconformist religion received strong support from local cultural and
political factors. Merfyn Jones explains in his study of the slate
quarriers that:

> Politics and religion sharpened and soured industrial relations in
> the quarries; every squabble was defined as a clash of cultures and
> traditions, of allegiances and values. The battle line was clear; on
> the one hand the quarrymen consciously upheld their brand of
> Radical Liberalism, their Nonconformity and their Welshness; on
> the other side the masters not only jealously guarded their profits,
> but also defended the ideology and institutions of an English
> squirearchy's Toryism and Anglicanism. . . . Religion provided

that massive sense of self-righteousness which characterized both quarryman and master.[11]

Religion also provided the slate workers with the terms in which they conceived their lives and struggles with the quarry owners, and so one is not surprised to find these Evangelicals invoking Exodus types. Jones reports, for instance, that at a meeting of Dinorwic quarrymen in 1885 one of the speakers urged: 'Do not go back to Egypt, my people'. Within the complex social, political, national-istic, and religious context of the Welsh quarrying regions, such citation of this commonplace passage does not comprise a secular or extended type at all. Rather the workers who urged their fellows not to return to Egyptian slavery were continuing the long Puritan tradition of conceiving contemporary events within the bounds of biblical typology. Since the quarriers so consciously opposed their own nationality, politics, class, and religion to those of the quarry owners, they could easily believe themselves to be in the condition of Israel in Egypt. These clear-cut oppositions encouraged them to see the Anglican Tories who owned the quarries – and always seemed to have little understanding of how they should be worked – in the position of Pharaoh and his cruel overseers.

In contrast, many working-class applications, such as those made by Gerald Massey, use this Exodus typology emptied of its christological import. Whereas Christian interpretations of the Exodus stress God's role in redeeming man, political secularizations of such types use it merely as a powerful means of stirring the oppressed to fight for their freedom. Whether or not he who applies the secularized type actually believes in a Christian God, he fre-quently emphasizes that aspect of the Exodus narrative in which a fierce vengeance falls upon the Egyptians trying to recapture their former slaves.

The working-class bias and the working-class associations of these types perhaps explain why Thomas Carlyle, who makes such major use of Exodus in *Sartor Resartus*, so rarely employs it in his political writings. On these occasions when he does employ secularized types derived from the Exodus narrative, he applies them in a manner very different from that found in Massey and other working-class radicals. 'Jesuitism', one of *The Latter-Day Pamphlets* (1850), thus bases an elaborate analogy of modern man's desire for freedom upon the Exodus account. But when Carlyle states, 'if it please Heaven, we shall all yet make our *Exodus* from Houndsditch', he is not concerned with freedom from political or economic oppression. Instead, this Victorian sage, who desires freedom from illusion, spiritual blindness, and the slavery of 'Consecrated Falsity', wants his contemporaries to make their 'Exodus into wider horizons, into God's daylight once more'. To free themselves from this form of Egyptian slavery, men of the nineteenth century, says Carlyle, must cast off an outmoded Old Testament religion (in which he apparently includes a great deal of Christianity as well). When men have grown enough to put aside such belief, they, 'immeasurably richer for having dwelt among the Hebrews, shall pursue their *human* pilgrimage. St. Ignatius and much other saint-ship, and superstitious terror and lumber, lying safe behind us (20.329–30). Like Swinburne writing two decades later, Carlyle masterfully uses typological images to attack the religion on which they are based.

Even when alluding to the departure from Egyptian slavery in an overtly political work, such as *The French Revolution* (1837), Carlyle gives this episode his own peculiar intonation. The chapter 'Give Us Arms', which relates the events of 13 July 1789 when the people of Paris obtained weapons, might seem the obvious context in which to make the usual political application of this type. Carlyle, however, instead uses it to argue that the urge to be free is essentially a spiritual fact, and he thus mentions the great 'moment, when tidings of Freedom reach us; when the long-enthralled soul, from amid its chains and squalid stagnancy, arises, were it still only in blindness and bewilderment, and swears by Him that made it, that it will be *free!*' According to this Victorian prophet who would on the contrary later in his career emphasize that men have a basic drive to be led, 'it is the deep commandment, dimmer or clearer, of our whole being, to be *free*. Freedom is the one purport . . . of all man's struggles, toilings, and sufferings'. Therefore, it is one of life's supreme moments when a man realizes that he can – that he must – be free. It is, says Carlyle, a 'first vision as of a flame-girt Sinai, in this our waste Pilgrimage, – which thenceforth wants not its pillar of cloud by day, and pillar of fire by night!' (2.183–4)

Carlyle obviously concentrates on the enslaved person's spiritual state and does not even mention the enslaving power, be it Pharaoh,

Satan, or the mill owners. His analogy hence does not serve the prime political purpose of sharply opposing groups or factions each of which immediately receives a predetermined moral status. Like many others who cite Exodus typology in a political context, he relies upon it to attach religious prestige, as it were, to an essentially secular matter. Similarly, in describing the mental state of a person awakening to the possibility of freedom, he employs this Exodus narrative to make that political awakening appear part of some essential principle of history. Nevertheless, he employs such imagery in neither the usual political or religious manner: although setting forth a political event, he concentrates upon the spiritual state of its participants; although claiming to perceive a universal spiritual principle in a historical event, and although casting that historical occurrence in terms of the Old Testament, he does not bring in Christ or Christian truth, directly or indirectly.

Like Rossetti, who employs secularized types in a non-political context, Carlyle draws upon the complex structure of the typological relation as a means of finding a meaning and order to human history. What makes the Carlylean application of the Exodus narrative function as an unorthodox, extended, and secularized type is not that the Old Testament events find completion in the lives of individuals. Such uses, as we have frequently observed, are considered to be entirely proper by leading Victorian exegetes. The crucial point is that Carlyle, who here sounds much like a preacher describing the way sinners suddenly desire freedom from Satan in Christ, has no room in his system for a Saviour. Thus, whereas Newman, in 'The Pillar of the Cloud' (1833), can pray: 'Lead, Kindly Light, amid the encircling gloom,/ Lead Thou me on!' Carlyle's pillars of fire and cloud are entirely subjective and internal. He believes that a universal principle makes all men capable of thus desiring liberty, but, like Swinburne, he holds that men themselves, and not God, must direct this Exodus.

Such fundamental spiritual attitudes explain in part why Carlyle does not make the usual applications of Exodus typology to politics and history in *The French Revolution*. Although he clearly believes in the forces of history, he does not accept that they guide men in a manner analogous to that of Moses or Christ. According to Carlyle, when societies base themselves upon what he terms 'Lies', such as ruling classes that do not govern and churches that do not guide, eventually the masses whom these false rulers oppress will revolt and sweep them away. Although Carlyle uses typology to spiritualize such forces, thus attempting to endow them with the spiritual prestige of a governing divinity, such rhetorical procedures only show how far he has moved from his earlier Evangelical faith. Like Ruskin, Newman, George Eliot, and many other Victorian writers who abandoned an early Evangelicalism, Carlyle always retained many habits of thought which that cast-off faith had originally created, and one of the most important of these involves his attitudes towards types and symbols. Like so many Victorians who learned to search biblical history for types and shadows of Jesus, Carlyle long retained the characteristic Evangelical delight in finding complex and unexpected meanings in the oddest events. He had become addicted, in other words, to the delights of interpretation. Furthermore, he had also learned both to manipulate individual types and to apply many of them to his own life and to those of the people about whom he wrote. He had become accustomed, in other words, to conceiving human lives in biblical terms; and no matter what the subject, biblical allusion, citation, and quotation came naturally to him. In Thomas Hood's 'Ode to Rae Wilson, Esquire' (1837), his satire on Evangelicalism, the poet announced:

> I do not hash the Gospel in my books,
> And thus upon the public mind intrude it. . . .
> On Bible stilts I don't affect to stalk;
> Nor lard with Scripture my familiar talk, –
>   For man may pious text repeat,
> And yet religion have no inward seat.

Unlike the author of 'The Song of the Shirt' (1843), Carlyle always spices his works with scriptural allusion, despite the fact that in him Christianity no longer has an 'inward seat'. He employs such 'pious texts' and the interpretive modes associated with them in part to reassure many in his audience about his lack of orthodoxy. He also uses such scriptural citation or allusion to suggest that his ideas grow forth naturally from traditional belief. But certainly the main reason Carlyle continued throughout his career to walk on 'Bible stilts' was that such had become part of his natural manner of proceeding.

None the less, he was always true to his beliefs, and he almost always presents such scriptural borrowings with a wry Carlylean twist. The two Carlylean uses of Exodus imagery at which we have looked suggest his characteristic handling of biblical history, language and symbolism.

Carlyle's allusions at two stages in his career to the episode from the twenty-first chapter of Numbers involving the brazen serpent exemplify additional Carlylean uses of commonplace types in political contexts. In *The French Revolution* he uses this event during the desert wanderings of the Israelites as a figure for France's representative assembly: 'The States-General, created and conflated by the passionate effort of the whole Nation, is there as a thing high and lifted up. Hope, jubilating, cries aloud that it will prove a miraculous Brazen Serpent in the Wilderness; whereon whosoever looks, with faith and obedience, shall be healed of all woes and serpent bites' (2.151). The Book of Numbers relates that after the Lord sent a plague of serpents to punish the Jews for their lack of faith, Moses interceded with God and was instructed: 'Make thee a fiery serpent, and set it upon a pole: and it shall come to pass, that every one that is bitten, when he looketh upon it, shall live' (Numbers 21:8). John 3:14, in which Christ proclaims 'And as Moses lifted up the serpent in the wilderness, even so must the Son of man be lifted up', taught Christians to see the brazen serpent as a divinely authenticated type of the Crucifixion, but commentators also emphasize that it is an image of saving faith. According to the usual reading of this type, the brazen serpent in the wilderness, which God gave to the people when they repented of their lack of faith, teaches man that he can be saved only by faith in Christ crucified.

Commentators like Thomas Scott emphasize that the brazen serpent is an image of saving faith precisely because the actions commanded by God were themselves so apparently unlikely to produce any beneficial result, and, similarly, without the eye of faith one would hardly think that salvation could conceivably come from gazing with belief at some person suffering painful execution.[12] The commentators also remark that Moses set up the brass image upon a pole in the midst of the Israelite camp, like a standard, and Carlyle employs all these elements of the original type when he explains with a characteristic blend of wry irony and sympathy that the Estates-

General will prove, if nothing else, 'a symbolic Banner' around which the 'exasperated complaining Twenty-five Millions, otherwise isolated and without power, may rally, and work – what it is in them to work. If battle must be the work, as one cannot help expecting, then it shall be a battle-banner' (2.151).

The Victorian sage follows his usual strategy of taking some historical fact, casting it in terms borrowed from the Old Testament or similar ancient mythos, and finally emphasizing its spiritual meaning. In this instance he once again reveals the presence in history of one of his most basic beliefs, that men require symbols to live and act. Carlyle, who knows the fate of the Estates-General and its members, uses the image of the brazen serpent to comment ironically upon this first attempt to cure the ills of misgovernment. For those Frenchmen who had lost faith in government, the political assembly seemed an act of faith that might cure their nation's ills; for those who believed that they or the nation had erred and fallen away from the ways of justice, it promised a means of earthly redemption. But the original brazen serpent was a divinely instituted type, whereas men alone made the Estates-General. Although both type and antitype seemed particularly unlikely to cure men's ills, they did so because they originated with God. By comparing the legislative assembly to the brazen serpent, Carlyle emphasizes both that it is equally unlikely to do good and that it does not derive from God. Furthermore, since the brazen serpent as a type was fulfilled by the Crucifixion, Carlyle's citation of the brazen serpent also suggests the eventual fate of the Estates-General. Carlyle, who was always sympathetic to any acts of faith, introduces the Estates-General to his reader in terms of a typological allusion which emphasizes this element of giving faith. His complex manipulations of the hermeneutic tradition associated with this type enables him to suggest the inevitable shortcomings of this governing body.

The potential for satire that obviously exists in Carlyle's use of the brazen serpent here in *The French Revolution* becomes fully realized in 'Hudson's Statue' (1850). In this *Latter-Day Pamphlet* he follows his usual satiric procedure and takes a contemporary phenomenon as an emblem of the nation's mind and soul. Like the typhus-ridden Irish widow, 'that great Hat seven-feet high, which now perambulates London Streets', and the 'amphibious Pope' and his 'Scenic Theory of Worship' from *Past and Present* (1843), the affair of Hudson's statue provides Carlyle with a grotesque satiric emblem of what is wrong with the age. He begins by drawing attention to the fact that whereas the people of England had not been able to make up their minds whether to build a statue of Oliver Cromwell, whom Carlyle takes to be one of the nation's greatest heroes, they readily subscribed £25,000 to erect one to the railway magnate and stock swindler, George Hudson (1800–71). After he was accused of having dishonestly recorded accounts and of having paid dividends out of capital invested by others, Hudson quickly lost his great wealth. He was not an entirely ruined man, for, although the public did not erect a monument to him after all, Sunderland continued to return him to Parliament until 1859.

Claiming that 'there was more of real worship in the affair of Hudson than is usual in such' monuments, Carlyle discovers that the people of England, who languish for better men to emulate, have chosen Hudson as one of their 'Pattern Men', a member of 'as strange a Pantheon of brass gods as was ever got together in this world'. According to Carlyle,

> Hudson the railway king, if Popular Election be the rule, seems to me by far the most authentic kind extant in this world. Hudson has been 'elected by the people' so as almost none other is or was. Hudson solicited no vote; his votes were silent voluntary ones, not liable to be false: he *did* a thing which men found, in their inarticulate hearts, to be worthy of paying money for; and they paid it. What the desire of every heart was, Hudson had or seemed to have produced: Script out of which profit could be made. They 'voted' for him by purchasing his script with a profit to him. Every vote was the spontaneous product of those men's deepest insights and most practical convictions, about Hudson and themselves and this Universe. (20.264–5)

George Hudson, whom many Victorians thought to be the new Saviour, turns out to be an incarnation of Mammon. Unlike Ruskin, who was later to charge that England worshipped the Goddess-of-Getting-On, Carlyle does not here importantly concern himself with the fact that his contemporaries worship such false divinities. Rather he finds in the entire affair an indictment of the nation's capacity to choose for itself.[13] He therefore asks:

After all, why was not the Hudson Testimonial completed? As Moses lifted up the Brazen Serpent in the wilderness, why was not Hudson's Statue lifted up? Once more I say, it might have done us good. Thither too, in a sense, poor poison-stricken mortals might have looked, and found some healing! For many reasons, this alarming populace of British Statues wanted to have its chief. The liveliest type of Choice by Suffrage ever given. The consummate flower of universal Anarchy in the Commonwealth, and in the hearts of men: was not this Statue such a flower . . . ? (20.275)

Carlyle's use of the type of the brazen serpent for satiric commentary upon a contemporary political question again demonstrates his complex manipulation of the interpretive tradition. For example, his initial parodic echo of John 3:14 not only reminds the reader of the usual reading of the brazen serpent but also underlines for him that Englishmen saw Hudson as a messiah. Carlyle's interpretation of this statue that was never constructed is appropriately marked by irony, and he begins setting forth his conceit by making clear that this Son of Man was in fact never lifted up. Thereupon in what seems to be a parody of typological exegesis, he suggests one explanation on the literal or historical level why Hudson's statue should have been erected. Since it represents what the nation really worships, and not what it pretends to worship, such a statue to the incarnation of Mammon would have been fitting. Considered in relation to the episode in the Book of Numbers, however, such a statue also 'might have done us good. Thither too, in a sense, poor poison-stricken mortals might have looked, and found some healing!' In other words, having before themselves such a Hudson's statue, Carlyle's contemporaries could look on the serpent which had plagued them and find their cure.

Of course, Carlyle is constructing a satiric emblem, not an orthodox typological reading, and important elements turn out to be inverted. One looks upon Hudson's statue as a brazen serpent, if one would be saved, not with faith but with necessary disbelief. The statue then becomes an emblem of saving skepticism and not saving faith. It instructs us, nevertheless, about two matters necessary for our 'salvation'. First, we learn to recognize the idolatrous nature of modern worship, and in so doing we also learn that we have fallen away from the true God. According to Carlyle, his is one of those epochs in which men 'keep a set of gods or fetishes, reckoned respectable, to which they mumble prayers, asking themselves and others triumphantly, "Are not these respectable gods?" and all the while their real worship . . . concentrates itself on quite other gods and fetishes, – on Hudsons and scripts, for instance'. This miserable epoch, which is 'in a manner lost beyond redemption', has added to its 'brutish forgettings of the true God . . . an immense Hypocrisy' (20.278), and perhaps such a putative Hudson's statue would state things so clearly that men would realize what they were worshipping.

The second great lesson according to Carlyle is that such a Hudson's statue would inform his contemporaries of the true nature of universal suffrage, which is the particular target of this *Latter-Day Pamphlet*. Carlyle, who had decisively turned from his earlier radical sympathies to embrace the reactionary political beliefs for which he is generally known, claims that giving the vote to everyone is but 'a scheme to substitute for the revelation of God's eternal Law, the official declaration of the account of heads! It is as if men had abdicated their right to attempt following the abovesaid Law, and with melancholy resignation had agreed to give it up, and take temporary peace and good agreement as a substitute' (20.274).

For Carlyle of *The Latter-Day Pamphlets*, the fact that Englishmen subscribed to build a statue of the Railway King means, in essence, that they have fallen away from God (or whatever it is that he defines as God). As he explains in terms which parody the New Testament,

> Know whom to honour and emulate and follow; know whom to dishonour and avoid, and coerce under hatches, as a foul rebellious thing: this is all the Law and all the Prophets. All conceivable evangels, bibles, homiletics, liturgies and litanies, and temporal and spiritual law-books for a man or people, issue practically here.

Carlyle, who devoted his later career to biographies of heroes such as Frederick, and Cromwell whom he could honor, uses 'Hudson's Statue', as he uses all *The Latter-Day Pamphlets*, to instruct his contemporaries 'whom to dishonour and avoid, and coerce under hatches, as a foul rebellious thing' (20.279). Since, unlike revolutionaries and working-class radicals, he is unwilling to follow the people, he must find someone else to honor and emulate, and the central problem of his later career is that he cannot find anyone in contemporary Britain worthy of his faith.

This central problem of Carlyle as a political sage appears in his use of extended types. Although he writes with the language and rhetoric of the Old Testament prophet – particularly when he lambasts his contemporaries for their 'brutish forgettings of the true God' – he lacks the one thing Jeremiah and Isaiah believed they had, the details of a specific religious ritual to which they could call back the Jews who had fallen away from the true God. He effortlessly dismisses all 'liturgies and litanies', just as he also brushes away 'respectable Hebrew and other fetishes' (20.278), but he cannot replace them with anything to which his contemporaries can give their allegiance. In the end, we realize that it is not the Railway King's non-existent monument which must be a true brazen serpent but Carlyle's *Latter-Day Pamphlet* entitled 'Hudson's Statue'. His pamphlet, which both warns the public about the consequences of false worship and instructs them in true belief, exists as the antitype, the true fulfillment, of the original brazen serpent. Unfortunately for Carlyle, the existence of an authentic typological relation requires both a God and a Christ, and he does not really believe in either one in anything like the normal sense – in the sense, that is, which typology requires. Consequently, Carlyle's wonderfully proficient manipulation of the brazen serpent results in the kind of complex image which arises only near the end of a tradition. Like many authors who employ secularized types, he uses them because they permit him to conjure up the imaginative power of a belief system without having to endorse it. Stated in the baldest possible terms, a secularized or extended type uses the materials of christological typology for effect. Hence it is a 'decadent' technique in so far as one defines that term to imply, not moral value, but something appearing near the end of an intellectual, artistic, or other tradition.

As one might expect from such self-reflective and often ironic handling of a tradition, Carlyle's brazen-serpent passage in 'Hudson's Statue', like many of his secularized types, demands that the reader be well acquainted with the fine points of typological exegetics. A second representative fact that becomes apparent when we look closely at the Carlylean secularized type is that this image comes to the reader laced with ironies and double meanings, not all of which he intended. Carlyle, whose exuberant love of language and symbolism colors all his writing, pushes such extensions of typology close to their limits. As a writer who wishes to use imagery for more than effect or mere emphasis, he tends to exploit the symbolic resonance of the original types as much as possible. But as he makes his secularized version of Christian symbolism ever more rich and complex, he unwittingly draws attention to the crucial fact that there is no Christ at the center of his typology; so, paradoxically, the more tightly Carlyle knits together his typological images, and the more elaborately he makes them resonate in the manner of the true typologist, the more likely he is to remind us that he employs, not something to which he grants full belief, but merely a powerful imaginative creation.

CHAPTER SIX

TYPOLOGICAL STRUCTURES: THE EXAMPLES OF GERARD MANLEY HOPKINS AND DANTE GABRIEL ROSSETTI

How a lush-kept plush-capped sloe
   Will, mouthed to flesh-burst,
Gush! – flush the man, the being with it, sour or sweet,
   Brim, in a flash, full!

                   Gerard Manley Hopkins, 'The Wreck
                        of the Deutschland'

Here dawn to-day unveiled her magic glass;
   Here noon now gives the thirst and takes the dew;
Till eve bring rest when other good things pass.
   And here the lost hours the lost hours renew.

                   Dante Gabriel Rossetti, *The*
                       House of Life

'Yet hear my paradox': Hopkins's typological allusions

As poetry, painting, and politics have shown, the Victorians employed both biblical typology and various unorthodox extensions of it. Many of their derivations, manipulations, and extensions take the form of abstracting one of typology's defining elements, such as its emphasis upon the literal truth of both type and antitype, and then applying it to a secular matter.[1] For instance, drawing upon typology's capacity to produce the entire Gospel scheme from a single image, authors will use types to create a defining moral context for political discourse or fictional narrative. When Mrs Browning, Swinburne, and others apply Exodus types to contemporary Italian politics, they abstract the entire structure of values contained in that biblical event and then employ it for an elaborate political analogy. Likewise, when authors use typology for characterization, they can employ it this way or they can borrow the typological pattern in which antitype completes type.

Gerard Manley Hopkins and Dante Gabriel Rossetti exemplify two additional forms of such extended typology. Rossetti abstracts a crucial feature of typological symbolism: its ordering of time in terms of prefigurations and their fulfillments. Then, emptying this structure of all christological import, he tries to use it to endow his own life with coherence. Like many other Victorians who make extensions of typology, Rossetti secularizes it. In contrast, Hopkins, the first poet at whom this chapter will look, does not secularize this divinely instituted form of symbolism, for he exemplifies a different kind of abstracted typology: instead of employing a single defining quality of the entive mode, he creates a powerful form of typological allusion by abstracting the essence – the defining conceit, idea, or structure – from individual scriptural types.

The major promise of exercises in scholarly recovery, such as this exploration of Victorian typology purports to be, is that they make an author and an age more accessible to us. They also promise us that we will better understand the relation of individual talents to the tradition or traditions within which they worked. In particular, such re-creation of the interpretive habits of a past age, say, that of the Victorians, purports to make us perceive the individual's debts and contributions to tradition and in this way helps us to understand the precise nature or originality of that individual's work. For example,

Ruskin, the Pre-Raphaelites, and Browning all become more accessible to the modern reader who understands Victorian typology. As it turns out, these artists and writers all influenced Hopkins to some degree, but the fact of such influence does not guarantee that our comprehending what is most important about typology will assist us in understanding what is most important about Hopkins's poetry.[2] Precise studies of his relation to his contemporaries are certainly needed; and when more about typology is generally known to Victorian scholars, such investigations will perhaps uncover unexpected connections and derivations. First, however, we must observe how Hopkins, a religious poet with a theologian's knowledge of the hermeneutic tradition, creates his own peculiarly effective mode of typological allusion. Without discussing all of Hopkins's poetry or even all his poems that employ types, the following pages will attempt to show how central such applications of typology are to his mind and art.

Hopkins develops his characteristic mode of abstracted typology by making refinements upon the more usual Victorian manner of citation practiced in earlier poems, such as 'Barnfloor and Winepress' (1865). In this poem, which draws upon George Herbert's 'The Bunch of Grapes', the poet cites a passage from scripture as an epigraph and also includes many biblical phrasings. Addressing the sinner and perhaps even the unbeliever, Hopkins, the Christian, announces the wonderful gifts that Christ purchased by means of His terrible sacrifice:

> Thou that on sin's wages starvest,
> Behold we have the joy in harvest:
> For us was gather'd the first-fruits,
> For us was lifted from the roots,
> Sheaved in cruel bands, bruised sore,
> Scourged upon the threshing-floor;
> Where the upper mill-stone roof'd His head,
> At morn we found the heavenly Bread,
> And, on a thousand altars laid,
> Christ our sacrifice is made!

Uniting them by a series of closely related paradoxes, Hopkins binds together an extraordinarily complex range of biblical allusions.

Most obviously, he cites the idea that the Eucharist, the 'heavenly Bread', came as the antitype of the Levitical 'first-fruits'. He also alludes to Genesis 3:15 when he mentions that Christ was 'bruised sore', but his central conceit, of course, is taken from the images of barnfloor and winepress that appear in the Bible from Numbers through the Revelation of St John the Divine. The poem's epigraph comes from 2 Kings 6:27: 'And he said, If the Lord do not help thee, whence shall I help thee? Out of the barnfloor, or out of the wine-press?' These lines telling the sinner that God is his only hope are taken from a rather grisly episode in the Bible. When the Syrians besieged Samaria, the people had nothing to eat:

> And as the king of Israel was passing by upon the wall, there cried a woman unto him, saying, Help, my lord, O king. And he said, If the Lord do not help thee, whence shall I help thee? out of the barnfloor, or out of the winepress? And the king said unto her, What aileth thee? And she answered, This woman said unto me, Give thy son, that we may eat him today, and we will eat my son tomorrow. So we boiled my son, and did eat him: and I said unto her on the next day, Give thy son, that we may eat him: and she hath hid her son. And it came to pass, when the king heard the words of the woman, that he rent his clothes. (2 Kings 6:26–30)

Hopkins serves several purposes by citing this grisly episode of biblical history in a poem about Christ's wonderful sacrifice. In the first place, this tale of cannibalism illustrates as forcefully as any could our fallen nature and consequent need of a Saviour. Second, although such an example of evil action cannot serve as a proper type, it does act as a powerful contrast between the true and false sacrifice of a son to preserve life. Third, the allusion to the linked terms, 'barnfloor and winepress', bring to mind the many complex associations they possess in the scriptures.

In Numbers 18: 26–7, the Lord, who is instructing Moses in the nature of the priestly office, tells him that when the Levites receive a tithe from the people, they must first offer up one-tenth of it as an offering to Him, after which they can retain the rest: 'And this your heave offering shall be reckoned unto you, as though it were the corn of the threshingfloor, and as the fulness of the winepress'. The priestly clan thus retains nine-tenths of the tithe as 'your reward for your service in the tabernacle of the congregation' (Numbers 18:31). This mention early in the Bible of the linked images of barnfloor (or here 'threshingfloor') and winepress bore several important significances for the Christian reader. First, barnfloor and winepress, the places where the making of bread and wine from natural growing things begins, stand for human sustenance; second, since they call to mind bread and wine, they prefigure the Eucharist; third, because this particular passage contains directions for priestly conduct, it prefigures Christian priesthood, tithing, and relations of priest to the congregation; fourth, since it mentions a sacrifice taken as a type of Christ, the passage also refers to Him and His sacrifice. Read in terms of Christian typology, then, the passage from Numbers, like so many others in the Pentateuch, provides anticipations of Christ as both priest and sacrifice.

In addition to presenting types of Jesus in these paradoxically opposing terms, barnfloor and winepress also suggest the ideas of slave and liberator, for in Deuteronomy 15:12–15 God instructs the Israelites to free all Hebrew slaves every seven years: 'And when thou sendest him out from thee, thou shalt not let him go away empty: Thou shalt furnish him liberally out of thy flock, and out of thy floor, and out of thy winepress'. As commentators point out, this law was meant in part to commemorate God's freeing the Israelites from slavery in Egypt and His leading them to prosperity. This connection of barnfloor and winepress to political liberation appears again in the Book of Judges. After the Jews had done evil in the sight of the Lord, He 'delivered them into the hand of the Midian seven years' (6:1), and the Midianites stole or destroyed their crops. Gideon, who 'threshed wheat by the winepress, to hide it from the Midianites' (6:11), is thereupon ordered by an angel of God to lead the people in battle, and, once again, the Israelites are victorious. In this passage from Judges, which provides a detailed contrast to that in 2 Kings, people again learn that falling away from God leads to punishment in the form of military defeat and consequent physical privation – but also, when the children of God are at their lowest state and most in need, God will send someone to save them.

As these examples have shown, the notion of divine punishment often appears in relation to the images of barnfloor and winepress, most frequently when God punishes man with dearth. Thus in Jeremiah 48:33, God causes 'wine to fail from the winepresses: none shall tread with shouting'. In another biblical usage, God punishes man by treading him in the winepress. In Lamentations 1:15 this application of the winepress image also echoes the idea of bruising or crushing from Genesis 3:15: 'The Lord hath trodden under foot all my mighty men in the midst of me: he hath called an assembly against me to crush my young men; the Lord hath trodden the virgin, the daughter of Judah, as in a winepress'. Similarly, in Isaiah 63:3, the Lord, who is angry because His people have not helped in the battle against evil, announces: 'I have trodden the winepress alone; and of the people there was none with me: for I will tread them in mine anger, and trample them in my fury; and their blood shall be sprinkled upon my garments, and I will stain all my raiment'. This passage prophesying divine punishment is then fulfilled in Revelation 14:19–20 when the angel gathers the 'vine of the earth' and casts it 'into the great winepress of the wrath of God. And the winepress was trodden without the city, and blood came out of the winepress, even unto the horse bridles, by the space of a thousand and six hundred furlongs'. These linked passages containing prophecies and types conflate, for the Christian exegete, an entire series of Christian paradoxes: Christ is both sacrificing priest and sacrificial victim; true, life-giving sustenance comes in feeding the soul with the Eucharist and not in feeding the body; Christ, who is both victim and conqueror, treads the winepress and is crushed by it; and more.

Hopkins, who draws upon all these meanings for 'Barnfloor and Winepress', adds others as well. James Finn Cotter correctly points out that as a reader it was Hopkins's 'custom to concentrate on an essential passage, gloss it exhaustively, and focus on a word or phrase that acted as key to the whole scene or meaning of the author'.[3] The phrase, conceit, or basic structure of ideas that informs this and so many other of his poems can be stated in the following form: true beauty, true life, true victory can only be achieved, as Christ has shown, by being bruised and crushed. Essentially, the basic Christian reading of Genesis 3:15, that Christ triumphs over sin and death by giving Himself to be bruised in the Crucifixion, remains one of Hopkins's central, organizing ideas. Stress, pressure, crushing, bruising, and similar terms that appear frequently in his poetry allude to the entire series of types presenting the Gospel scheme.

In 'Barnfloor and Winepress' Hopkins emphasizes how Christ,

'Sheaved in cruel bands, bruised sore' brought man new life, the Tree of Life, by His sacrifice then and His continuing sacrifice now, which is the sacrament of Holy Communion:

> For us by Calvary's distress
> The wine was rackèd from the press;
> Now in our altar-vessels stored
> Is the sweet Vintage of our Lord.

Emphasizing the element of paradox that derives from Christ's combination of being conquered and conqueror, Hopkins first tells us that He was 'Sheaved in cruel bands' and later, near the poem's close, that Christ has saved all men and 'sheaved us in His sheaf'. The poem's epigraph, which Hopkins addresses to those whom the Saviour does not include among the saved, employs the darker side of the barnfloor-winepress and bruising types; the body of the poem emphasizes that Christ has saved the believer. The type's basic structure, in other words, contains both threat and promise of hope, and Hopkins need only employ part of his basic structure to convey the type's full Christian message.

'Barnfloor and Winepress' uses other types as well, but they all join to this central structure of paradox. In this and similar early poems Hopkins's typological allusions take the form of easily recognized quotation and citation of scripture. Later, he relies increasingly upon the basic structure, rather than the specific language, of the biblical type. For instance, he organizes 'The Windhover: to Christ Our Lord' (1877) with this conceit that being bruised and crushed produces higher beauty. The octet magnificently conveys the beauty and mastery of the bird's physical conquest of the air – of the natural elements – and the sestet then proceeds to the far higher beauty that springs forth when the kestrel and plough, soil, and even mere ember endure pressure. As in most of his complex poems, Hopkins supports this form of allusion with others. For example, his address to Christ at the poem's close – 'and blue-bleak embers, ah my dear,/ Fall, gall themselves, and gash gold-vermillion' – also brings to mind Christ's descent into human flesh, the gall offered Him on the Cross, and the colors of the bird as well.[4]

This notion that bruising produces highest beauty appears in both early and late poems. 'Rosa Mystica', for example, asks,

What was the colour of that blossom bright? –
White to begin with, immaculate white.
But what a wild flush on the flakes of it stood
When the rose ran in crimsonings down the cross-wood!

In contrast to this rather baroque seventeenth-century conceit, that in 'Felix Randal' (1880) hovers beneath the surface of the lines relating how a 'heavenlier heart' came to this powerful man as sickness broke him. The related idea that pressure produces the Word of God, thus creating what is in essence another incarnation of the Word, appears both in 'The Wreck of the Deutschland' (1876) and in his undated fragment on the death of the Catholic martyr Margaret Clitheroe, who was pressed to death calling the name of Jesus. In 'That Nature is a Heraclitean Fire and of the comfort of the Resurrection' (1888) Hopkins makes, not martyrdom, but conversion or illumination embody this central structure. Here the pressure of God turns mere earthly materials into precious ones, as the poet draws upon the physical process by which diamonds are created from carbon as an analogy for spiritual metamorphosis:

In a flash, at a trumpet crash,
I am all at once what Christ is, since he was what I am, and
This Jack, joke, poor potsherd, patch, matchwood, immortal
    diamond,
            is immortal diamond.

Because divine pressure, force, or illumination can transform all men, they can be – if only for brief instants – Christ:

For Christ plays in ten thousand places,
Lovely in limbs, and lovely in eyes not his
To the Father through the features of men's faces.
            ('As kingfishers catch fire', c. 1881)

But, as Hopkins shows us in the 'terrible sonnets', such as 'Carrion Comfort' (1885) and 'Patience, hard thing!' (1885), man, who has so much evil in him, must be bruised by God to create good – to release that transient likeness to Christ. Thus, the abstracted type of bruising, like that drawn from barnfloor and winepress, embodies

185

both Christ's triumph over evil and a specific application of it to the condition of the individual sinner.

In addition to appearing in scriptural references to bruising and to barnfloor and winepress, Hopkins's favorite structure of ideas is embodied in the idea of crushing olives to produce oil. As we have already observed, Gethsemane, the location of Christ's agony, means the 'place of the olive-press', and he several times draws upon this fact. For example, in 'A Soliloquy of one of the Spies left in the Wilderness' (1864) he reinforces the ironic self-revelation that occurs when the speaker mentions the smitten rock in Horeb using what appears to be such an allusion. The rebellious, ungrateful speaker would willingly sacrifice his freedom for the Egyptian slavery of the past:

> Give us the tale of bricks as heretofore;
> To plash with cool feet the clay juicy soil.
> Who tread the grapes are splay'd with stripes of gore,
>   And they who crush the oil
> Are spatter'd. We desire the yoke we bore,
> The easy burden of yore.

This rebellious Israelite, who serves as a type for all those who reject Christ's dearly purchased gift of freedom, also prefigures those who crucified Christ during His Incarnation and still crucify Him with their sins. Delighting in the idea of splashing about in the Nile mud, he also delights in the thought of being splashed by the crushed oil and grape juice, both of which are images of Christ. In contrast to this characteristic use of a type within a dramatic monologue, 'God's Grandeur' (1877) employs Hopkins's later, abstracted form of allusion, for the grandeur of God 'gathers to a greatness, like the ooze of oil/ Crushed'. Despite the fact that trade and labor have smudged the earth, 'nature is never spent' because the Holy Ghost continually infuses 'the dearest freshness deep down things'. This freshness is dearest because it is both precious and very costly, purchased, in fact, by Christ's descent into human flesh. Hopkins, who draws upon Ruskin's and Keble's notions that physical beauty symbolizes divine spiritual attributes, here suggests that the Holy Ghost ceaselessly repeats the miracle of the Incarnation by inspiriting the world and thus making it bear that beauty which symbolizes

God. Moreover, the mention of oil being produced from the press reminds us that this beauty embodies the specific spiritual principle (or structure) that Hopkins believes to underlie all existence: that beauty and life were purchased only by Christ's enduring the pressure, bruising, and crushing of the descent into human flesh and subsequent Crucifixion. Finally, it is also possible that the mention of the oil press, when combined with the Holy Ghost brooding over a fallen word, is meant to recall Christ's Agony in the Garden: in both cases contemplating the results of fallen man leads to new life and beauty.

Hopkins can thus cite the same basic structure of ideas in poems about earthly beauty, conversion, spiritual agony, martyrdom, and biblical events, because he obviously believes that it contains the essence of Christian truth. Our realizing that he derives this structure from commonplace types does serve to make many of his poems more accessible, because it reveals both a common procedure and a common theme that might otherwise not be perceived. Such recognitions also suggest that much of what is most characteristic – and perhaps also what is most difficult – in his poems can be explained primarily by reference to Victorian typology. Indeed, one suspects that much of his manner and matter that has been explained in other terms, such as traditions of Christian Gnosticism, can be more accurately comprehended when his poems are placed in the historical context of contemporary British Bible reading.[5] At the same time as we recognize the Victorian commonplaces underlying his unique art, we can also better appreciate how brilliant, how original, are the poems he raises upon these foundations. Or, using Hopkins's own favorite conceit, we can thus better enjoy the way his poetic, imaginative pressure bruises common grapes to release unexpected beauties and greater triumphs.

'Life touching lips with immortality': Rossetti's temporal structures

Throughout his career as painter and poet Dante Gabriel Rossetti drew upon biblical typology. In his early career this unbeliever used it chiefly to endow orthodox Christian devotional images and poems with greater power, while later he drew upon it for those structures of nostalgia and regret that characterize his particular form of

Victorian Romanticism. Having already observed that Rossetti, Hunt, and their Pre-Raphaelite associates employed typology to create a symbolic realism, we shall now examine the way Rossetti moves beyond these orthodox applications of typological symbolism by abstracting from it two basic structures. In the first, which is most closely related to orthodox Christian usage, he employs one event to prefigure a second which completes it. Rossetti was apparently intrigued by the fact that prefigurative symbolism provides a means of redeeming human time, a means of perceiving order and causality in human events. Those familiar with his continual examination of the problems of time and loss in his poetry will immediately perceive how crucial such an idea could be to him. The other structure derived from typology is constituted by an event and its connections with eternity. In other words, typology provides repeated instances of situations in which the eternal brushes up against or reaches into human time. On each occasion that a divinely instituted type, say, Joseph, Aaron, or Samson, pre-enacts a portion of Christ's life and message, a privileged situation occurs, one which exists on a double temporal scale, that of the earthly and that of the eternal. Rossetti continually searches for analogous secular moments in life and art that could give human existence the same kind of meaning and essential coherence that types furnish for sacred history. Finding an event or instant when time and eternity supposedly interpenetrate, Rossetti discovers a point at which 'Life touches lips with immortality' and metamorphoses into something greater, something beyond human limits and limitations.

Although Rossetti did not possess the faith of Holman Hunt or his own sister Christina, typology remained important to him because it offered an example of the way the human imagination could organize written discourse to show that time had meaning. Therefore he continues to draw upon the language and habits of mind associated with typology in 'The Burden of Nineveh', 'Troy Town', and *The House of Life*, even though he ultimately has to admit that love (or the beloved) cannot, like Christ, serve as a center to human history. Although his upbringing in a High Church household did not provide him with Christian belief, it did leave him with a sincere yearning for the order and coherence that such a belief could offer. Many of his poems seek a replacement for that unavailable faith, something which will provide continuity for the self, but he fails to find one, and the closing portions of *The House of Life* show the poet accepting death.

A somewhat atypical application of typology (because it does not appear in the context of this personal quest) marks 'The Burden of Nineveh' (1856), in which Rossetti takes the ancient kingdom to be a prefiguration of Victorian England. In *The Stones of Venice* (1851–3), which the poet read and liked, Ruskin had presented Tyre and Venice as types of England that would prefigure the nation's downfall if it did not heed the warning offered by its predecessors. Such use of typological readings of history to draw conclusions about one's own time were common among seventeenth-century Puritans and nineteenth-century Evangelicals, among those, for example, who would have written that 'zealous tract "Rome, – Babylon and Nineveh" ', at which Rossetti smiles in the course of his poem.

A secularized political typology had long been associated with the idea of Rome: the Italian city-states of the Renaissance, France during the period of Revolution and First Empire, and fascist Italy and Germany during the twentieth century all turned to the shadow of ancient Rome as authority and goal for their programs. Here one is talking of a relation between two times, a prefiguring and fulfillment, which is more a permanent part of Western thought than a derivation of Christian readings of history. Such attitudes towards secular history assisted the popularity of Christian typology, one suspects, far more than Christian typology gave birth to them. Rossetti's beloved Dante, it is true, did set forth in the *Purgatorio* the notion that Roman history could be incorporated into the divine scheme of salvation: just as the Old Testament types and prophecies led up to Christ, preparing His way in spiritual matters, so the Roman Empire had done in terms of political, purely secular order. Such habits of mind thus would have been familiar to Rossetti.

The irony with which he hypothesizes this relation between Nineveh and England is entirely in keeping with the attitudes of the poem. The speaker encounters workmen hoisting in the Assyrian bull-gods just as he is leaving the sanctity of the British Museum, where he has retreated to admire the beauties of Greek art. Now, finding himself once more in the noise and bustle of modern London, he comes upon the ancient statues and quickly moves into a meditation upon time and loss. Finally, he thinks of that distant era when some future archeologists, perhaps the descendants of some now still-primitive tribe, will excavate London as Layard had Nineveh. Encountering the massive idols in the ruins of a once proud city, these latter-day explorers will assume that the English had worshipped such gods. 'The smile rose first,– anon drew nigh/ The thought':

> Those heavy wings spread high,
> So sure of flight, which do not fly;
> That set gaze never on the sky;
>   Those scriptured flanks it cannot see;
> Its crown, a brow-contracting load;
> Its planted feet which trust the sod: . . .
> (So grew the image as I trod:)
> O Nineveh, was this thy God, –
>   Thine also, mighty Nineveh? [Ellipsis in original]

As the meditator elaborates upon the bull-god's appearance, one gradually perceives that it effectively provides a satiric catalogue of a presumed British deity, not, as Ruskin put it in 'Traffic', that which men pretend to worship on the Sabbath but that to which they offer themselves the other six days of their weekly existence. In fact, Rossetti's closing description much resembles Ruskin's later creation of the English – and one must add, European and American – Goddess-of-Getting-On.

Another, more characteristic example of Rossetti's oblique use of ideas associated with typology appears in 'Troy Town'. The critical history of this poem centers upon the fact that many readers have assumed the refrain has no effect other than to stress that Rossetti has cast classical myth in ballad form. If, however, one examines 'Troy Town' from the vantage point of his many attempts to provide a connection between various times, one perceives that the prefigurative refrain has an important function indeed. The poem opens with a stanza describing the beauty of Helen, whom the second stanza portrays standing before the altar of Venus and praying for the love of Paris:

> Helen knelt at Venus' shrine,
> (O Troy Town!)

Saying, 'A little gift is mine,
A little gift for a heart's desire.
Hear me speak and make me a sign!'
(O Troy's down,
Tall Troy's on fire!)

After the first line of each stanza, then, Rossetti inserts a lament for Troy, one that is generalized and timeless, while each stanza ends with the more specific statement that Troy is burning *now* while the speaker is telling the tale, while the prayers are being directed at Venus. The poem, in other words, proceeds by juxtaposing two facts and two times stanza after stanza until they are understood to merge into each other. The refrain is thus a poetic or verbal parallel to Rossetti's use of multipaneled pictures in *Paolo and Francesca* (1849–62) and *The Seed of David* (1860–4). Thus, Helen's beauty and desire are repeatedly set side by side until we recognize that they are all but equivalent: Helen's desire, Helen's beauty *are* the destruction of Troy, and they become so implicated in the fate of Paris's home that they function proleptically. As the ballad progresses, it builds a momentum of gathering doom. The first nine stanzas depict Helen's prayers for the love of Paris; and the next two Venus's approval of the desire that she herself has created; and the eleventh and twelfth, Cupid sending his burning arrow on its way. The last stanza shows that Helen's prayer has been answered, for Paris lies 'Dead at heart with heart's desire', and the stage is set for the tragedy to be enacted. Within the poem, which thus juxtaposes two times, the end is implicit in the beginning, and this is precisely what Rossetti has managed to emphasize so effectively. If such a poetic strategy sounds familiar, it is because Yeats repeats it with far greater artistry in 'Leda and the Swan', a poem for which 'Troy Town' is almost certainly the model and source. While Yeats manages to conflate his times with more brevity and without the need for archaizing language, Rossetti's poem manages most powerfully to make its point about the tragic power of human desire.

A related, if far different effect appears in two of his best long poems, 'Jenny' (1848–58) and 'The Last Confession' (1849). Like Swinburne's 'The Triumph of Time' (1866), both incorporate what can be termed a meditative structure; that is, they each begin with a single point, a single event, and continually find themselves led back to it. We do not find out until the closing lines of 'The Last Confession' that this event was the speaker's murder of his beloved, and the entire poem moves towards the point at which we learn this fact and then perceive that for the dying man this murder has become the center of his life, the significant moment towards which he moved and which still obsesses him. I am not trying to argue, of course, that such a concern with time is in any sense an example of typology. Rather, I merely wish to show that the poet's interest, or perhaps obsession, with time led him continually to look for ways to organize his poems to find such temporal centers. Indeed, one could accurately define Rossetti's verse in terms of the recognition that since Christ as a center of human history is no longer available or even relevant to him, man must search for other poetic and spiritual solutions.

One recurrent solution is to capture a moment which in some way captures the eternal, the timeless. 'For a Venetian Pastoral' (1849), one of his most famous sonnets, attempts to preserve one of these centers to time when the eternal brushes against the temporal, just as it does in the typological image. As in his sonnet 'For An Annunciation, Early German' (1849), he makes use of his ability to create a poetry of sensation and experience, a poetry which can capture the sensory edge of things, their sound, their look. For a long time critics of Pre-Raphaelite poetry assumed that Rossetti and other writers associated with the young painters wrote a visually oriented poetry, a verse characterized by sharp visual impressions and carefully composed scenes – analogues, as it were, to Ruskin's word-painting and to hard-edge Pre-Raphaelitism. In fact, a large portion of Rossetti's poetry takes the form of meditations that are conceived non-visually or that make a major use of conceits and other non-visual devices. None the less, he did have a fine talent for writing such visual poetry. It is just that he rarely finds the attractions of such a method compelling enough to make it the center of an entire poem, as do, say, Morris and Tennyson.

'For a Venetian Pastoral' represents one of his comparatively rare attractions to this kind of verse. Reading Giorgione's painting as a moment of secular and sensual illumination, he recreates that moment by detailing the things whose touch and sound make it so perfect. His speaker, here as always an observer outside the picture-space, comments upon the figures' actions by means of imperatives that serve in the manner of stage directions. The sonnet begins with a yearning for water, which can ease the thirst of summer's longest day, and then we hear the water flow so quietly into the jar the woman holds. He directs this nude woman sitting at the fountain or well, 'dip the vessel slowly, – nay, – but lean/ And hark how at its verge the wave sighs in/ Reluctant'. We are then turned from the quiet sound of the water filling the vessel to greater quiet, greater absence of motion: 'Hush! Beyond all depth away/ The heat lies silent at the brink of day'. Now the players cease their music and 'brown faces cease to sing,/ sad with the whole of pleasure'. They are sad, we soon realize, because all things, all beings, all moments must pass. Rossetti underlines this inevitable loss when he returns our gaze to the woman, against whose naked side we are meant to feel 'the shadowed grass'. He asks us – or those in the painting – not to break the spell in which she finds herself enclosed, nor later attempt to recall or categorize it:

> Say nothing now unto her lest she weep,
> Nor name this ever. Be it as it was, –
> Life touching lips with immortality.

According to Rossetti, then, the woman (who has, in effect, become one of his own Fair Ladies) experiences one of those perfect moments, one of those centers to time, that offer a pattern and order to our lives. Unfortunately for the poet, the only such moment of which he knows that could last is that one at which Christ was supposed to have appeared on earth, thereafter providing a center to all history for those who believed in Him. Since Rossetti, like so many Victorians, cannot accept such a divine irruption into the human, these centers to time and other aspects of typology can only appear in his most personal poetry in a truncated form. This description is not meant to criticize his poetry for a deficiency. Rather, I wish merely to show how Rossetti remains fascinated with those moments at which life touches immortality. Here it is the quality of the moment, its sensory perfection, which raises it above the flux of ordinary minutes and hours – and the fact that a great painter chose to immortalize it in color and form. None the less, however powerful the experience, however intense the illumination, it passes all too quickly, and hence the major tone of the sonnet is elegaic as we are left with a sense of piercing loss, of pain at recognizing the transience of things, of ourselves.

The most important example of Rossetti's concern with time occurs in *The House of Life* (1870–81), the complex gathering of sonnets which is his poetic masterpiece. It ends with his acceptance of time and death; but before arriving at that conclusion the poet makes many attempts to conquer or evade the temporal and its painful destructions. Throughout the first portion of *The House of Life*, he tries to find or create centers to time, something that can provide a core and a meaning to his existence as man, lover, and poet. In section twenty-seven, for instance, he replaces Christ with the beloved at the center of human existence:

> Sometimes thou seem'st not as thyself alone,
>   But as the meaning of all things that are;
>   A breathless wonder, shadowing forth afar
> Some heavenly solstice hushed and halcyon.

The problem for Rossetti, as for all secular poets, is that the beloved is not in fact divine, she is not all that much like Christ, and it is only at odd moments that she 'seem'st' to be the center of all things.

The poet's tendency to treat either love or his beloved as spiritual saviour appears most strikingly in some of the sonnets written earliest for *The House of Life*. For example, in its earlier version, section three, 'Love's Testament', was entitled 'Love's Redemption', and it employed explicit imagery of the sacrament of communion:

> O thou who at Love's hour ecstatically
>   Unto my lips dost evermore present
>   The body and blood of Love in sacrament;
> Whom I have neared and felt thy breath to be
> The inmost incense of his sanctuary;
>   Who without speech hast owned him, and intent
>   Upon his will, thy life with mine hast blent,
> And murmured o'er the cup, Remember me! –

Such an obvious and almost blasphemous transference of things associated with Christ to Rossetti's own incarnation of romantic love apparently dissatisfied him, for he later removed the imagery of the Eucharist, thus making the second and third lines read: 'Unto my heart dost evermore present,/ Clothed with his fire, thy heart his testament'. The effect of this slight change was reinforced by his further removal of the last line of the octet, which echoed the words of Christ to His disciples at the Last Supper, and which apparently elevated the lovers to the status of Christ Himself: 'And murmured o'er the cup, Remember me!–' These alterations in the first part of the sonnet change the effect of what follows, for the sestet in the later version no longer so obviously alludes to the harrowing of Hell. It is difficult to determine precisely why Rossetti made these modifications, but at least one reason would seem to be his growing realization that he could not sincerely make his earlier identifications of love and Christ.

The first part of *The House of Life* contains other attempts to make the beloved the center of his life. Sonnet thirty-four thus opens with the assertion that he himself cannot plumb the limits of his love, adding,

> How should I reach so far, who cannot weigh
>   To-morrow's dower by gage of yesterday? . . .
>   And shall my sense pierce love, – the last relay
> And ultimate outpost of eternity?

Such a claim, which works perfectly if this greater love equals Christ, as it does in the work of religious poets, becomes problematic and desperate in this context – as it is supposed to be. The speaker remains sure at this point, none the less, that through the beloved's eyes Love 'grants me clearest call/ And veriest touch of powers primordial/ That any hour-girt life may understand'. The beloved, in other words, provides a point at which the eternal enters human time, acting analogously to Christ's presence in history. Rossetti's use of terms conventionally associated with typology, such as 'shadowing' and 'fulfillment', demonstrates that his attempted solutions to the problem of time derive ultimately from this Christian mode of thought.

More commonly in *The House of Life* Rossetti makes not the loved one nor even love itself but some perfect moment serve as the yearned-for center to time. His attempts to create such moments provide the burden of several of his other poems, including 'For a Venetian Pastoral', 'The Woodspurge' (1856), and 'Sudden Light' (1854). 'Parted Presence' similarly relates how a moment of perfect love can redeem us from time:

> The hourglass sheds its sands
> All day for the dead hours' bier;
> But now, as two hearts draw near,
> This hour like a flower expands.

There are several such instances of frozen or stopped time in the earlier parts of *The House of Life*, and characteristically they are achieved by means of Rossetti's visual, rather than his abstract, style. Sonnet nineteen, 'Silent Noon', begins with the poet's word-painting and then proceeds to draw from it a moral about the lover's temporal existence. The opening lines convey the speaker's sight of his beloved's hands in the green of nature:

> Your hands lie open in the long fresh grass, –
> The finger-points look through like rosy blooms.

The poet then moves his glance from her hands upward to her eyes, which 'smile peace', and next looks around them, first to the pasture in which they find themselves and then at the 'billowing skies that scatter and amass'. The movement of his eyes, which provides the drama and structure of the sonnet, scans a full circle, thereby sketching the pasture in more detail:

> All round our nest, as far as the eye can pass,
> Are golden kingcup-fields with silver edge
> Where the cow-parsley skirts the hawthorn-hedge.

Then, in the final line of the octet he draws his preliminary moral, his *sententia*, as if he were unable to exist for long on the level of the purely sensory and sensual, but were driven inevitably to reflect upon his joy. ' 'Tis visible silence, still as the hour-glass', he tells his beloved, and then having obliquely reminded himself of the effect of time, he looks once again at their surroundings that now speak to him of its inevitable movement:

> Deep in the sun-searched growths the dragon-fly
> Hangs like a blue thread loosened from the sky: –
>   So this wing'd hour is dropt to us from above.

Now fully aware of the destructions of time, he pleads, he demands, that they hold on to this perfect moment:

> Oh! clasp we to our hearts, for deathless dower,
> This close-companioned inarticulate hour
>   When twofold silence was the song of love.

Thus, even in the lines that apparently capture this moment of joy, Rossetti finds himself driven first to reflect upon it and then to yearn desperately, almost helplessly, to still the onrush of hours and days. In fact, his use of 'was', rather than 'is', in the closing line thrusts him (and the reader) imaginatively forward into the future when this moment will have long disappeared.

In section thirty, 'Last Fire', he tells his beloved once again that they have, together, lived through a day of happiness. Now the consolation must be, not that they can retain that time in any way, but that it existed at all:

> Many the days that Winter keeps in store,
>   Sunless throughout, or whose brief sun-glimpses
>   Scarce shed the heaped snow through the naked trees.
> This day at least was Summer's paramour,
>   Sun-coloured to the imperishable core
> With sweet well-being of love and full heart's ease.

Earlier, in sonnet fourteen, 'Love's Spring-Tribute', he had captured the erotic joys shared by the lovers in the awakening spring. The speaker's only awareness of time, if one may even term it that, appears in his mention that spreading his beloved's hair about the 'newborn woodflowers' occurs at 'the hour of Love's sworn suit-service'. By making his kisses analogous to the April sun that is warming the earth into new life, he, like Lucretius and other classical authors, makes his own actions subject to the universal eros awakening the world. In other words, he is so much a part of nature, so much in harmony with the world, that he is only aware that this is *the* time for loving, and not that time itself will pass on to autumn and winter.

In this poem, as in 'Last Fire' and 'Silent Noon', he creates a sonnet truly 'a moment's monument'. But monuments both preserve a memory and mourn a passing, and, as we have observed, the speaker in *The House of Life*, whom we may take to be Rossetti himself, increasingly realizes that he cannot hold on to these moments. The confidence that he can capture the passing instant found in 'The Portrait' and 'Last Fire' becomes replaced by the recognition of transience, and the poet's attempts to retain his joys become increasingly desperate.

Transience provides the subject of many of Rossetti's other poems, including his translations from Villon, because it was something he found compelling throughout his poetic career. Even in a supposedly optimistic poem, such as 'Possession', it is the loss, rather than the joy, that comes through, and his more usual emphasis falls upon the loss itself. Thus, 'Dawn on the Night-Journey' uses the language of typology and prophecy, schemata which create temporal order, only to emphasize a final lack of that order:

> When the last
> Of the sun's hours to-day shall be fulfilled,
>   There shall another breath of time be stilled
> For me, which now is to my senses cast
>   As much beyond me as eternity,
>   Unknown, kept secret.

Even as the day begins he is aware that the hour will be given 'as sheer as chaos to the irrevocable Past'. Such recognitions of man's helplessness in the waters of time serve as the burden of many sections of *The House of Life*. For example, section twenty-four, 'Pride of Youth', quickly dramatizes the lover's consciousness of time, for even while rejoicing in new love he must admit that 'there is a change in every hour's recall'. He first mentions the happy side of change, perceiving that even as the last cowslip fades away, the first corn-poppy springs to life. Immediately afterwards, however, the implications of such succession force their way upon him.

> Alas for hourly change! Alas for all
> The loves that from his hand proud Youth lets fall,
> Even as the beads of a told rosary!

In sonnet forty-three, 'Love and Hope', such recognition of inevitable change and loss makes the speaker place a more desperate emphasis upon that kind of perfect moment he had presented hopefully in 'Silent Noon' and 'Youth's Spring-Tribute'. Moreover, the speaker now becomes explicitly retrospective. Whereas the earlier sonnets begin in the present, portraying the perfect moments as they unfold before the poet, 'Love and Hope' leads up to such a moment by recognizing that others have already eluded him and his beloved:

> Full many a withered year
> Whirled past us, eddying to its chill doomsday;
> And clasped together where the blown leaves lay,
> We long have knelt and wept full many a tear.

Suddenly, they come upon a perfect hour once again: 'Yet lo! one hour at last, the Spring's compeer,/ Flutes softly to us from some green byeway'. The poet consoles himself and his beloved with the thought that although those times are already dead, the lovers remain. But even as he asserts this 'comfort', he asks her not to demand of 'this hour' if they shall awake together after death in the 'sunshine of the imperishable land' – in essence, a denial of the lover's desires in 'The Blessed Damozel'.

'Stillborn Love', section fifty-five, makes an even more desperate claim that capturing such a perfect hour is still possible, for here the only place it can be found is after death. Describing the failure to realize their potential perfection of love in 'the hour which might have been yet might not be', the poem draws the lovers themselves as parents of that 'little outcast hour', which treads some unknown shore against which breaks 'Time's weary sea'. But by the close of the sonnet the speaker can envision the two lovers, now united once again, at last capturing that hour of joy on the 'immortal strand'. The context of this part of *The House of Life* suggests, not that the speaker has achieved new faith, but that he has become more desperate, placing his hope on those things that he has already indicated will not come to pass. The lovers thus displace God as the center and creator of their scheme of salvation, revelation, and culmination, but by now in the sonnet sequence the speaker is presenting a poetry, not of belief, but of hypothesis that serves primarily to communicate the intensity of his desire.

By sonnet eighty-three, 'Barren Spring', only the awareness of transience and loss remains. At this point in *The House of Life*, imagery of natural fertility no longer can represent the poet's mood. Spring thus awakens no echoing, answering smile from the poet, 'whose life is twin'd/ With dead boughs that winter still must bind'; and when he sees the new life springing from the earth, he no longer has his beloved with him to quicken into an echoing vitality. Instead, he perceives, like that last great Victorian poet, that April is the cruelest month for one who has no capacity for joy and new life within him. Hence the flowers he sees remind him only of what he has lost:

> Behold, this crocus is a withering flame;
> This snowdrop, snow; this apple-blossom's part
> To breed the fruit that breeds the serpent's art.

These lines invert the earlier joyful centers of time he had portrayed, because now the juxtaposition of the two moments only underlines how much time has taken from him. The 'changed year's turning wheel' becomes, then, not an image of nature's eternal cycle of growth but of fortune's wheel; for without his beloved he is now but fortune's fool.

Increasingly pessimistic, the speaker devotes several sonnets to the difficulty of seizing and holding on to anything of importance to him. In particular, 'Hoarded Joy', eighty-two, dramatizes the impossibility of catching the right instant, the point of fullness, so that the final result of the poet's meditation is not a memory of having captured something beautiful that can sustain him, but of being captured by the memory that he has allowed that precious moment to slip away. Whereas Rossetti had written with sharp visual detail earlier in 'Silent Noon' and similar sonnets that optimistically present the possibility of preserving such moments, now he writes in his more characteristic abstract style. 'A Superscription', ninety-seven, one of the closing sections of *The House of Life*, again emphasizes the impossibility of retaining anything of value. Here we have an address by 'Might-have-been/ I am also called No-more, Too-late, Farewell'– all denied potential – who tells the lover that his longed-for center to life and time, his moment of culmination, will not come to pass. Even when one recalls moments of joy, 'Might-have-been' transforms them into 'a shaken shadow intolerable'. Even if the poet should find 'one moment' when peace enters his soul, the realization of what he has lost, of what has not been achieved, will turn his tranquillity to suffering, his dream to sleepless misery. When the speaker was sitting next to his beloved, such moments appeared sufficient to console him for any loss that might follow; but once she is lost to him such brief instants merely intensify his loss. Moments are not enough.

'He and I', ninety-eight, the next sonnet, shows that he has lost more than his beloved – he has lost his old self. Discontinuity of the self is the final result of living within this meaningless, eroding time; for just as Rossetti finds he cannot hold on to love, so, too, he finds he cannot hold on to his memories and experiences, and so at last he becomes a different person, a stranger to his earlier being. Rossetti's attempt to recapture things past ends, unlike those of Ruskin and Proust, with resignation and not the triumphant resurrection of an earlier self. The final two sonnets accept death as the inevitable creation of life, as Rossetti's version of *In Memoriam* becomes, in effect, an anti-*In Memoriam*.[6] He enforces his acceptance of death-as-the-end-of-life with 'Newborn Death', sonnet ninety-nine, in which he creates what seems to be a parody of a Nativity or Adoration scene: the 'worn mother Life' places Death upon his knee 'to grow my friend and play with me'. None the less, Rossetti ends not with despair, for the final sonnet ends on a note of hope, though one for which Rossetti can provide no reason except desire.

In conclusion, the explicit and skillful use of typology that Rossetti displayed in his early poetry had several major effects upon his career. It provided him with a means of making poetry and painting into sister arts, while at the same time it permitted him to solve some of the problems inherent in all realistic styles of painting. Because he could not accept the validity of Christian belief necessary for a sincere use of christological typology, he could not employ it in his most personal works, as could Hunt, Browning, Tennyson, Newman, and Keble. Instead, he makes use of typology's various capacities to organize time, and they have a major effect upon his tone and manner of proceeding. In *The House of Life* he writes about a present, which (he hopes) has been prefigured by perfect moments of the past, and his search for these organizing prefigurations provides his poem with its introspective, elegaic tone.

CHAPTER SEVEN

THE PISGAH SIGHT –
TYPOLOGICAL STRUCTURE
AND TYPOLOGICAL IMAGE

What says the Scripture? 'As many as are led by the Spirit of God, they are the sons of God.' (Rom. viii. 14.) . . . It is the Spirit who leads them to Sinai, and first shows them the law, that their hearts may be broken. It is He who leads them to Calvary, and shows them the cross, that their hearts may be bound up and healed. It is He who leads them to Pisgah, and gives them distant views of the promised land, that their hearts may be cheered.

–John Charles Ryle, 'Are You an Heir?'

Faith is the Christian's Pisgah. Here he stands
Enthroned above the world; and with the eye
Of full belief looks through the smiling sky
Into the Future, where the Sacred Lands
Of Promise . . . are brought nigh,
And he beholds their beauty.

–Charles Sangster (1822–93, known as
the 'Father of Canadian Poetry'), 'Faith'

The wanderings of the Israelites end when Joshua leads them into Canaan after the death of Moses. Before the prophet dies, God commands him to ascend Mount Pisgah and there He grants him a sight of the Promised Land, a glimpse which provides a particularly complex and interesting type:

> And Moses went up from the plains of Moab unto the mountain of Nebo, to the top of Pisgah, that is over against Jericho. And the Lord shewed him all the land of Gilead, unto Dan.
>
> And all Napthali, and the land of Ephraim, and Manasseh, and all the land of Judah, unto the utmost sea,
>
> And the south, and the plain of the valley of Jericho, the city of palm trees, unto Zoar.
>
> And the Lord said unto him, This is the land which I sware unto Abraham, saying, I will give it unto thy seed: I have caused thee to see it with thine eyes, but thou shalt not go over thither.
> (Deuteronomy 34:1–4)

Since Moses's vision of the Promised Land takes place in a complex situation marked by punishment and reward, success and failure, it is fraught with many potential ironies that authors can either suppress or develop. Like other portions of the Exodus narrative which Victorians applied as types to their own deepest personal and political concerns, the Pisgah sight appears in orthodox christological, extended religious, and completely secularized forms. Its particular significance for the student of Victorian culture lies in the fact that it possesses a complex structure, each of the parts of which can be employed for a different intonation of the basic type.

The Pisgah sight is a coming together, a confrontation, of the human and the divine, the temporal and the eternal, that occurs immediately before the death of the prophet who had given his life to serving God and His chosen people. Therefore it stands simultaneously as the culmination, reward, and punishment for the acts of that life. As the Lord explains to Moses when instructing him to climb the mountain of vision, 'Because ye trespassed against me among the children of Israel at the waters of Meribah-Kadesh, in the wilderness of Zin; because ye sanctified me not in the midst of the children of Israel. Yet thou shalt see the land before thee; but thou shalt not go thither unto the land which I give the children of Israel'

(Deut. 32:51–2). Like the Rabbis, Christian interpreters explained God's apparently harsh punishment as His means of emphasizing that no man, no matter how powerful or blessed, can ever be above the law of God.

Furthermore, Christian exegetes discovered a complex reference to Christ in this divine action. 'Why, after bringing the people out of Egypt, might he not settle them in Canaan?' asked Henry Melvill. 'Why, except that Moses was but the representative of the law, and that the law, of itself, can never lead us into heavenly places? The law is as "a schoolmaster, to bring us unto Christ"; it may discipline us during our wanderings in the wilderness; but if, when we reach the Jordan, there were no Joshua, no Jesus – for the names are the same – to undertake to be our guide, we could never go over, and possess that good land.'[1] Melvill also argues that God punished Moses as a way of underlining that his earlier action in defying God's instructions and striking the rock a second time was wrong. The first time Moses struck the rock in Horeb and produced water for the wandering Israelites, his action symbolized the fact that law had to strike – crucify – Christ to bring forth the waters of grace and salvation. Thereafter only prayer was necessary, but by becoming impatient and striking the rock, Moses threatened to muddle the divine scheme of salvation and obscure the complex web of significant events God intended to adumbrate it. In addition, says Melvill, since Moses later appears during the transfiguration of Jesus, it was necessary to the prophet's later symbolical value that he should not enter the Promised Land in life.

Finally, according to this great Evangelical Anglican preacher, Moses was granted his Pisgah sight as a means of instructing Christians how to die in God:

> We must die on the summit of Pisgah: we must die with our eye upon Bethlehem, upon Gethsemane, upon Calvary. It was not . . . the gloriousness of the Canaanite landscape, which satisfied the dying leader, and nerved him for departure. It was rather his view of the Being by whom that landscape would be trodden, and who would sanctify its scenes by His tears and His blood. And, in like manner when a Christian comes to die, it is not so much by view of . . . the paradise of God . . . that he must look to be comforted: his eye, with that of Moses, must be upon the manger,

the garden, and the cross. . . . O that we may all . . . lie down with Moses on Pisgah, to awaken with Moses in paradise. (186–7)

According to Melvill, then, Moses's dying vision on Mt Pisgah serves as a divinely intended prefiguration of the kind of Christian death so frequently urged by Evangelical preachers, tract writers, and poets, for Mt Pisgah stands as a type of the deathbed of the true believer who leaves this life confident in his faith, and Moses's sight from that mountain prefigures the Christian's dying sight of his Saviour.

Evangelical hymns and devotional poetry made such readings of the Pisgah sight commonplace to Victorian worshippers. Thus, 'Jerusalem, my happy home' (1801), an anonymous hymn which Palmer includes as number 110 in *The Book of Praise* (1863), asks,

> Why should I shrink from pain and woe,
>   Or feel at death dismay?
> I've Canaan's goodly land in view,
>   And realms of endless day.

Unlike Melvill, who takes the rather extreme position of assuming that Moses was granted literal visions of the Christian future, this hymn takes Canaan itself in its commonplace acceptation as a type of heaven. Similarly, Isaac Watts's 'There is a land of pure delight' (1709) used the parallel between the Promised Land of Israelites and Christians as a basis for making the Pisgah sight a type of the Christian's happy death. Describing the land of pure delight which awaits all believers, Watts explains that 'Death, like a narrow sea, divides' it from us and that 'timorous mortals' fear to attempt its waters.

> O! could we make our doubts remove,
>   These gloomy doubts that rise,
> And see the Canaan that we love
>   With unbeclouded eyes;

Could we but climb where Moses stood,
  And view the landscape o'er;
Not Jordan's stream, nor death's cold flood,
  Should fright us from the shore.

Unlike 'Jerusalem, my happy home', Watts's hymn only implicitly takes the Pisgah sight as a type of the Christian's hoped-for death; whereas the other hymn asserts that its speaker has 'Canaan's goodly land in view', Watts only wishes that we might be in a similar position. Yet another way of creating an implicit type within a hymn appears in Augustus Montague Toplady's 'Deathless principle, arise!' (1777). Unlike the two previous examples, Toplady's lines are extensions of the original type, since he employs the secular analogue of the Pisgah sight, which is the prospect, rather than the original literal vision from Mt Pisgah. After describing both 'the haven full in view' and the necessity of traveling across water to reach it, he closes his hymn:

> Such the prospects that arise
> To the dying Christian's eyes;
> Such the glorious vista faith
> Opens through the shades of death.

These lines, which remind us that the biblical type of the vision from Mt Pisgah can exchange values with the secular prospect or view from a high place, explain part of the complexity of this particular typological image.

A similarly extended version of the basic type occurs in the closing pages of Kingsley's *Alton Locke*, whose hero, dying of consumption, realizes that he will never live to set foot on American shores. 'Yes! I have seen the land!' he tells us in his dying moments. 'Like a purple fringe upon the golden sea . . . there it lay upon the fair horizon – the great young free new world! and every tree, and flower, and insect on it new!– a wonder and joy– which I shall never see'. Immediately after admitting that he has known all along that he would never 'reach the land', Locke hears the happy voices of his fellow emigrants on deck as they greet their new home and he exclaims that they and all workers should 'come out of Egypt and the house of bondage, and the waste and howling wilderness of slavery and competition, workhouses and prisons, into a good land and large, a land flowing with milk and honey'. His citation of the Exodus type in a political context reminds us that Kingsley's hero, who is certainly no Moses, none the less provides us with a figure in some ways analagous to him: a member of an enslaved people, he has acquired an unusual consciousness of his position, and though tempted to follow the usual course and move upward to the middle classes, he chooses, like Moses, to remain with his people and advance their cause. He also makes an exodus, though it takes the milder form of emigration; and he is no leader – except in so far as his writings will inspire other workers.

Locke's dying words come in response to his hearing his fellow emigrants singing 'the grand lilt of the "Good Time Coming" ', which he describes as 'a fitting melody to soothe my dying ears!' He thereupon asks, 'Ah! how should there not be A Good Time Coming? – Hope, and trust, and infinite deliverance! . . . coming surely, soon or late, to those for whom a God did not disdain to die!' Unlike Toplady's hymn, which only implicitly refers to the Pisgah sight, this closing section of Kingsley's novel surrounds a dying vision of a promised land with types. It thus insures that we perceive that Locke's glimpses of America exist in an antitypical relation to Moses's sight of Canaan.[2] Furthermore, the fact that his last words are about Christ and 'infinite deliverance' makes us perceive that Kingsley has given his hero a Broad Church version of the Evangelical 'happy death'.

Locke's tranquil, accepting death reminds us of another aspect of its Christian significance. However strong the punitive element in God's commands to Moses, He clearly grants him a vision of the Promised Land as both solace and as reward, for He rewards His prophet for faithful service and He solaces the pain of punishment with a vision. The Pisgah sight therefore provides a powerful image of divine mercy, but in *Alton Locke* another implication almost emerges. Since the dying hero only glimpses a land he cannot live to enter, we are reminded that the Pisgah sight also provides an image of man's failure to achieve his goals – be they following the moral law or attaining true freedom. However, the Pisgah sight's intrinsic capacity for irony, which appears in so many works of nineteenth-century literature, is here suppressed by Kingsley's emphasis upon Locke's final acceptance and belief. For all the political applications that the Broad Church novelist makes of types, the final emphasis of his novel is still Christian. In terms of the Pisgah sight itself this final emphasis appears in the fact that although we are partially aware of the irony in Locke's dying before he can set foot in his promised land, we realize that it is far more important to Kingsley that his hero have dying visions of both Christ as deliverer and the salvation He brings. These are the true Pisgah sights, and they serve to de-emphasize the importance of America as a literal promised land and to lessen the effect of any irony generated by Locke's sight of it in his last hours.

Since his hero's Christian acceptance of such a potentially painful vision contrasts so strongly with an earlier mention of an explicit Pisgah sight in the context of political violence, this closing passage permits Kingsley to demonstrate that Locke has grown beyond his once dangerously radical views. At the close of 'Tailors and Soldiers', the novel's fourth chapter, Locke explains that hundreds of thousands of the working classes, convinced that they have been denied basic rights, 'live on a negation' and

> have to worship for our only idea . . . the hatred of the things which are. Ay, though one of us here and there may die in faith, in sight of the promised land, yet is it not hard, when looking from the top of Pisgah into 'the good time coming' to watch the years slipping away one by one, and death crawling nearer and nearer, and the people wearying themselves in the fire for very vanity, and Jordan not yet passed, the promised land not yet entered? While our little children die around us . . . of cholera and typhus and consumption, and all the diseases which the good time can and will prevent; which, as science has proved, and you and the rich confess, might be prevented at once, if you dared to bring in one bold and comprehensive measure, and not sacrifice yearly the lives of thousands to the idol of vested interests, and a majority in the House. Is it not hard to men who smart beneath such things to help crying aloud – 'Thou cursed Moloch-Mammon, take my life if thou wilt; let me die in the wilderness, for I have deserved it; but these little ones in mines and factories, what have they done? If not in their fathers' cause, yet still in theirs, were it so great a sin to die upon a barricade?'

Locke's powerful indictment of the way England treats her workers, which draws heavily upon Carlyle's 'Chartism' (1839) and *Past and Present* (1843), closes with an ironic call to the English clergy for leadership. He asks, 'my working brothers, is it true of our promised land, even of that Jewish one of old, that the *priests'* feet must cross the mystic stream into the good land and large which God has prepared for us?' If such is the case, he concludes, why in the name of God don't the clergy – 'ye priests of His' – awake and lead the people 'over Jordan'. Up until this point in his remarks Kingsley, the Broad Church clergyman, has been speaking through his character, but here he seems to address his fellows in his own voice. Certainly, despite his elaborately Evangelical vocabulary, tone, and rhetoric, Locke is not speaking as a believer. Rather, like so many working–class radicals, he applies the devices of the Evangelical preacher to the needs of the labor organizer, strike leader, and revolutionary. Locke argues implicitly that both owners and workers, rich and poor, follow false gods: the desperate working and unworking poor worship only 'hatred of the things which are' and as they become less hopeful of improving their painful lot, they inevitably become attracted to violent solutions. The rich, who worship a 'Moloch-Mammon', sacrifice the poor to their false god and do not understand that men who know they will die as offerings to such an obscene god will soon enough realize that they might as well 'die upon a barricade'. Kingsley's first use of the Pisgah sight in *Alton Locke* thus emphasizes that neither rich nor poor have found Christ. His uses of the type later in the novel show us, in contrast, that at least one member of the lower classes has found Him and thereby gained a true vision of the Promised Land.

Alton Locke's various skillful intonations of this biblical type suggest its range of literary possibilities. Unlike many commonplace types, the Pisgah sight is not secularized solely by replacing a reference to Christ with one to some other entity or idea, such as 'the people'. Seven basic elements comprise the Pisgah scene, and it may be modified (and is usually secularized) by manipulating any of these: (1) the presence of God to the one who has the Pisgah sight; (2) the time in the viewer's life when such a sight occurs; (3) the physical position, usually a mountain top or high place, from which the prophet gazes; (4) his removal from the viewed object, his separation from the promised land; (5) his isolation from other people; (6) the content of the vision, the nature of the promised land, and the kind or degree of compensation they offer; and (7) the nature of the viewed object to human time – whether, in other words, it is something to be attained in time (in the future) or outside time (in eternity).

Paradoxically, much of the Pisgah sight's power and richness as an allusive device appears to derive from the fact that it is so difficult to employ literally.[3] As we have observed in the case of Locke's dying glimpse of the American coast, the ironies intrinsic in the original scene threaten to overpower whatever religious meaning one wishes to find in it. Kingsley solves this problem by having his dying hero receive additional metaphoric Pisgah sights which compensate for this first one. Even Melvill, who usually places chief importance upon following the literal narrative, feels impelled to replace the sight of the Promised Land of Canaan with a supposed vision of the Christian future. Melvill and other Christian interpreters transform a simple glimpse of a geographical area into a prophecy, a glimpse of the future. True, the biblical account does contain a slight futuristic element, since God tells Moses that the land he sees will be given to the Israelites, but the prophet knows that they will become the property of the chosen people soon after his death. Christian interpreters, on the other hand, entirely transform the Pisgah sight by adding this temporal element and thus making the vision a matter of a distant future. By juxtaposing a literal and a metaphorical Pisgah sight, Kingsley manages to create a close parallel to the Old Testament original and then solve the problems it produces. But this example suggests that the intrinsic difficulties of the original type require that almost any any application of the last events of Moses's life to a Christian purpose requires modifying or adjusting the scriptural narrative.

The most common orthodox application of the Pisgah sight, which the hymn 'Jerusalem, my happy home' exemplifies, takes the position of Moses on the mountain as a literal prefiguration of the believer's deathbed. But such applications redefine the geographical vision of Moses, transforming it into a spiritual vision: Canaan becomes Heaven. Such spiritualizing portions of the Old Testament figure in the antitype follows the strictest orthodox exegetical practice, but as soon as one wishes to employ this compelling image of a person catching sight of the distant promised land at any other time in a character's life than at its end, one necessarily creates an extended version of the basic type. Furthermore, as Toplady's mention of 'prospects' in 'Deathless principle, arise!' reminds us, another major source of the Pisgah sight's richness and complexity as a literary device is that it often merges with a secular tradition of visions from mountains, hilltops, and other high places.[4] In fact, the particular additions Henry Melvill makes to the original Pisgah sight when he grants Moses a full sight of the Christian future owes as much to Milton and the prospect tradition as it does to the Bible.

In *Paradise Lost* Adam receives a vision of the future of mankind which, like that of Moses, serves as instruction, solace, and reward. At God's command, Michael leads the father of mankind up to a place of divine vision, as

> both ascend
> In the visions of God: it was a hill
> Of Paradise the highest, from whose top
> The hemisphere of earth in clearest ken
> Stretched out to the amplest reach of prospect lay. (11,376–80)

Under angelic guidance Adam learns both the horrific results of his fall and the coming salvation through Christ which will redeem man. Milton, who combines the classical and religious traditions to create a new Christian poetry, draws upon biblical and secular sources for this Adamic prospect vision. In particular, he draws upon the vision that Vergil grants Aeneas. In *The Aeneid*, during the hero's descent to the underworld, he receives a vision of the future of Rome which simultaneously provides a goal for his life and offers comfort in its many trials. This political vision, which is directed at the future, differs thus significantly from Vergil's Homeric sources, which present a fixed, static conception of time rather than a progressive theory of history.[5] The Roman poet, for example, transforms *The Iliad*'s description of the shield of Achilles, which presents an image of human life as it is, into a vision of the future which will see dramatic changes in human existence. His vision contains the Roman version of the earthly paradise – the *imperium* with its *Pax Romana*. Rather than being able to return to a past existence (as can Odysseus), Aeneas must create a new one, and his vision of the future is intended to comfort him for what he has lost.

Similarly, in *Paradise Lost* Adam receives his vision as both consolation and as something for which to strive. Like Aeneas, the father
of mankind receives an overview of the race he will sire, but, unlike
the father of Rome, Adam is learning how he has introduced evil into
the world, and not solely that he is the father of ultimate good. Like
Moses, Adam has the prospect sight shortly before leaving his
former existence, and although the father of mankind does not die
when he and Eve depart from Paradise, they both leave behind the
potential immortality of Eden and the Tree of Life. Adam thus
changes from being a potential immortal to a mortal, and he now
must await Christ before he can attain to this higher state. None the
less, his vision of a Christian future with its promise of salvation
compensates for his loss.

In the Miltonic extension of the Pisgah sight, a divinely sponsored
imaginative vision of truth compensates for the loss of an original
Edenic state. A rather different religious extension of the original
type occurs when nineteenth-century religious poets attempt to
catch glimpses of the promised land during the course of life and not
at its end. James D. Burns's 'O time of tranquil joy and holy feeling!'
(1855), which exemplifies such an extended Pisgah sight, makes the
Sabbath appear a window into eternity:

> Even now I see the golden city shining
> Up the blue depths of that transparent air:
> How happy all is there!
> There breaks a day which never knows declining;
> A Sabbath, through whose circling hours the blest
> Beneath Thy shadow rest!

By making the earthly Sabbath a type of an eternal heavenly one,
Burns thus employs the futuristic element implicit in all prefigurative images and events to lead the believer to a sight of the promised
land of heaven. Similarly, the anonymous 'Ere another Sabbath's
close' (1841), which is number 320 in Palmer's *The Book of Praise*,
implores:

> Let these earthly Sabbaths prove
> Foretastes of our joys above;

214

While their steps Thy pilgrims bend
To the rest which know no end!

Newman's 'The Haven' (1832) makes a bolder extension of the notion of types, for he takes, not some divinely ordained institution like the Sabbath, but a rare moment of perfect earthly peace as a means of glimpsing a lost paradise:

Sinner! thou hast in this rare guest
Of Adam's peace a figure blest;
'Tis Eden seen, but not possess'd,
Which cherub-flames still keep.

Unlike most such use of types as implicit Pisgah sights, Newman here makes his image serve as the antitype of Edenic bliss and only implicitly as the type of heavenly peace. In 'The Month of Mary' (1850), which he wrote after his conversion to the Roman Church, Newman makes the more usual application of earthly phenomena to heaven:

The green green grass, the glittering grove,
The heaven's majestic dome,
They image forth a tenderer bower,
A more refulgent home;
They tell us of that Paradise
Of everlasting rest,
And that high Tree, all flowers and fruit,
The sweetest, yet the best.

Newman's use of earthly things, rather than biblical events, as materials for typological interpretation follows frequent High Church and Roman Catholic practice.[6] When used specifically as a type of heaven, which exists outside time, these images serve as windows into eternity. Whereas the characteristic type chiefly refers to something which exists at a specific moment of future time, this particular extended version refers instead to something which is essentially atemporal. Furthermore, when Keble, Newman, Faber and other High Anglican and Roman Catholic authors use earthly phenomena as types of something outside human time, they have abandoned most of the defining characteristics of this form of symbolism. In fact, frequently when they use the term 'type' they mean little more than 'symbol', though much of the time, it is true, they assume that the symbolical relation is divinely instituted.

Such extension of typology to natural symbols, which comprises an important current of nineteenth-century Romanticism, of course involves far more than situations derived from the Pisgah sight or analogous to it. Such extensions, however, provide a paradigm of what happens to this form of biblical interpretation during the course of the century. One of the first points to note about such modifications and transferences of typology is that they occur in the works of believers from all denominations. For instance, Ruskin, who was raised as an Evangelical Anglican, bases his theory of beauty upon such a conception of type as divinely instituted symbol. According to his reasoning, all phenomena which we find beautiful, such as proportioned curves, symmetry, and pure colors, act as types of divinity. Ruskin, one should add, is not concerned that people habitually use beautiful objects for the element of the divine in them. Rather, in his search for an objective basis for aesthetic emotions, he simply argues – like Fairbairn explaining the existence of scriptural types – that this symbolic relation grows forth naturally from the essential laws of the universe: since God is the highest good in the universe, anything that humans perceive as delightful will turn out to echo some aspect of divinity.

A manuscript which Ruskin originally planned to include in the second volume of *Modern Painters* (1846) reveals the significant fact for us that he derived his conception of beauty as theophany upon an intense experience of Alpine beauty – upon an experience, more-over, which he casts in the form of a vision of heaven from a mountain height. One dark, still July evening he lay beside a fountain midway between Chamouni and Les Tines under a sky 'dark not with night, but with storm. The precipice above me lost itself in the air within fifty feet of my head – not in cloud – but in the dark, motionless atmosphere' (2.363). As he lay beneath a sky which was like a 'roof' or 'one level veil, as of God's Holy Place',

> Suddenly, there came in the direction of Dome du Goûter a crash – of prolonged thunder; and when I looked up, I saw the cloud cloven, as it were by the avalanche itself, whose white stream

came bounding down the eastern slope of the mountain, like slow
lightning. The vapour parted before its fall, pierced by the
whirlwind of its motion; the gap widened, the dark shade melted
away on either side; and, like a risen spirit casting off its garments
of corruption, and flushed with eternity of life, the Aiguilles of the
south broke through the black foam of the storm clouds. One by
one, pyramid above pyramid, the mighty range of its companions
shot off their shrouds, and took to themselves their glory – all fire
– no shade – no dimness. Spire of ice – dome of snow – wedge of
rock – *all* fire in the light of the sunset, sank into the hollows of the
crags – and pierced through the prisms of the glaciers, and dwelt
within them – as it does in clouds. The ponderous storm writhed
and moaned beneath them, the forests wailed and waved in the
evening wind, the steep river flashed and leaped along the valley;
but the mighty pyramids stood calmly – in the very heart of the
high heaven – a celestial city with walls of amethyst and gates of
gold – filled with the light and clothed with the Peace of God. And
then I learned – what till then I had not known – the real meaning
of the word Beautiful. With all that I had ever seen before – there
had come mingled the associations of humanity – the exertion of
human power – the action of human mind. The image of self had
not been effaced in that of God . . . it was then that I understood
that all which is the type of God's attributes . . . can turn the
human soul from gazing upon itself . . . and fix the spirit . . . on
the types of that which is to be its food for eternity; – this and this
only is in the pure and right sense of the word BEAUTIFUL.
(4.364–5)

Ruskin's mountain vantage point, his isolation, and his description
of the mountain glory unveiling itself before him in terms of the
heavenly city all suggest that he cast his experience in forms learned
from Evangelical hymns, sermons, and scriptural meditation. He
describes the mountains standing calmly 'in the very heart of the
high heaven', and it is not clear if, at this moment, Ruskin means
they exist in the midst of the earthly sky, in heaven itself – or if he
distinguishes between these states. He describes 'the mighty
pyramids' as a 'celestial city with walls of amethyst and gates of gold'
much in the manner of countless Evangelical hymns, and his description of the mountains first appearing 'like a risen spirit casting off

its garments of corruption, and flushed with eternity of life' similarly enforces his elaborate parallel between his mountain experience and Evangelical visions of heaven. Ruskin's comments upon his experience at the end of the quoted passage make clear that in calmer, more analytic moments he understood the mountain glory to be a type of heaven and not a vision of heaven itself. But in narrating his experience, Ruskin essentially collapses the type into the antitype, the earthly into the celestial, to convey how the beautiful in fact serves as a window into eternity. Like Milton's extension of the Pisgah sight in the last two books of *Paradise Lost*, Ruskin's manipulation of this type has the viewer – here Ruskin himself – receive religious knowledge essential to his earthly enterprise. Moreover, like Adam who is instructed in the meaning of types by Michael, Ruskin learns that they adumbrate a God whom we shall encounter only at a later time.

Ruskin's use of the Pisgah-sight structure as a form to present a natural type that is also a metaphorical Pisgah sight has important precedents in the poetry of Wordsworth and Coleridge. For instance, Wordsworth's 'The Simplon Pass', which he wrote in 1799 but did not first publish until 1845, makes a similar use of the tumult and peace of a mountain landscape; for after describing it with powerful word painting the poet concludes that its elements were 'The types and symbols of Eternity,/ Of first, and last, and midst, and without end'.[7] Coleridge's 'Hymn before Sun-Rise, in the Vale of Chamouni' (1802) parallels even more closely Ruskin's description of his experience in a nearby Alpine location. Coleridge contrasts tumult and a calm, silent mountain, the sight of which leads to an experience of heaven. He moves from an initial struggle to find adequate perceptions of the scene before him to a combined perceptual and spiritual state that subsumes what he sees into a vision of something out of space and time. He thus begins his address to 'sovran Blanc' with the perception that 'thou, most awful Form!/ Risest from forth thy silent sea of pines' silently as if an alien force were piercing the 'dark, black, substantial' air surrounding its peak. But when he looks at Mont Blanc with higher vision, Coleridge recognizes that it belongs in this setting, and this sight in turn brings him beyond vision:

> But when I look again
> It is thine own calm home, the crystal shrine,
> Thy habitation from eternity!
> O dread and silent Mount! I gazed upon thee,
> Till thou, still present to the bodily sense,
> Didst vanish from my thought: entranced in prayer
> I worshipped the invisible alone.

Coleridge, who believed that 'we receive but what we give,/ And in our life alone does Nature live' ('Dejection: An Ode', 1802), appropriately concerns himself with the reciprocal relation of perceiver and perceived object. He therefore addresses the mountain with the claim that it has blended with his own thought and 'secret joy',

> Till the dilating Soul, enrapt, transfused,
> Into the mighty vision passing – there
> As in her natural form, swelled vast to Heaven!

Although Ruskin's experience of Alpine beauty and sublimity may have been just as subjective as Coleridge's earlier fictional 'experience' of Mont Blanc, he still claims that the scene before him comprised an objectively existing type of God. Coleridge, whose experience of a sublime mountain landscape also brings him an experience of heaven, does not state any such precise symbolic equivalence between landscape and eternity. Rather, the natural scene – his version of the Pisgah sight itself – acts as a stimulus for a spiritual change which occurs in him, for by some mysterious process of imaginative empathy he and the mountain interpenetrate until his soul passes into 'the mighty vision' and there 'As in her natural form, swelled vast to Heaven!' Coleridge's phrasing does not make it easy to ascertain if his soul passed into the form of the mountain and, like it, rose up to heaven, or if it entered the entire vision of mountain and sky and swelled vast, and in this form entered heaven. Part of the difference between the two accounts of a mountain vision as a window into eternity lies in the sensibilities of the two men. Whereas Ruskin, who accepted an entirely visual epistemology and psychology, presents his spiritual experience in terms of the landscape, Coleridge tries to demonstrate that experience in the inadequate terms of what happened to him.

In emphasizing the role played by his own powers of perception, Coleridge exemplifies a major strain in English Romanticism. God brings Moses to Mt Pisgah and there permits him to look at the Promised Land of his people, and, similarly, in the Miltonic extension of the Pisgah sight, God also has Adam brought to 'a hill/ Of Paradise the highest' from where the father of mankind receives a divinely sponsored vision of the future that compensates, to some degree, for the loss of Eden. Ruskin, like the writers of Evangelical hymns, speaks as though he too receives his sight of heaven in the presence of God. But despite the fact that Coleridge devotes the last two-thirds of his poem to urging the mountain and other elements of the neighboring scene to 'Utter forth God, and fill the hills with praise', his Pisgah sight does not seem to take place in the presence of God. His deity seems to reside either hidden or at one remove from this natural landscape. Unlike Ruskin and Newman, Coleridge does not encounter some fact of nature which turns out to be a divinely instituted symbol capable of furnishing a sight of heaven. Instead, this poet encounters Mont Blanc, and after it blends with his 'Thought,/Yea, with my Life and Life's own secret joy', he finds that his soul 'swelled vast to Heaven'. Having been enraptured, he returns to something like his usual perception of things and urges the landscape to speak forth the God who created it. The very fact that in the course of his address to the landscape he appropriates the voice of God in the whirlwind from the Book of Job suggests how much, perhaps, of the divine role he has had to assume in this endeavor. Part of the difference between Ruskin and Coleridge's mountain visions lies in the fact that Ruskin writes as a visionary and Coleridge as a mystic; that is, the author of *Modern Painters* casts his experience in the form of a detailed visually patterned scene, while the poet attempts to describe changes taking place in his soul. The most important point of difference, however, appears in the fact that Ruskin writes under the belief that God is present at his Pisgah sight, whereas Coleridge does not.

Although orthodox Pisgah sights have the direct sanction and sponsorship of God, characteristically romantic and modern ones seek the same education, solace, and reward in His absence. As M. H. Abrams has pointed out, such transference of Christianity's ideas to relatively secular matters provides a central theme of British and German Romanticism.

The tendency in innovative Romantic thought (manifested in proportion as the thinker is or is not a Christian theist) is greatly to diminish, and at the extreme to eliminate, the role of God, leaving as the prime agencies man and the world, mind and nature, the ego and the non-ego, the self and the not-self, spirit and the other, or (in the favorite antithesis of post-Kantian philosophers) subject and object. . . . The notable fact, however, is that this metaphysical process does not delete but simply assimilates the traditional powers and actions of God, as well as the overall pattern of Christian history. . . . In this grandiose enterprise, however, it is the subject, mind, or spirit which is primary and takes over the initiative and the functions which had once been the prerogatives of deity.[8]

Furthermore, according to Abrams, post-Kantian philosophical systems share a characteristic 'plot form' which 'parallels the exemplary lyric form which Wordsworth, following the instance of Coleridge's *Frost at Midnight*, established in *Tintern Abbey*: an individual confronts a natural scene and makes it abide his question, and the interchange between his mind and nature constitutes the entire poem, which usually poses and resolves a spiritual crisis.' Attempting, in the absence of a deity, to reproduce or reinterpret a structure originally based upon the coming together of man and God has certain obvious problems, the most basic of which is that one party must do all the work.

Although the leading figures of the first Romantic generations for a time believed they were up to such a task, few in the generations which followed had such grandiose conceptions of man and poet. Most of the artists and writers who employed typology during the reign of Victoria retained some form of Christian belief and hence prove extremely conservative within the context of Romanticism as defined by Professor Abrams. Those like Rossetti, Swinburne, and George Eliot, whose major works were written while they were non-Christians, had, however, a knowledge of typology and the habits of mind associated with its use at earlier stages in their careers. In relation to the Pisgah sight the religious condition of Victorian authors produced two very different effects: those with relatively firm belief employ the orthodox and extended forms of this type to describe dying visions or to create images which are windows into eternity; those without such belief, unable to pursue the grandiose enterprise of the early Romantics, employ the Pisgah sight and its analogue, the prospect, for the ironies potential in the situation, and even believers, such as Tennyson, will use them in this way when dramatizing troubled faith.

For example, Tennyson closes *The Idylls of the King* by granting Bedivere, the last of Arthur's knights, a consolatory vision which is yet tinged with ironies. Bedivere is directly assisted by no divine or angelic voice, and his mount of vision is appropriately an iron crag in a wasteland. Having loyally obeyed his dying king at last, he finds that both the words and the higher faith which he has never been able to comprehend now spontaneously come to him, bringing comfort. Turning from the water on which Arthur has begun his voyage to Avilion, the good knight slowly climbs an 'iron crag', which Tennyson transforms into a mountain of vision, to catch a last sight of the departing boat. As he climbs, this knight, who had once so easily discounted tales of Arthur's miraculous origin, cries out: 'He passes to be King among the dead,/ And after healing of his grievous wound/ He comes again'. Though mixed with doubt, which for Tennyson is the condition of all belief, this faith comes as a consolation and reward for Bedivere. Building to a climax of vision, Tennyson next permits the last survivor of the Round Table to have two more experiences that will support his faith in the difficult times to come. First,

> from the dawn it seemed there came, but faint
> As from beyond the limit of the world,
> Like the last echo born of a great cry,
> Sounds, as if some fair city were one voice
> Around a king returning from his wars.

Thereupon he climbs once more, as Tennyson ends *The Idylls of the King* with a vision of the rising sun which intentionally echoes Moses's vision from Mt Pisgah and Adam's vision of the future in *Paradise Lost*.

> Thereat once more he moved about, and clomb
> Even to the highest he could climb, and saw,
> Straining his eyes beneath an arch of hand,

Or thought he saw, the speck that bare the King,
Down that long water opening on the deep
Somewhere far off, pass on and on, and go
From less to less and vanish into light.
And the sun rose bringing the new year.

Like Tennyson's own mystical experience in *In Memoriam*, the sight
of Arthur moving toward Avilion is stricken through with doubt
even as it occurs; and yet it still suffices to provide faith for life.[9]
Good Sir Bedivere, the first made and last left of Arthur's men, has
managed to keep faith with his lord after great trials, and as a reward
he becomes aware of mystical and magical dimensions of existence
which before were beyond his ken. Most important, his experiences
on the mountain crag, however mysterious they may be to him, yet
give him faith to live in a faithless age. 'The Passing of Arthur', while
making it clear how the Round Table failed, offers some cause for
hope when it presents the trials, conversion, and Pisgah sight of the
ordinary man, Bedivere.

Although the content of Bedivere's vision is inherently ambiguous, Tennyson is still using the high vantage point in a completely
traditional manner. Bedivere does not see Arthur enter heaven but
Avilion, and he is not himself dying – though he has lost his former
defining role and purpose as Arthur's knight. None the less, he
clearly receives a privileged spiritual vision from this mountain
height, and so the general features of the Pisgah sight are either
present or suggested by analogues, such as Arthur's isle of rest.

In contrast, when Matthew Arnold's protagonist reaches a
mountain height in 'Empedocles on Etna' (1852), his vision is
screened by the volcano's vapour, and rather than receiving a Pisgah
sight, the philosopher remains conscious only of his own spiritual
fatigue, isolation, and longing for release. Such uses of cloud or fog
to symbolize a spiritual condition– particularly man's inability to
reach beyond his limitations and attain spiritual truth – are, of
course, common in literature. For example, the world which had
been clear and sunlit during Arthur's first battle becomes foggy and
darkened during his last one in 'The Passing' as

A deathwhite mist slept over sand and sea:
Whereof the chill, to him who breathed it, drew

Down with his blood, till all his heart was cold
With formless fear; and even on Arthur fell
Confusion, since he saw not whom he fought.
For friend and foe were shadows in the mist,
And friend slew friend not knowing whom he slew. (95–101)

And saddest were 'the shrieks/ After the Christ, of those who falling down/ Looked up for heaven, and only saw the mist' (110–12).

As one might expect, devotional poets make use of the same image. Thus, James Montgomery's 'For ever with the Lord!' (1853) first presents the implicit Pisgah sight which occurs when 'faith's foreseeing eye' glimpses the 'golden gates' of 'The bright inheritance of saints,/ Jerusalem above'; after which it laments, 'Yet clouds will intervene,/ And all my prospect flies'. Similarly, Toplady's 'I saw, and lo! a countless throng' (1759–74), which begins with the speaker's yearning for a vision of heaven, mentions also that too 'soon the clouds return' as

Damp vapours from the valley rise,
And hide the hill of Sion from my view.

Standing on his mountain, Empedocles's beclouded spirit finds no divine sponsor, since he has grown beyond gods, and he hence receives no vision of the future, since he has come after any possible future. 'No, thou art come too late, Empedocles', he tells himself, 'And the world hath the day, and must break thee,/ Not thou the world' (2, 16–18). Like Moses, Empedocles possesses much knowledge and wisdom in advance of his time, but he does not lead his people, and those two contemporaries who recognize something of his abilities do not really understand him. He has, in other words, no people, no Aaron, and no Joshua. When the seer comes to the top of the mountain to die, to achieve final rest, he must die without consolation.

Since Arnold's poem contains so many ironic intonations of the Pisgah-sight structure, it seems possible that he consciously intended these echoes of the last moments of another, greater sage; but one of the problems we encounter in thus tracing extended secularized types through the literary tradition is that unless they are surrounded by other types or contain language quoted from the biblical text, we cannot be certain that any particular example is an extended type rather than a purely secular analogue. We are here exploring the hazy, ill-defined borders between religious and secular discourse in an age when these territories continually shifted – within the entire culture, within economic and social classes, and within the life and experience of the individual. In exploring these territories, we encounter the entire problem of the Victorian audience. Whereas the student of the seventeenth century can assume that Milton's audience, or audiences, were aware of typology, the student of twentieth-century culture has to assume that such knowledge is found only in Evangelical popular culture and the work of specialists. The problem for the student of Victorian thought and the arts is to determine to what extent typology remains the property of 'high culture' as well as 'low', and for how long. One obvious approach to such a desired archeology of ideas lies in identifying the materials particular authors both read and drew upon for their writings; and in the case of certain authors, such as Ruskin, Browning, Newman, Keble, Hopkins, and Eliot, the results are easy to obtain. Another approach lies in a more complete investigation than has been possible in these pages of various elements of Victorian popular culture. We have examined hymns and sermons, like those of Spurgeon, which constitute a part of such culture, and for a more complete picture it will also be necessary to investigate middle- and working-class autobiography, political writings, and literature aimed particularly at the poor and less educated. Of course, even after these and other approaches have been clearly established, they will not necessarily lead us to a promised land in which every image and every work fits neatly into its assigned category, but the student of the last century's ideas and culture will have a much more accurate notion of how various segments of that image's or work's audience would have perceived it.

Swinburne's 'Evening on the Broads' (1880) exemplifies a prospect poem with a particularly problematic relation to the tradition of the Pisgah sight. Indeed, if the poet alludes to this type, he does so even more distantly than does Arnold. Here we cannot solve the problem of the author's intention by reference to either his knowledge or audience, since we already know that Swinburne, the aggressive atheist, frequently employs secularized and ironic typological allusions that would have been immediately recognized by most of his readers. Therefore, perhaps it is best to consider 'Evening on the Broads' as a secular analogue to the Pisgah sight and use it to determine the nature of an extreme counter-example to the situation, structure, and imagery of the type.

Swinburne's poem takes place at that instant immediately before sunset when the sun apparently hovers above the horizon before plunging the world into darkness with its disappearance. Swinburne, who is the poet of borders and transition states, stands at the point where sea and land meet and contemplates the transition from light to dark, making that transition a metaphor for his spiritual state.[10] Whereas the Pisgah sight and traditional prospect take place high on a mountain, the traditional location of moments of revelation, 'Evening on the Broads' unfolds with the speaker–narrator standing upon a sandbank. God gave Moses the Commandments on Horeb and his view of the Promised Land on Pisgah; at God's command, Michael leads Adam to the highest point in Paradise and there he receives a vision of the future. Similar experiences of revelatory vision occur to Petrarch on Mount Ventoux, Dante on the mount of Purgatory, Spenser's Red Cross Knight on the mount of Contemplation, Rousseau's St Preux in the Valois, Wordsworth on Mount Snowdon, and Coleridge, Shelley, and Ruskin in the Alps. In contrast, Swinburne stands on a low rise between two bodies of water, and his spatial position turns out to be emblematic of his vision of bleakness which contains no promised land. Like the speakers in Heine's 'Fragen' (1827), Arnold's 'Dover Beach' (1867), Mallarmé's 'Brise Marine' (1887), Pessoa's *Ode Marìtima* (1915), and so many other works of the past hundred or so years, Swinburne descends to the level of the sea; and, like so many other would-be visionaries, daydreamers, and questers at sea level, he discovers that his prospect includes shipwreck.

Swinburne attempts a complete fusion or interpenetration of speaker and landscape, for, as Bruce Redford has pointed out, he 'dissects his tortured mind in terms of the natural phenomena, the sun, the lagoon, and the wind, on which he broods'.[11] We later discover that the speaker is standing upon a sandbank with a salt lake at his back as he looks across the ocean. When the poem opens, however, all we discover is an apparently shipwrecked sun hovering above a wasteland:

Over two shadowless waters, adrift as a pinnace in peril,
Hangs as in heavy suspense, charged with irresolute light,
Softly the soul of the sunset upholden awhile on the sterile
Waves and wastes of the land, half repossessed by the night.

This introductory sentence sets forth the symbolic topography of
the poem and introduces its chief images which are those of shipwreck, darkness and light, and the wasteland. Redford explains:

> These image systems simultaneously reflect and communicate the
> poem's central themes: indecision, weariness, angst, and a
> pervasive death-wish. . . . The preliminary quatrain dramatizes
> the speaker's lack of balance, structure expressing thought. The
> syntax underlines the twin themes of division and anxious
> ambiguity: participial phrases float free from the central core of
> subject-verb-predicate, 'the soul of the sunset hangs softly,' itself
> split up and adrift in the quatrain as a whole.

After sketching in the content of the vision – what he sees –
Swinburne probes his metaphor again and again, denying and then
affirming the likeness of the sunset to shipwreck. It soon becomes
apparent that although the speaker purports to be describing the
exterior world, he is doing so in terms that make his description an
image of himself, an elaborate *paysage intérieure* of a man and an age
suspended between past and future, day and night, life and death –
and fearing both. Thus, although 'Evening on the Broads' does not
contain a literal deathbed scene or dying vision, its fusion of the
speaker with the hesitantly dying day creates much the same effect as
this one component of the Pisgah sight.

As the poem unfolds, Swinburne, who has made time stand still
by expanding the instant of sunset, paints a wasteland waiting to be
inspirited. Drawing upon the imagery of the Gospel of St John and
of Genesis, the poem leads up to the return of chaos and night as
though the spirit will move once again upon the face of the deep; but
in a final irony no such creative inspiriting takes place, for the only
wind that blows upon the waters is masterless. In 'Evening on the
Broads' the isolated and troubled speaker looks out from his
mountain of vision and receives only a prospect of universal death.

His attempt to commence a perceptual, visionary voyage brings him only an encounter with himself in a view of metaphorical shipwreck.

Swinburne's dark landscape meditation reminds us how much the nature of the perceived object in such works can vary. Depending upon the spiritual condition of the figure standing on mountain or shore, the Pisgah sight and its secular analogues may take the form of Christ, a true promised land, a true but transitory vision, a natural object which serves as either a symbol of eternity or an escape into it, a mere hidden reef or other dangerously illusory goal, self-reflection or self-encounter, or simply the blackness or blankness of an essentially opaque nature. Since Moses alone could literally see the Promised Land of Canaan from Mt Pisgah, all later applications of this structure must solve the problem of how to find suitable equivalents to that literal geographical vision. What is so compelling about the vision that Moses received on Mt Pisgah is how close it comes to joining present and future, desire and fulfillment. If it were any closer, the prospect would no longer be in the future at all. It would be something presently enjoyed and would lose most of its appeal. By turning the Pisgah sight into an essentially spiritual, atemporal situation, Christian authors often try to make up for the new temporal distance of fulfillment with reassurance that one can escape time at any time.

Would-be voyagers and visionaries without belief also try to escape present time, but, as the example of Swinburne reveals, they abandon attempts to reach some objectively existing eternity and withdraw into the self. Meditation and reverie become the vehicles of the inward voyager who usually journeys without hope.[12] The image seen from the mountain is essentially an image of hope and faith – an image, that is, of matters not present in either physical or chronological senses. Even Moses does not possess or fully experience what he observes. To reach something not present one must move across or through time, and for this defining human situation the ancient topos of the ship voyage presents an obvious metaphor.[13] But for Baudelaire's 'Le Voyage' (1859), Arnold's 'A Summer Night' (1852), and so many of Swinburne's poems, the idea of voyage immediately brings to mind the possibility of shipwreck: hope calls into being ideas of failure, and the search prompts one to envisage a prospect of disaster.[14] Indeed, except for Coleridge's assurance that some supernatural force validates his discovery of self in a vision of the mountain, his landscape meditation is not very different from that one Swinburne composed almost eighty years later. All turns on that supposed supernatural link or authentication, for without it the mind of the poet remains a visionary castaway trapped on a Crusoe island of self. No matter how – or where – it attempts to explore, the imagination ends up exploring the self if it does not have such a divinely guaranteed way up and way out. Christian poets who employ the Pisgah sight and its analogues found their enterprises on the assumption that some divine factor binds together man looking and what man perceives. Without such a guarantee, the poet encounters the threat of radical solipsism; and, as Abrams, Bloom, and Hartmann have argued, the exploration of this problem constitutes the core of a major tradition in European, British, and American literature.[15]

Even those Victorian authors who do not concern themselves with such problems occasionally draw upon the Pisgah sight as a means of conveying the difficulties of the artistic imagination. For example, both Elizabeth Barrett Browning and her husband Robert emphasize that the poet, like Moses, is set apart from other people. The prophet is literally exalted – raised above – other men because his Pisgah sight, like his earlier reception of the Law, takes place on a mountain height, and both Brownings take this physical condition to represent the essential isolation from other men which is the condition of prophet and poet. Whereas Donne and Milton had employed Moses as a figure for the divinely inspired poet as a means of claiming special status for their own works, these Victorian poets do so to underline the ironies and costs of their position. When Robert Browning compares himself to Moses in 'Pisgah Sights' he does so, for example, to state that since the divinely inspired vision comes just before death, it comes too late to communicate; and in earlier poems that use Moses as a figure for himself as poet, such as 'One Word More' (1855), he had long stressed that the poet's vision separated him from those for whom it was intended. Like Baudelaire in 'L'Albatross' (1859), Browning believes that the poet's vision, that which makes him a poet, makes it hard for him to feel comfortable with other men who do not understand him. As Elizabeth Barrett Browning asks in *Aurora Leigh* (1856):

Who, getting to the top of Pisgah-hill,

Can talk with one at bottom of the view,
To make it comprehensible?

The Romantic conception of the artist as an inevitably isolated figure received added life and appeal during the Victorian period when so many self-conscious prophets and sages were torn by the occasionally opposing pressures of self and audience.[16]

John Ruskin, who frequently felt the painful position of the isolated prophet, employs another element in the Pisgah-sight structure – the perceiver's separation from the land of promise – when telling the tale of his own life. In Deuteronomy God solaces Moses with a distant vision of the Promised Land, and so the sight of the unreachable goal becomes an image, an example, of divine mercy. But the very fact that Moses finds himself in a situation in which he is told, in effect, 'look but don't touch' has obvious potential for ironic commentary upon man's ability ever to achieve his goals. When poets therefore take the Pisgah sight as a paradigm of either human existence or the human imagination, they suggest that the best man can hope to do is catch sight of an unobtainable goal.[17] Thus, Newman's 'Day-Labourers' (1833), which appears as 'The Prospects of the Church' in The Lyra Apostolica (1836), argues that 'E'en Moses wearied upon Nebo's height' and that, therefore, only Christ, 'of GOD's messengers to man,/ Finish'd the work of grace, which he began'. In contrast, Ruskin concerns himself in his autobiography Praeterita (1886–8), not with failed goals, but with the cost of learning to see with the cleared eye of an artist and prophet. He therefore arranges his autobiography in a series of juxtaposed Paradises Lost and Pisgah sights, thus implying that vision has been his reward or consolation for loss of Edenic childhood joy. Ruskin includes a series of deaths and losses in the first part of Praeterita, and, having lost so much to death and time – so many people, so many objects, so many sources of joy – he implies that he gains reward only in the ability to see. Throughout Praeterita Ruskin presents the many stages through which he passed as he ascended his ladder of vision. Some of these stages take the form of descriptions of how experiences at Norwood and Fontainbleau taught him to draw and hence see better; but many of the most important ones, such as his first sight of the Alps, take the form of visionary glimpses of a distant paradise which are presented as Pisgah sights. But the cost is that

Ruskin, who presents himself as the Spectator of his own life, must always remain at a distance from the promised land that exists only as an image and not as a reality. Like the Lady of Shalott, Ruskin can weave his tapestries only by contenting himself with images.

NOTES

Introduction

1 See, for instance, Basil Willey, *Nineteenth Century Studies* (N.Y., 1950) and *More Nineteenth Century Studies* (N.Y., 1955); Walter E. Houghton, *The Victorian Frame of Mind, 1830–1870* (New Haven, 1957); A. O. J. Cockshut, *The Unbelievers: English Agnostic Thought, 1840–1890* (London, 1964); J. Hillis Miller, *The Disappearance of God: Five Nineteenth-Century Writers* (Cambridge, Mass., 1963); and Hans W. Frei, *The Eclipse of Biblical Narrative: A Study in Eighteenth and Nineteenth Century Hermeneutics* (New Haven, 1974).

2 George P. Landow, *The Aesthetic and Critical Theories of John Ruskin* (Princeton, 1971), pp. 321–457; and Robert Hewison, *John Ruskin, The Argument of the Eye* (London, 1976), pp. 26–7, 58–63.

3 Although Herbert Sussman's 'Hunt, Ruskin, and *The Scapegoat*', *Victorian Studies,* 12 (1968), pp. 83–90, points out that Hunt had read the second volume of *Modern Painters* and that the artist was interested in symbolism, it does not recognize that typology is a central issue.

4 George P. Landow, *William Holman Hunt and Typological Symbolism* (New Haven and London, 1979), pp. 2–7, examines the role of Ruskin's interpretation of the Scuola di San Rocco *Annunciation* in Hunt's career. For a more detailed examination of the relationship between the artist and critic, see George P. Landow, ' "Your Good Influence on Me": the Correspondence of John Ruskin and William Holman Hunt', *Bulletin of the John Rylands University Library of Manchester,* 59 (1976–7), pp. 95–126, 376–96.

5 For Rossetti's knowledge and use of christological typology, see my *William Holman Hunt and Typological Symbolism,* pp. 148–61.

6 See Chapters Four and Six for Rossetti's various uses of this symbolic mode.

7 Compare this speech by Conrad of Marpurg, the Pope's Commissioner

for the suppression of heresy, in Charles Kingsley's *The Saint's Tragedy* (1848):

> Ah! poor wordlings!
> Little you dream what maddening ecstasies,
> What rich ideals haunt, by day and night,
> Alone, and in the crowd, even to the death,
> The servitors of that celestial court
> Where peerless Mary, sun-enthroned, reigns,
> In whom all Eden dreams of womanhood,
> All grace of form, hue, sound, all beauty strewn
> Like pearls unstrung, about this ruined world,
> Have their fulfilment and their archetype.
> Why hath the rose its scent, the lily grace?
> To mirror forth her loveliness, for whom,
> Primeval fount of grace, their livery came:
> Pattern of Seraphs! only worthy ark
> To bear her God athwart the floods of time! (Act 1, sc. 2)

8 For the application of typology to contemporary politics by Mrs Browning and Swinburne, see Chapter Five, below.

9 'Hopkins' Imagery and Medievalist Poetics', *Victorian Poetry*, 15 (1977), pp. 99–119.

10 'The Two Kingdoms in *In Memoriam*', *Journal of English and Germanic Philology*, 58 (1959), p. 240.

11 Although Newman does not apply typology to biological evolution, he, like the Evangelical Fairbairn, believes that

> The whole Bible, not its prophetical portions only, is written on the principle of development. . . . Revelation is . . . a process of development: the earlier prophecies are pregnant texts out of which the succeeding announcements grow; they are types. It is not that first one truth is told, then another; but the whole truth or large portions of it are told at once, yet only in their rudiments, or in miniature, and they are expanded and finished in their parts, as the course of revelation proceeds. The Seed of the woman was to bruise the serpent's head. (*An Essay on the Development of Christian Doctrine*, London, 1845, pp. 103, 1–3)

12 'Personal Myth: Three Victorian Autobiographers', in *Approaches to Victorian Autobiography*, ed. George P. Landow (Athens, Ohio, 1979), p. 217.

13 'Biblical Typology and the Self-Portrait of the Poet in Browning', in *Approaches to Victorian Autobiography*, pp. 235–68.

Chapter One: Typological Interpretation in the Victorian Period

1 For examples of the difficulties Victorian art critics had in interpreting individual works, see George P. Landow, 'There Began to be a Great Talking about the Fine Arts', in *The Mind and Art of Victorian England*, ed. Josef L. Altholz (Minneapolis, 1976), pp. 124–45, especially pp. 131–3; and George P. Landow, *William Holman Hunt and Typological Symbolism* (New Haven and London, 1979), pp. 163–5.

2 J. B. Schneewind, *Backgrounds of English Victorian Literature* (N. Y., 1970), which contains an excellent brief overview of Victorian religion and a useful annotated bibliography, accepts the essential accuracy of these statistics and a related contemporary estimate of the allegiances of Anglican clergymen. Robert Lee Wolff, *Gains and Losses: Novels of Faith and Doubt in Victorian England* (N. Y., 1977), which also provides an excellent summary of religious doctrine and Church-party conflict during the period, points out that the survey of clerical allegiance much underestimates the number of Evangelicals. The one essential volume remains Owen Chadwick, *The Victorian Church* (London, 1966). Alec R. Vidler, *The Church in an Age of Revolution: 1789 to the Present Day* (Harmondsworth, 1961), vol. 5 in the Pelican History of the Church, provides a useful summary examination of Victorian developments in a broader context.

3 'The Cross', in *A New Birth* (Grand Rapids, 1977).

4 In ch. 4 of *Barchester Towers,* Trollope tells us that the Rev. Mr Obadiah Slope, a graduate of Cambridge,

> is tolerant of dissent, if so strict a mind can be called tolerant of anything. With Wesleyan-Methodists he has something in common, but his soul trembles in agony at the iniquities of the Puseyites. His aversion is carried to things outward as well as inward. His gall rises at a new church with a high pitched roof; a full-breasted black silk waistcoat is with him a symbol of Satan; and a profane jest-book would not, in his view, more foully desecrate the church seat of a Christian, than a book of prayer printed with red letters and ornamented with a cross on the back. Most active clergymen have their hobby, and Sunday observances are his. Sunday, however, is a word which never pollutes his mouth – it is always 'the Sabbath.' The 'desecration of the Sabbath,' as he delights to call it, is to him meat and drink: – he thrives upon that as policemen do on the general evil habits of the community.

It is the loved subject of all his evening discourses, the source of all his eloquence, the secret of all his power over the female heart.

5 George Eliot's 'Janet's Repentance' (from *Scenes of Clerical Life,* 1858), which bases its tale of the saintly Rev. Mr Tryan on an actual Evangelical clergyman, John Edmund Jones of Stockingford Chapel, Nuneaton, provides one of the rare instances in Victorian fiction of a favorably presented minister with this Church allegiance. Such stories of effective preaching appear in biographies of all major Evangelicals and in histories of the movement. See, for example, Hugh Evan Hopkins, *Charles Simeon of Cambridge* (Sevenoaks, 1977), pp. 63–5, and Charles Haddon Spurgeon, *Autobiography: The Early Years, 1834–1859,* eds Susannah Spurgeon and Joseph Harrald (Edinburgh, 1962), pp. 87–8 (the preacher's own conversion at a sermon in a little Primitive Methodist chapel), 196–9, 265–7, and *passim.*

6 The continuing attempt on the part of High Church designers, architects, and clergy to make worship a complete aesthetic experience that would appeal to all of man's higher nature later in the century drew many Aesthetes and Decadents into both the high Anglican and Roman Catholic churches. Augustus Welby Pugin (1812–52), John Ruskin, and the Cambridge Camden Society (later known as the Ecclesiological Society) were the seminal forces in this aspect of the Gothic Revival. See Phoebe Stanton, *Pugin* (London, 1971); James E. White, *The Cambridge Movement, the Ecclesiologists and the Gothic Revival* (Cambridge, 1962); Shirley Bury, *Copy or Creation, Victorian Treasures from English Churches,* Catalogue of an exhibition organized by the Worshipful Company of Goldsmiths and the Victorian Society (London, 1967); *Victorian Church Art,* Catalogue of an exhibition at the Victoria and Albert Museum (London, 1971).

Just as both old and new adherents of the High Church party scorned Evangelical emotionalism and hymns, the Evangelicals, in their turn, scorned Puseyite aestheticism. Ryle, for example, pointedly contrasts High and Low Church approaches to religion: 'There are thousands of religious books published in our times, in which there is everything except the Cross. They are full of directions about sacraments, and praises of the Church. They abound in exhortations about holy living, and rules for the attainment of perfection. They have plenty of fonts and crosses both inside and outside. But the real Cross of Christ is left out' ('The Cross', in *A New Birth,* p. 21). George Eliot's 'A College Breakfast-Party' (1874) presents the common view that such High Church aestheticism had little to do with true religion and often proved an adolescent fad. Her main character is attracted to Hinduism one day and the next,

Finding the fount of grace in sacraments,
And purest reflex of the light divine
In gem-bossed pyx and broidered chasuble,
Resolved to wear no stockings and to fast
With arms extended, waiting for ecstasy;
But getting cramps instead, and needing change,
[Became] A would-be pagan next.

7 Trollope, an obviously hostile witness, explains that both the High Church Dr Grantly and the Evangelical Rev. Mr Slope 'are eager, much too eager, to support and increase the power of their order. Both are anxious that the world should be priest-governed. . . . Both begrudge any other kind of dominion held by man over man' (ch. 4, *Barchester Towers*). Friendlier witnesses would point out that the Tractarians, who often battled with the Evangelicals, resembled them in zeal and earnestness.

8 Thomas Vargish, *Newman: The Contemplation of Mind* (Cambridge, 1970) demonstrates, for instance, that Newman's conceptions of the human mind were formed during his Evangelical phase and remained essentially unchanged during his movement from Tractarianism to the Roman Church.

9 During Ruskin's 1851–2 stay in Venice, he several times wrote to his parents at their London home, thanking them for copies for Melvill's sermons in *The Pulpit* or requesting additional ones be sent to him. See Ruskin's *Letters from Venice, 1851–1852,* ed. John Lewis Bradley (New Haven, 1955), pp. 89, 92, 100. One of Amos Barton's few achievements as a preacher, we recall, is that he had a sermon printed in *The Pulpit.*

10 In 'Janet's Repentance', George Eliot alludes to Keble's Tractarian attacks on dissenting Protestantism when she remarks that 'Milby, in those uninstructed days, had not yet heard that the schismatic ministers of Salem were obviously typified by Korah, Dathan, and Abiram; and many Church people there were of opinion that Dissent might be a weakness, but, after all, had no great harm in it' (ch. 2). She alludes to the political use of this type again in her essay 'The Modern Hep! Hep! Hep!'

11 'Notes on Psalm Ll' (1851), *Sermons Preached at Brighton* (N. Y., nd), pp. 297–8.

12 *Sermons,* ed. C. P. M'Ilvaine, 2 vols (N. Y., 1851), 1 pp, 10–11.

13 'Caiaphas's View of Vicarious Sacrifice' (1848), *Sermons Preached at Brighton,* p. 117. See also pp. 497, 596.

14 'Evangelical Religion', *Knots Untied. Being Plain Statements on Disputed Points in Religion, from the Standpoint of an Evangelical Churchman,* 13th edn. (London, 1891), p. 40.

15 'David and Goliath: Part I', *Ninety-One Short Sermons for Family Reading:*

Following the Course of the Christian Seasons: Second Series, 2 vols (Oxford, 1867), 2, p. 519.

16 *Sermons,* 1, p. 13.

17 'Satan Falling from Heaven', *Sermons (Preached in Cambridge)* (London, 1859), p. 197.

18 *The Book of Psalms . . .,* 2 vols (London, 1817), 1, p. xv. Hereafter cited in text.

19 3 vols (London, 1832), 1, p. viii. Hereafter cited in text. Interestingly, Morison, who claims to represent orthodoxy, employs the term 'irradiate', which is one of Hutchinson's favorites.

20 'Simon the Cyrenian', *Sermons,* 2 vols (London, 1843), 2, p. 263–4. Subsequent passages from this sermon are cited in text by page number alone.

21 'The Well of Bethlehem', *Sermons,* 2, p. 196.

22 *Mimesis: The Representation of Reality in Western Literature* (Princeton, 1953), p. 196.

23 'Preface; containing especially a compendious view of the evidences that the Holy Scriptures, and every part of them, as they stand in our Bibles, were given by inspiration from God', *A Commentary on the Holy Bible containing the Old and New Testaments . . . arranged for family and private reading . . .* 5 vols (Philadelphia, 1858), 1, pp. ii–iii.

24 Quoted by John William Colenso, *The Pentateuch and the Book of Joshua Critically Examined,* Part I (London, 1862), p. 6.

25 'David and Goliath: Part II', *Short Sermons,* 2, p. 521–2. The following quotation appears on p. 522.

26 In George Eliot's 'Evangelical Teaching: Dr. Cumming'), which first appeared in the 1855 *Westminster Review,* she took this clergyman to task for such views:

> According to Dr. Cumming, Abel had so clear an idea of the Incarnation and Atonement, that when he offered his sacrifice 'he must have said, "I feel myself a guilty sinner, and that in myself I cannot meet thee alive; I lay on thine altar this victim, and I shed its blood as my testimony that mine should be shed; and I look for forgiveness and underserved mercy through Him who is to bruise the serpent's head, and whose atonement this typifies." '

Chapter Two: The Smitten Rock

1 'The Death of Moses', *Sermons* (London, 1836), 2, pp. 163–4.

2 Curiously, the Evangelical Fairbairn rejects the standard nineteenth-century reading of this incident as a type of the Crucifixion on the

grounds that no literal equivalence existed between rock and Christ:

There was not only no *seeming*, but also no *real* aptitude in the rock to yield the water; while in Christ, though He appeared to have no form or comeliness, there still was everything that was required to constitute Him a fountainshead of life and blessing. Then the smiting of the rock by Moses with the rod could not suggest the idea of anything like violence done to it; nor was the action itself done by Moses as the lawgiver, but as the mediator between God and the people; while the smiting of Christ, which is commonly held to correspond with this, consisted in the bruising of His soul with the suffering of death, and that not inflicted, but borne by Him as Mediator. There is no real correspondence in these respects between the type and the antitype; and the manner in which it is made out, is nothing more than a specious accommodation of the language of the transaction to ideas which the transaction itself could never have suggested. (2, pp. 67–8)

Fairbairn, who takes to task Toplady's famous hymn 'Rock of Ages' for confounding things which 'essentially differ' (2, p. 69n), argues that the typologist must concern himself with the stream of water flowing from the rock, for that is what prefigures Christ.

3 Such close examination of Old Testament names for symbolic meaning, which owes something to contemporary theories of language and its origins, is the source of Ruskin's etymological word play. Keble's 'The Saving Name' contains a more restrained High Church version of such symbolic interpretation of biblical name (*Sermons*, 2.183, 2.311).

4 To this Evangelical emphasis upon preaching the word of God we may compare Keble's remarks upon reading the scriptures: 'If you will really keep these three or four simple rules, To read thoughtfully and regularly, a little at a time, of the sayings and doings of our dear Lord in the Gospels; praying also regularly, and abstaining from bad books and bad company; a blessing, be sure will be upon you; *it will be as when the rock was smitten;* the dry, hard, barren place will break out in springs of water' (2. p. 137; emphasis added).

5 I am grateful to Professor Karlfried Froelich of the Princeton Theological Seminary for pointing out this second allusion to me.

6 This illustration is contained in the large volumes, apparently assembled to provide a running record of the firm's work, which are now in the Print Room of the British Museum (C247 c12; 1913–4–15–205 [389]). This particular wood engraving appears in a volume for 1882–3, but I have been unable to identify the edition of Mrs Hemans's poems for which it seems to have been cut.

7 The picture in the Vatican Logge is reproduced in S. J. Freedberg,

Painting of the High Renaissance in Rome and Florence, 2 vols (Cambridge, Mass., 1961), 2, p. 368. For Poussin's depictions of the subject and his concern with typology, see Anthony Blunt, *Nicholaus Poussin*, 2 vols (New York, 1967), 1, pp. 179–81; 2, plates 116, 198, 258. The *Illustrated Handbook* of the Museum of Fine Arts, Boston (1976), p. 271, illustrates the Van Leyden.

8 The City of York Art Gallery *Catalogue of Paintings* (1961), which contains an illustration of this interesting painting (1, plate 18), provides a brief discussion and bibliography of it, though it does not relate it to Moses striking the rock.

9 An anonymous hymn dated 1855, which begins 'Lord! may the inward grace abound', provides one of the few examples of a nineteenth-century application of the older reading of the stricken rock:

> Type of the Spirit's living flow,
>   In faith we pour the hallow'd stream;
> We sign the cross upon the brow,
>   The solemn pledge of truth to Him,
> Who shed for us His precious Blood
> To seal the covenant of God.
>
> Baptized into the Trinity,
>   Adopted children of Thy grace,
> O help us, Lord, to live to Thee.

Roundell Palmer includes this hymn as no. 282 in his *Book of Praise* (1863).

10 According to Robert Collinson, *The Story of Street Literature: Foreruner of the Popular Press* (ABC-Clio: Santa Barbara–Oxford, 1973), p. 116, *The New Pictorial Bible* 'included two small and indifferently printed woodcuts on each page, below each of which it gave the Biblical reference, accompanied by the actual text'. It devoted six woodcuts to the Creation and another twenty-three to the remainder of the Old Testament, and among these last were several events conventionally read as types: Moses striking the rock, Abraham and Isaac, Joseph cast into the pit, Samson pulling down the temple, and David killing Goliath.

11 Bonar, who makes extensive use of types in his poetry, uses the same image in 'The Desert Rock', *The Song of the New Creation* (N. Y., 1872); and, more obliquely, in 'The Rod', *Hymns of Faith and Hope* (N. Y., 1857), pp. 122–6.

12 This emphasis upon the central importance of this type to the poet suggests that Hopkins may have begun 'Soliloquy' with it; and the evidence of his 1864 diaries would seem to confirm this supposition,

since he changed every line of the stanza in which it appeared except 'Who would drink water from a stony rock?' See *Journals and Papers of Gerard Manley Hopkins*, eds H. House and G. Storey (London, 1959), p. 29.

13 *The Complete Poetry of Henry Vaughan*, ed. French Fogle (Garden City, N. Y., 1964), p. 137. The pictorial emblem is illustrated opposite p. 384.

14 Quoted in Morison, *An Exposition of the Book of Psalms*, 3 vols (London, 1832), 2, p. 77.

15 The untitled ninth hymn in the second book of the Olney Hymns, which begins 'Now may fervent pray'r arise', may have inspired Miss Rossetti to her greater effort. Its third stanza contains some of the elements of her 'Good Friday':

> Shepherd of thy blood–bought sheep!
> Teach the stony heart to weep;
> Let the blind have eyes to see,
> See themselves and look on thee!

16 John D. Rosenberg, 'The Two Kingdoms of *In Memoriam*', *Journal of English and Germanic Philology*, 58 (1959), p. 238, quotes and comments upon the poet's remarks. He also argues that 'The progression from death to life is again implicit in the reference to the "spiritual rock" from which Moses struck water in the desert and which Paul called the rock that "was Christ" – the same rock from which man partakes of the baptismal waters of rebirth and on which Tennyson bases his faith that we shall *"close* with all we loved . . . soul in soul" ' (p. 238). Professor Rosenberg here refers to the Pauline interpretation of the stricken rock as a type of baptism, a reading of the image which does not seem to work as well in this case as the interpretation I have suggested.

17 This type, one should add, also well prepares the reader for the epilogue's concluding emphasis upon Hallam's role as a prefiguration of both Christ and the higher race of men.

18 One may also note that since the deer hunt is also an old allegorical image of both the Crucifixion and Christ's hunting down the sinner to save him, Dickinson may also be using the opening lines in the way she does the type to create sharper emphasis. For the deer hunt, see Howard M. Helsinger, 'Images on the Beatus Page of Medieval Psalters', *Art Bulletin*, 53 (1971), pp. 161–76.

19 See Linda H. Peterson, 'Biblical Typology and the Self Portrait of the Poet in Robert Browning', *Approaches to Victorian Autobiography,* ed. George P. Landow (Athens, Ohio, 1979), pp. 243–64, both for discussion of earlier poetic applications of this type and for an analysis of Browning's complex use of it and related ones. David also constitutes an

important type of the artist, and nineteenth-century psalm commentaries contain a wealth of information about the nature of the divinely inspired prophet, poet, and singer.

20 Hopkins quotes other poems from Browning's *Men and Women* in his *Journals* about this time, thus demonstrating that he was familiar with the volume. Of course, any study such as this one which emphasizes the role of the commonplace image or rhetorical *topos* in literary tradition tends to cast doubt on the notion that any one particular antecedent example by itself influenced a poet. I assume that after reading 'One Word More' Hopkins, already well aware of the traditional type, was prompted to use it in a more purely Christian sense than did Browning.

21 In contrast, George Meredith's use of this type in ch. 31, 'Sir Willoughby Attempts and Achieves Pathos', of *The Egoist* (1879) clearly relies upon the reader's recognizing the christological sense even though he is making a completely secular application: 'We cannot quite preserve our dignity when we stoop to the work of calling forth tears. Moses had probably to take a nimble jump away from the rock after that venerable Law-giver had knocked the water out of it'. The allusion achieves its full effect only if one recognizes the traditional association of Christ's calling forth tears of repentance from the sinner.

Chapter Three: Typology in Fiction and Non-fiction

1 As the example of Robert Calder Campbell's love sonnet reminds us, amatory verse frequently employs conceits in which the beloved replaces God as the reigning divinity. Campbell's poem, at which we looked in the previous chapter, applies types in such a situation as a means of complimenting the beloved. In contrast, Brontë's Jane Eyre applies types to herself once she realizes the consequences of idolatrous love.

2 Just as Jane compared her dwelling in a state of sin to that of the Egyptians who enslaved the Jews, thus disobeying God's will, so now she seems to compare herself to the Virgin Mary, on whom grace begot the divine word. Gerard Manley Hopkins uses precisely such a conceit in 'The Wreck of the Deutschland'.

3 See Introduction, above.

4 'The Apostasy and Death of St. Praxed's Bishop', *Victorian Poetry*, 8 (1970), p. 216.

5 Charles T. Phipps, 'The Bishop as Bishop: Clerical Motif and Meaning in "The Bishop Orders His Tomb at St. Praxed's Church" ', *Victorian Poetry*, 8(1970), p. 207, points out:

The Bishop seems to parallel further Christ's ultimate sacrifice and his own ironic hope for ultimate aggrandizement when he instructs his sons to dig for his absconded *lapis lazuli* in 'the white-grape vineyard where the oil-press stood' (37). The suggestiveness of this latter bit of rural detail may possibly have been a happy accident. But it is not inconceivable that Browning remembered that the garden on the slope of the Mount of Olives where Christ suffered his Agony was called Gethsemane, which is Aramaic for 'olive-press'. If so, he has subtly suggested that the Bishop's hopes are soon to dissolve into a bizarre and fruitless imitation of Christ's redemptive Agony.

6 In the light of St Augustine's own changing attitude towards symbolic interpretation of the Bible, ch. 21 of Kingsley's *Hypatia or New Foes with an Old Face* (1851) makes an especially interesting fictional use of one of his sermons: although at first completely skeptical of Augustine's way of interpreting the Bible, Kingsley's character Raphael gradually finds it convincing. The novelist draws upon St Augustine's encounter with other Fathers of the Church as a model for Raphael's encounter with him.

7 Although Richard D. Altick and James F. Loucks II, *Browning's Roman Murder Story: A Reading of 'The Ring and the Book'* (Chicago, 1968) does not raise the issue of typology, it shows many of the other uses of scripture made by Browning. The fourth chapter of Linda H. Peterson's 1977 Brown University PhD dissertation, 'Robert Browning and Biblical Typology', sets forth the poet's uses of types for characterization and literary structure.

8 Owen Meredith's *Lucile* (1860) similarly glorifies its heroine:

> The mission of woman on earth! to give birth
> To the mercy of Heaven descending on earth.
> The mission of woman: permitted to bruise
> The head of the serpent, and sweetly infuse,
> Through the sorrow and sin of earth's registered curse,
> The blessing which mitigates all: born to nurse,
> And to soothe, and to solace, to help and to heal
> The sick world that leans on her. This was Lucile.

9 See, for example, W. W. Robson's 'The Dilemma of Tennyson' and E. J. Chiasson's 'Tennyson's "Ulysses" – a Re-interpretation', in *Critical Essays on the Poetry of Tennyson*, ed. John Killham (London, 1960); and B. R. Jerman's 'Browning's Witless Duke' and Laurence Perrine's 'Browning's Shrewd Duke' in *The Browning Critics*, eds Boyd Litzinger and K. L. Knickerbocker (Lexington, 1967).

10 Linda H. Peterson convincingly argues that Browning thus employs typology as part of his career-long concern with the problems of

meaning and interpretation. She demonstrates, furthermore, that he organizes *The Ring and the Book* around such questions. Thus, the first and last books employ typology in relation to the role of the poet himself. Then,

> In the first triad [Books 2–4] the monologuists interpret the Franches-chini case by correlating its participants and events directly with the Old Testament *types*. In the second triad, however, the monologuists do not correlate their experiences with the type but instead link themselves directly with the New Testament *antitype*. Almost as if they have heard Rome speak, they complete the pattern of prefiguration and fulfillment, presenting either Guido or Pompilia as the 'fulfillment' and thus making the structural arrangement of the first two triads resemble the relationship of Old and New Testaments (pp. 167–8). . . . If by Book VII we have already judged the case and established the 'spiritual guilt' of the participants, as Chesterton puts it, what is Browning's concern in the remainder of the poem? Quite simply, in Books VIII through XI he tests the validity of the typological method itself, of the patterns it considers authoritative and of the Christian view of history it implies (p. 182).

11 *Victorian Conventions* (Athens, Ohio, 1975), pp. 20–1. See also Paul J. Korshin, 'The Development of Abstracted Typology in England, 1650–1820', in *Literary Uses of Typology from the Middle Ages to the Present*, ed. Earl Miner (Princeton, 1977), pp. 147–203.

12 *George Eliot and the Visual Arts* (New Haven and London, 1979), p. 96.

13 *George Eliot and the Visual Arts*, pp. 75–6.

14 *Victorian Conventions*, p. 5.

15 John Holloway's pioneering *The Victorian Sage* (1953), which does not discuss Ruskin, properly emphasizes the secular prophets' rhetorical and poetic devices but does not succeed in defining a coherent genre. *The Art of Victorian Prose*, eds George Levine and William Madden (N. Y., 1968), contains many valuable contritutions to the still-necessary critical theory of Victorian non-fiction.

16 See George P. Landow, *The Aesthetic and Critical Theories of John Ruskin* (Princeton, 1971), pp. 243–93.

17 See George P. Landow, 'The Rainbow: a Problematic Image', in *Nature and the Victorian Imagination*, eds U. C. Knoepflmacher and G. B. Tennyson (Berkeley, 1977), pp. 341–69.

18 See Landow, *The Aesthetic and Critical Theories of John Ruskin*, pp. 370–442.

19 I have discussed Ruskin's application of the legal types from Leviticus to architecture in *The Seven Lamps of Architecture* and shown how he draws

upon sermons which he had heard as a child in *The Aesthetic and Critical Theories of John Ruskin*, pp. 336–41.

20 George Allan Cate's 'Ruskin's Discipleship to Carlyle: A Revaluation', in *Carlyle and His Contemporaries: Essays in Honor of Charles Richard Sanders*, ed. John Clubbe (Durham, N. C., 1976), pp. 227–56, provides an excellent introduction to the relationship between the two men.

Chapter Four: Typology in the Visual Arts

1 See George P. Landow, 'J. D. Harding and John Ruskin on Nature's Infinite Variety', *Journal of Aesthetics and Art Criticism*, 28 (1970), pp. 369–80.

2 10 August 1870; Jerusalem. Entire letter quoted in William Bell Scott, *Autobiographical Notes . . . and Notices of His Artistic and Poetic Circle of Friends, 1830–1882*, ed. W. Minto, 2 vols (London, 1892), 2, p. 95.

3 The story of Hunt's attempts to draw upon Hogarth and other artistic predecessors for means of renovating outmoded iconographic conventions is told in George P. Landow, *William Holman Hunt and Typological Symbolism* (New Haven and London, 1979), pp. 19–59. This work, which provides some of the detailed background for this chapter, will be cited in the notes as *William Holman Hunt*. Herbert Sussman, who was one of the first to perceive the importance of the *Tintoretto Annunciation* passage in *Modern Painters*, volume 2, to the early Pre-Raphaelite Brotherhood, also discusses the influence of typology upon these young painters in his recent *Fact into Figure* (1979), a work that unfortunately appeared too late for me to see it before this present discussion went to press.

4 Such a claim does not, of course, deny that the Pre-Raphaelites may have either used photographic processes or been influenced by them in various ways. Aaron Scharf, *Art and Photography*, rev. edn (Harmondsworth, 1974) contains some interesting speculations on this subject.

5 Compare, for instance, Albrecht Dürer's *Man of Sorrows with Hands Raised* (*c.* 1500), an engraving upon which Hunt may have drawn in designing *The Shadow of Death*. According to Hunt, he and his friends studied such earlier engravings in the British Museum Print Room, and so he and Millais could have encountered various versions of the subject.

6 Alastair Grieve, 'The Pre-Raphaelite Brotherhood and the Anglican High Church', *Burlington Magazine*, 111 (1969), pp. 294–5, suggests Tractarian readings of this painting.

7 See G. B. Tennyson, 'Tractarian Aesthetics: Analogy and Reserve in Keble and Newman', *Victorian Newsletter*, 55 (1979), pp. 8–10.

8 For a detailed analysis of the fascinating poem, see Landow, *William Holman Hunt*, pp. 141–7.

9 In *William Holman Hunt and His Works: A memoir of the Artist's Life, With Description of His Pictures* (London, 1860), which the painter's friend F. G. Stephens wrote at the request of Gambart, the art dealer, several pages are devoted to explaining Hunt's elaborately detailed psychological portraits (pp. 63–70). As I have argued elsewhere, one can assume that Stephens followed Hunt's explicit interpretations of his own work.

10 See Lotte Philip, *The Ghent Altarpiece and the Art of Jan van Eyck* (Princeton, 1971), pp. 56–7, 61–4; and Shirley Neilsen Blum, *Early Netherlandish Triptychs: A Study in Patronage* (Berkeley, 1969). Landow, *William Holman Hunt*, pp. 101–2, 129, 131, explains this Victorian's attempt to find equivalents to older applications of this form of symbolism.

11 'Striking the Rock', *The Art-Journal*, 31 (1869), p. 60. All subsequent quotations are taken from this page. The fountain was dismantled in about 1972 as part of the construction of new offices on the west side of Guildhall Yard, and the stonework was dispersed while the bronze plaque by Durham was transferred to the temporary care of the Museum of London. The precise location of the plaque remains obscure, and therefore I have been unable to inspect it personally or have photographs of it made. I am most grateful to Andrew Saint of the Survey of London, Greater London Council Director-General's Department, who provided this information, for his strenuous exertions on my behalf.

12 See Chapter Five: Political Types.

13 The painter also wrote an interpretation of *Early Christians Rescuing A Priest from the Persecution of the Druids* (1850) for his friend Thomas Combe, who purchased the picture, and he wrote explanations for owners of other works, including *The Hireling Shepherd* (1851). He also published pamphlets for most of his later major works.

14 See the item mentioned in note 7, above.

15 Although Richard L. Stein, *The Ritual of Interpretation: The Fine Arts as Literature in Ruskin, Rossetti, and Pater* (Cambridge, Mass., 1975) does not discuss the role of typology, he makes some interesting comments on this Victorian genre.

16 As we have observed in George Eliot's application of this type to Amos Barton, such uses outside a devotional context appear presumptuous, and, unlike European art at 1300, Victorian religious art created few elaborate devotional objects for the individual worshipper.

17 This object is illustrated and described in *Victorian Church Art* (1971), the catalogue for an exhibition at the Victoria and Albert Museum, pp. 123–4. I have drawn heavily upon this valuable compendium of original research for much of the information cited in the text about such art forms.

18 Illustrated, *Victorian Church Art*, p. 44

19 Albert Gilbert's bronze *St Michael* (1899–1900), which he created for the memorial to the Duke of Clarence at Windsor, exemplifies a somewhat different application of this image. The 1978 catalogue for the *Victorian High Renaissance* organized by the Minneapolis Institute of the Arts contains Richard Dorment's description of the entire program (pp. 192–203; illustrated, p. 200).

20 Illustrated in A. Charles Sewter, *The Stained Glass of William Morris and His Circle* (New Haven and London, 1974), plate 431.

21 Illustrated, *Victorian Church Art*, p. 100.

22 See *Works*, 7, pp. 397–422. Writing of Turner's *The Garden of the Hesperides* (1806), Ruskin comments that 'the reader may have heard, perhaps, in other books of Genesis than Hesiod's, of a dragon being busy about a tree which bore apples, and of crushing the head of that dragon' (7, p. 398). Ruskin's interpretation of this painting and of Turner's *Apollo and Python* (1811), to each of which he devotes a full chapter of *Modern Painters*, vol. 5, begins with the implicit assumption that they embody the prophetical type from Genesis 3:15. For the significance of this set of interpretations in the context of Ruskin's career see Landow, *The Aesthetic and Critical Theories of John Ruskin* (Princeton, 1971), pp. 420–57.

23 As long as one abandons the common mediaeval belief that pagan gods were devils, one can allow that the true God permitted other people besides the ancient Israelites to catch glimpses of the coming Messiah. Dante's adulation of ancient Rome led him to make examples from its history prefigure Christian virtues in the *Purgatorio*, and Milton draws upon this tradition throughout *Paradise Lost*. For a discussion of such treatment of classical narrative as a source of types in *The Ring and the Book*, see Linda H. Peterson, 'Biblical Typology and the Poetry of Robert Browning', 1977 Brown University PhD. dissertation, pp. 183ff.

24 In Hunt's original conception of the picture, the Lady was dominated by a circular mirror derived from Van Eyck's *Arnolfini Portrait*, which, like its source, surrounded the reflecting surface with scenes from the life of Christ. Hunt's point here seems to have been that Tennyson's figure of the artist should observe the life around her with a spiritual eye, and his painted versions of the subject and the Moxon illustration both still make this emphasis, though they reduce the scenes to a few, less obtrusive bas-reliefs. Hunt's painting, which serves as the statement of his artistic credo, is particularly interesting because it shows him applying typological imagery to a subject not drawn from sacred history.

25 I am grateful to the Rev. Mr Colin Bennetts, Chaplain of Jesus College, Oxford, and the Rev. Mr Dennis Whitley, the former Chaplain, for providing me with the date of this stained glass.

26 ALS to C. E. Norton, July 1858; London. *Letters*, eds Oswald Doughty and John Robert Wahl, 4 vols (Oxford, 1965–7), 1, p. 338.

27 For the Burgess flagon, see *Victorian Church Art,* pp. 44–5; and for the piece by Powell, see p. 80. For contemporary French work, see *The Second Empire: Art in France under Napoleon III* (1978), the catalogue for the exhibition shown jointly at the Philadelphia Museum of Art, the Detroit Institute for the Fine Arts, and the Grand Palais, Paris, 1978–9, p. 146.

28 *Victorian Church Art,* pp. 36, 130–1.

29 For an examination of this work within the context of the problems confronting the Victorian artist who would apply typology to a realistically conceived scene, see George P. Landow, 'The Rainbow: A Problematic Image', in *Nature and the Victorian Imagination,* eds U. C. Knoepflmacher and G. B. Tennyson (Berkeley, 1977), pp. 341–69.

30 The painting by Gale is illustrated in *The Art-Journal,* 31 (1869), p. 373, and in *William Holman Hunt,* p. 120. When I cited Gale's picture in my study of Hunt, I was unaware of the symbolic implication of the plough. Now I would probably suggest that the shoes doffed by the mother of Jesus, like those in the *Arnolfini Portrait,* symbolize that the setting is holy ground. The bird above Christ's head would appear to be an emblem of the Holy Spirit, such as is found in works by Hunt, Rossetti, and Millais.

Chapter Five: Political Types

1 For example, one such contrast of doctrine occurs in the fourth stanza from the poem's close when Keble denies the Roman Catholic notion of transubstantiation:

> O come to our Communion Feast:
> There present in the heart,
> Not in the hands, th'eternal Priest
> Will his true self impart.

2 'Note A. Liberalism', *Apologia Pro Vita Sua,* ed. A. Dwight Culler (Boston, 1956), p. 271.

3 Reginald Heber (1783–1826), Bishop of Calcutta, who is probably best known for his hymn 'From Greenland's icy mountains', makes a somewhat different reading of Psalm 137 in his prize poem, 'Palestine', for rather than holding that it prefigures the agony and triumph of Christ, he sees it as an appeal to the Messiah for restoration to their homeland:

> And their sad lyres, which, silent and unstrung,
> In mournful ranks on Babel's willows hung,
> Would oft awake to chant their future fame,
> And from the skies their lingering Saviour claim.

Morison's commentary, on the other hand, interprets Psalm 137 as referring to Christ Mystical or the Church: 'Let us . . . cheer ourselves with the prospect of that utter discomfiture which awaits all the enemies of God and his church. As the literal Babylon fell, by reason of its idolatry and cruel persecution, so every power which follows in its footsteps shall ultimately share its fate; till over the ruins of them all the triumphant church shall exclaim, "Babylon the great is fallen, is fallen, and shall rise no more for ever" ' (3, pp. 200–1).

4 See, for example, Massey's 'The Cry of the Unemployed'. Hoxie Neale Fairchild, who includes Massey in his section on 'Seers and Seekers' with similar social-protest poets of the working classes, suggests the odd inconsistencies in his position when he points out that in some poems Massey attempts to 'give to Chartism something of the flavor of Kenelm Digby and the Young England Movement' ('Young England Movement', Religious Trends in English Poetry (New York, 1957), 4, pp. 176–7).

5 Locke, the worker-poet, had been raised in a dour Evangelicalism, and he here makes an application of the Exodus to political phenomena which had been orthodox among the seventeenth-century Puritans whom many Evangelical sects honored as predecessors. At other points in the novel, the hero, who exchanges his early faith for Kingsley's Broad Church Anglican views, treats the Bible with the broadly symbolic approach characteristic of the liberal wing of the Church. For instance, in the novel's opening chapter Locke tells the reader that he learned from reading the scriptures that the 'old Jewish heroes . . . were patriots, deliverers from that tyranny and injustice from which the child's heart . . . instinctively, and, as I believe, by a divine inspiration, revolts. Moses leading his people out of Egypt; Gideon, Barak, and Samson, slaying their oppressors; David, hiding in the mountains from the tyrant, with his little band of those who had fled from the oppressions of the aristocracy of Nabals; Jehu, executing God's vengeance on the kings – they were my heroes, my models'. Later Locke interprets all biblical history along these lines, claiming that 'the Bible is the history of mankind's deliverance from all tyranny, outward as well as inward, of the Jews, as the one free constitutional people among a world of slaves and tyrants; of their ruin, as the righteous fruit of a voluntary return to despotism; of the New Testament, as the good news that freedom, brotherhood, and equality, once confided only to Judaea and to Greece, and dimly seen even there, was henceforth to be the right of all mankind' (ch. 30, 'Prison Thoughts').

6 Christ is often spoken of as having been crushed in the winepress at the Crucifixion or as then having to endure the hard labors of working the winepress; at the Last Judgment He will reverse his role and tread upon,

crush, or bruise evil. Massey applies what we may term the passive version of this image from Isaiah 63:3 and Revelation 14:19–20 in 'Anathema Maranatha':

> They have broken our hearts for their hunger, and trod
> The wine-press for Death, with the grapes of our God;
> And ye lick their feet, red with your blood, like dumb cattle.

One of the more famous applications of this set of biblical texts to God's punishment of political oppressors appears in Julia Ward Howe's 'Battle Hymn of the Republic' (1862).

7 Fairchild points out, like Mr Lyons in *Felix Holt*, the father of Ebenezer Elliott, author of the famous *Corn-Law Rhymes* (1831), had been 'both a Methodist and a radical; but as the century moved on this combination, fairly common between Peterloo and the passage of the Reform Bill, became much more difficult to maintain' (*Religious Trends in English Poetry*, 4, p. 77). After many who had begun as both Evangelicals and radicals abandoned their original nonconformist beliefs, they still expressed their political views with Evangelical vocabulary, imagery, and rhetoric.

8 Ebenezer Elliott thus complains that the Evangelicals forget that charity begins at home:

> Their Bibles for the heathen load our fleets;
> Lo! looking eastward, they inquire, 'What news?'
> 'We die,' we answer, 'foodless in the streets,'
> Oh, 'they are sending bacon to the Jews!' (*Corn-Law Rhymes*, 1831)

9 The implications of Sabbatarianism, which has so often been described by Victorian autobiographers and novelists, are drawn out by Trollope in *Barchester Towers* (1857). He explains that Mrs Proudie, wife of the Bishop of Barchester,

> is in her own way a religious woman; and the form in which this tendency shows itself in her is by a strict observance of Sabbatarian rule. Dissipation and low dresses during the week are, under her control, atoned for by three services, an evening sermon read by herself, and a perfect abstinence from any cheering employment on the Sunday. Unfortunately for those under her roof to whom the dissipation and low dresses are not extended, her servants namely and her husband, the compensating strictness of the Sabbath includes all' (ch. 3, 'Dr. and Mrs. Proudie').

Thomas Hood's 'Ode to Rae Wilson, Esq.', which makes all the usual charges against the Evangelicals, remarks that unlike 'Those pseudo Privy Councillors of God',

No solemn sanctimonious face I pull,
Nor think I'm pious when I'm only bilious –
Nor study in my sanctum supercilious
To frame a Sabbath Bill.

10 Ford K. Brown, *Fathers of the Victorians: The Age of Wilberforce* (Cambridge, 1961) provides a valuable detailed study of Evangelical social and political policy.

11 'Y chwarelwyr: the slate quarrymen of North Wales', in *Miners, Quarrymen and Saltworkers,* ed. Raphael Samuels (London, 1977), p. 129. The quotation following is from the same location.

12 'Nothing could *in itself* be less suited to give relief than this expedient: but it was the Lord's appointment; and by this token the sufferers must express their entire dependence on him, and submissively expect a cure from him alone. . . . This forms a very significant type of our salvation by Jesus Christ. . . . For faith in a crucified Saviour is the appointment of God, and rendered effectual by his grace: and though man's reasoning pride considers it as foolishness, all believers experience it to be "the power of God to salvation" ' (Scott's note on Numbers 21:6–9).

13 Since several poems in the Tractarian *Lyra Apostolica* (1836), including 'The Religion of the Majority', 'National Property', and 'National Degradation', use types to charge contemporary England with worship of Mammon and deciding spiritual matters by ballot, Carlyle had ample precedent here.

Chapter Six: Typological Structures: The Examples of Gerard Manley Hopkins and Dante Gabriel Rossetti

1 For related notions of 'abstracted' typology, see Paul J. Korshin, 'The Development of Abstracted Typology in England, 1650–1820', in *Literary Uses of Typology from the Middle Ages to the Present*, ed. Earl Miner (Princeton, 1977) pp. 147–203.

2 Wendell Stacy Johnson, *Gerard Manley Hopkins: The Poet as Victorian* (Ithaca, 1968) and Alison G. Sulloway, *Gerard Manley Hopkins and the Victorian Temper* (N. Y., 1972) both make interesting attempts to place Hopkins, a poet too often thought to be *sui generis*, within the context of contemporary thought. Unfortunately Sulloway, who makes several game attempts to show the influence of Ruskin upon the poet, begins

with such a limited view of the critic's main ideas that her results are very disappointing. In particular, she fails to perceive either the nature or importance of Victorian conceptions of biblical or literary symbolism.

3 *Inscape: The Christology and Poetry of Gerard Manley Hopkins* (Pittsburgh, 1972), p. xxi.

4 There had been ample poetic precedent in seventeenth-century religious poetry for such use of derived or abstracted structures based upon Genesis 3:15 and related passages. For example, George Herbert's 'The Banquet' thus provides an earlier instance of Hopkins's favorite organizing conceit:

> But as Pomanders and wood
>   Still are good,
> Yet being bruised are better scented:
> God, to show how farre his love
>   Could improve,
> Here, as broken, is presented.

5 I am thinking of Cotter's interesting discussion of 'Poetry and Gnosis' in his *Inscape: The Christology and Poetry of Gerard Manley Hopkins*, and I should emphasize that I do not necessarily disagree with many of his conclusions. Rather, I believe that many of Hopkins's basic attitudes towards Christianity and poetry are to be found in contemporary typological exegesis and related attitudes, such as Tractarian conceptions of the necessity of 'reserve', and that therefore one need not go so far afield to explain this Victorian writer. Just as Carlyle, who knew the work of Comte and the St Simonians, turns out to have been most influenced by his native Scottish Puritanism, so Hopkins and many other major Victorians seem best understood by first relating them to ideas most easily accessible to them. In many cases, one suspects, apparently novel or alien schools of thought appeal to particular authors only because they have important similarities to ideas and attitudes acquired from contemporary thought.

6 See William E. Fredeman, 'Rossetti's "In Memoriam": an Elegaic Reading of *The House of Life*', *Bulletin of the John Rylands University Library of Manchester*, 47 (1965), pp. 298–341. Professor Fredeman, who kindly read an earlier version of this section on Rossetti, has suggested in a private communication that 'Perhaps in the secular typology of *The House of Life* Rossetti is writing about a present, which has been prefigured by specific events (monumental moments) in the past, and it is this introspective element that gives the poem its elegaic tone'. This interpretation strikes me as convincing, and I have adopted it below. For the context of Rossetti's attitudes towards time, see Jerome Hamilton

Buckley, *The Triumph of Time: A Study of Victorian Concepts of Time, History, Progress, and Decadence* (Cambridge, Mass., 1966).

Chapter Seven: The Pisgah Sight– Typological Structure and Typological Image

1 'The Death of Moses', *Sermons* (London, 1836), 2, p. 185. Succeeding quotations are taken from pp. 186–7.

2 Kingsley, a patriotic Englishman, does not here take advantage of the venerable typological tradition that takes America as the new Canaan and true promised land. For a discussion of such applications of Old Testament history to the New World, see Mason I. Lowance, 'Typology and Millennial Eschatology in Early New England', in *Literary Uses of Typology from the Middle Ages to the Present*, ed. Earl Miner (Princeton, 1977), pp. 228–73.

3 Newman, who frequently employs types of the Pisgah sight, bases 'The Death of Moses' (1832) on the literal fact of the prophet's dying in sight, but not in possession, of the Promised Land. Moses is the speaker in the poem, and after he has mentioned in successive stanzas that he has finally reached the hope of his fathers, is dying while still strong and energetic, and yearns to test the reality of the 'Blest scene . . . And prove the vision true', he realizes that God, 'Who chastens whom He loves', justly prevents his entering the Promised Land. Newman thereupon presents the dying vision of Moses:

> Ah! now they melt . . . they are but shades. . . .
> I die! – yet is no rest,
> O Lord! in store, since Canaan fades
> But seen, and not possest? (Newman's ellipsis)

In addition to drawing upon this realistic psychological portrayal of the prophet's last moments for the moral lesson that one should accept God's punishments, Newman seems to be employing this literal version of the narrative to demonstrate that even the greatest Old Testament figures died unsatisfied and unfulfilled because Christ had not yet come. In making this Christian emphasis, Newman also probably distorts the original story and adds an undue emphasis upon the prophet's dissatisfaction.

4 For the nature and tradition of the prospect poem and landscape meditation, see Earl R. Wasserman, *The Subtler Language: Critical Readings of Neoclassical and Romantic Poems* (Baltimore, 1959); Alan Roper, *Arnold's Poetic Landscapes* (Baltimore, 1969); and M. H. Abrams, *Natural Supernaturalism: Tradition and Revolution in Romantic Literature* (N. Y., 1971).

5 Aeneas's descent into the underworld is, of course, in imitation of Odysseus's similar descent into Hades, and the vision itself ultimately derives from the shield of Achilles in *The Iliad*. The shield of Achilles presents an archetypal and essentially static picture of human life, while Odysseus enters the lands of death in order to learn what he must do to return to a past existence, for in the Homeric scheme of things he must return to Ithaca and resume his defining roles as father, husband, and king if he is to be himself. Although Vergil elsewhere writes as if nature and man inevitably decline from a golden age, in the epic of Rome he presents history progressing in the sense that it builds towards the founding of Rome and the subsequent *imperium*.

6 Such applications of types to natural objects also appears frequently in the works of Keble and of Frederick William Faber, an Anglican convert to the Roman Church. G. B. Tennyson, 'The Sacramental Imagination', in *Nature and the Victorian Imagination*, eds U. C. Knoepflmacher and G. B. Tennyson (Berkeley, 1977), pp. 370–90, contains a valuable discussion of such conceptions of natural symbols.

7 Richard E. Brantley, *Wordsworth's 'Natural Methodism'* (New Haven, 1975), pp. 156–70, offers an important discussion of Wordsworthian applications of typology to natural fact.

8 *Natural Supernaturalism*, pp. 91–2.

9 See Carlisle Moore, 'Faith, Doubt, and Mystical Experience in "In Memoriam" ', *Victorian Studies*, 7 (1963), pp. 155–69; and George P. Landow, 'Closing the Frame: Having Faith and Keeping Faith in Tennyson's "The Passing of Arthur" ', *Bulletin of the John Rylands University Library of Manchester*, 56 (1974), pp. 423–42.

10 Jerome J. McGann, *Swinburne: An Experiment in Criticism* (Chicago, 1972), pp. 171, 174. One may add that Spurgeon, the great Baptist preacher, provides an example of the religious uses of this favorite Swinburnean landscape situation:

Reflect a moment, man. Where art thou standing now?

> 'Lo, on a narrow neck of land,
> 'Twixt two unbounded seas I stand;
> An inch of time, a moment's space,
> May lodge me in yon heavenly place,
>   Or shut me up in hell.'

I recollect standing on the seashore once, upon a narrow neck of land, thoughtless that the tide might come up. The tides kept continually washing up on either side, and, wrapped in thoughts, I still stood there, until at last there was the greatest difficulty in getting on shore. You and I stand each day on a narrow neck, and there is one wave coming up there; see, how near it is to your foot; and lo! another follows at every tick of the clock ('The Bible', *Sermons*, 1.38).

11 I am quoting from Bruce R. Redford, ' "A God with the world inwound": Structure and Theme in Swinburne's Landscape Poetry', an unpublished Brown University undergraduate honors thesis. Mr Redford has published the portions of his topic concerned with Swinburne's use of Stoicism in the similarly titled ' "A God with the world inwound": Swinburne's "A Nympholept" and Classical Stoicism', *Victorians Institute Annual*, 7 (1978), pp. 35–55.

12 With characteristic irony the Roumanian-French philosopher E. M. Cioran comments upon the way such meditation allows us to escape from time and yet throws us back into it:

> By meditation we perceive the inanity of the diverse and the accidental, of the past and the future, only to be *engulfed* more readily in the limitless moment. A thousand times better to take a vow of madness or to destroy oneself in God, than to prosper by means of such simulacra! One articulate prayer, repeated inwardly to the point of hebetude or orgasm, carries more weight than any idea, than all ideas. To *prospect* any world but this one, to *sink* into a silent hymn to vacuity, is to indenture oneself to *elsewhere* ('The Tree of Life', in *The Fall into Time*, trans. Richard Howard [N. Y., 1970], pp. 46–7; the final ellipsis and emphasis on *elsewhere* are Cioran's).

Clearly, he still employs the same concerns and images as did Swinburne a century before: the prospect, the shipwreck of self, the sea of time.

13 The conventional combination of Pisgah sight or prospect and a ship voyage derives in part from Evangelical hymns which turn the passage of the River Jordan into a full-fledged ship voyage.

14 See George P. Landow, 'Shipwrecked and Castaway on the Journey of Life: an Essay Towards a Modern Iconography', *Revue de Littérature Comparée*, 184 (1972), pp. 569–96.

15 Harold Bloom, 'The Internalization of Quest-Romance' and Geoffrey H. Hartman, 'Romanticism and "Anti-Self-Consciousness" ', in *Romanticism and Consciousness: Essays in Criticism*, ed. Harold Bloom (N. Y., 1970), pp. 3–23, 46–56; and M. H. Abrams, *Natural Supernaturalism*.

16 The classic statement of such a view of Victorian literature is made by E. D. H. Johnson, *The Alien Vision of Victorian Poetry: Sources of the Poetic Imagination in Tennyson, Browning, and Arnold* (Princeton, 1952).

17 'Thyrsis' (1866), Arnold's elegy for Clough, employs a secularized

version or analogue to the Pisgah sight when he finds he not only cannot reach the goals the Scholar Gypsy set for himself, he cannot even join the quest. What is more, he at first cannot even find the tree which, to him and Clough, had represented that higher life of the Scholar Gypsy. Finally, just before the sun disappears, casting the world into darkness, he catches a brief, tantalizing distant sight of the elm tree. That brief consolatory glance, which is so much like the one Bedivere receives, is all there is and it must suffice.

INDEX

Abrams, M. H., 220–1, 229, 252n4
Aeneas, 213, 253n5
Altick, Richard, D., 242n7
Annunciation, 122, 125
Apollo, 137
Apostles, 139
Apostolic succession, 19
Arnold, Matthew, 81, 160, 223–4,
    226, 228, 254–5n17
Art-Journal, 129–9
audience, problem of identifying,
    75–6, 129–30, 225–6
Auerbach, Erich, 54
Augustine, St, 6, 54, 104, 242n6
Antichrist, 37, 161
autobiography, and typology,
    11–12, 225, 230

Baptists, 18, 19, 27
Bassius, Junius, tomb of, 75
Baudelaire, Charles, 228–9
Bennetts, Rev Mr Colin, 246n25
Bentley, John Francis, 137
Bible: Broad Church attitudes
    towards, 20; Christ at centre of,
    32–3, 39; centre of Evangelical
    Protestantism, 17, 54, 55;
    commentaries on, 15, 21–2, 57;
    how Victorians learned to
    interpret, 3, 15, 21–2, 67–72;

imaginative experience of, 26,
    60; language and phrasing
    means of appealing to audience,
    114; literally the word of God
    (Verbal Inspiration), 55–6;
    reading of, a religious duty,
    21–2; system of progressive
    revelation, 35; types
    characteristic feature of, 32–3,
    38; passages discussed:
    Deuteronomy 15:12–15, 182,
    34:1–4, 205, 35:51–2, 207,
    Exodus 12, 99–100, 17:6,
    67–72, 128, 25:9, 104, 33:22–3,
    74, 205–6, Genesis 3:15, 7–10,
    32–3, 47, 101–2, 105, 183,
    242n8, 251n4 (contains
    fundamental principle of
    universe, 32, problems of
    treating visually, 132–7,
    political applications, 153–4,
    163), Hebrews 5:3, 36, Isaiah,
    20:2, 31, 63:3, 163, 183,
    Jeremiah 48:33, 182–3, John
    3:14, 170, 173, Joshua 7:12, 98,
    Judges 6:1, 11, 182,
    Lamentations 1:15, 183,
    Leviticus 1:3, 27, Malachi 3:1,
    131, Matthew 27:32, 47,
    Numbers 18:26–7, 181–2,

257